# Social Media Commerce

### FOR

# DUMMIES®

# by Marsha Collier

WILEY

John Wiley & Sons, Inc.

**Social Media Commerce For Dummies®**

Published by
**John Wiley & Sons, Inc.**
111 River Street
Hoboken, NJ 07030-5774

www.wiley.com

Copyright © 2013 by John Wiley & Sons, Inc., Hoboken, New Jersey

Published by John Wiley & Sons, Inc., Hoboken, New Jersey

Published simultaneously in Canada

For general information on our other products and services, please contact our Customer Care Department within the U.S. at 877-762-2974, outside the U.S. at 317-572-3993, or fax 317-572-4002.

For technical support, please visit www.wiley.com/techsupport.

Wiley publishes in a variety of print and electronic formats and by print-on-demand. Some material included with standard print versions of this book may not be included in e-books or in print-on-demand. If this book refers to media such as a CD or DVD that is not included in the version you purchased, you may download this material at http://booksupport.wiley.com. For more information about Wiley products, visit www.wiley.com.

Library of Congress Control Number: 2012950498

ISBN 978-1-118-29793-3 (pbk); ISBN 978-1-118-29943-2 (ebk); ISBN 978-1-118-46150-1 (ebk); 978-1-118-53195-2 (ebk)

Manufactured in the United States of America

10  9  8  7  6  5  4  3  2  1

WILEY

# About the Author

**Marsha Collier** spends a good deal of time online. As a blogger, the author of the best-selling *Dummies* books on eBay, and a radio host, she shares her love of the online world with millions.

Before her eBay career took off, Marsha owned and operated her own marketing and advertising firm, a company that won numerous awards and earned her "Small Business of the Year" accolades from several organizations. She got started online during the Internet's early years and quickly mastered the art making friends online.

Marsha is one of the foremost eBay experts and educators in the world and the top-selling eBay author. In 1999 Marsha created the first edition of *eBay For Dummies,* the bestselling book for eBay beginners. She followed up the success of her first book with *Starting an eBay Business For Dummies,* a book targeting individuals interested in making e-commerce their full-time profession, These books are updated regularly to keep up with site and market changes.

Marsha's books have sold over one million copies (including the special editions in foreign countries — two in Australia, two in Canada, and two in the United Kingdom — as well as translations in Spanish, French, Italian, Chinese and German).

Along with her writing, Marsha is an experienced e-commerce and customer service educator speaking at conferences all over the world. Embracing social media has earned Marsha awards as an influencer and author:

- 2011 Forbes: Top 10 Women Social Media Influencers
- 2012 Small Business Book Award Winner: *Starting an eBay Business For Dummies*
- 2012 Forbes: Top 50 Social Media Power Influencers
- 2012 The 100 Most Powerful Women on Twitter
- 2011 One of the Top 10 LA Tech & Twitter Voices in the Los Angeles Tech Scene by Ranker.com
- 2011 PeerIndex #1 Customer Experience Online Influencers
- 2011 #1 Most Influential in Customer Service MindTouch

She hosts Computer & Technology Radio on iTunes and on the web at www.computerandtechnologyradio.com. Marsha currently resides in Los Angeles, CA. She can be reached via her website, at www.marshacollier.com.

# Dedication

This book is dedicated to all the small businesses and entrepreneurs who have a zest for knowledge and the gumption to follow through. It's dedicated also to those who have figured out that get-rich-quick schemes don't work and that, in the long run, hard work and passion for what you do leads to financial achievement and contentment. Those who run small businesses are a special breed, and I salute you. This book was written to lighten your load, and maybe make social media a pleasant respite from your day.

Finally, I dedicate this book to my many friends in social media. Our morning chats and Tweets help me to start my day with a smile.

# Author's Acknowledgments

This book couldn't have been written without the input from thousands of my Twitter and Facebook friends (who are also on Google+) from all over the world. Thank you for answering my silly polls, for helping me with words when I can't think of just the right one, and for just being there to brighten my day. You inspire me to work harder and do my best to help everyone succeed.

I particularly want to thank the crew at Wiley: my project editor, Susan Pink, who endured my feistiness while helping me produce a better book (and who really needs a Facebook page); my bad-ass tech editor (and friend) TJ McCue, whose smart ideas and encouraging words helped me through this project; my acquisitions editor, Amy Fandrei, who had no idea what she was getting in to *Tweet* but was a real help centering my bazillion ideas; to executive editor Steve Hayes, with whom I've worked long before he hit the big time (and I might note has never copped a highfalutin' tone); and to Andy Cummings, publisher and vice president, who I've worked with for over a decade but yet we still don't have time for a second cigar.

On the home front: Thanks to my very successful, smart, and charming daughter, Susan Dickman. Susan was there when I was stuck in limbo, helping with suggestions and sitting with me while I worked late on edits (even after her own full day at work). I believe she thinks it was payback for the many childhood dioramas, but I know she was just being kind. For sure, without Curt Buthman's support (and hot meals), writing this book would have been a whole lot less fun than it was. Thank you, Curt, for putting up with my long hours (I know you got to watch a lot more UFC) . . . it's time we go dining and dancing (until the next book).

Whoa! Can't forget my agent, Matt Wagner who helped me climb (finally) out of my eBay box and expand my horizons. Thanks, pal!

Thank you all!

## Publisher's Acknowledgments

We're proud of this book; please send us your comments at http://dummies.custhelp.com. For other comments, please contact our Customer Care Department within the U.S. at 877-762-2974, outside the U.S. at 317-572-3993, or fax 317-572-4002.

Some of the people who helped bring this book to market include the following:

### Acquisitions and Editorial

**Project Editor:** Susan Pink

**Acquisitions Editor:** Amy Fandrei

**Copy Editor:** Susan Pink

**Technical Editor:** TJ McCue

**Editorial Manager:** Jodi Jensen

**Editorial Assistant:** Leslie Saxman

**Sr. Editorial Assistant:** Cherie Case

**Cover Photo:** © VOLODYMER GRINKO/ iStockphoto and © sureyya akin/ iStockphoto

**Cartoons:** Rich Tennant (www.the5thwave.com)

### Composition Services

**Sr. Project Coordinator:** Kristie Rees

**Layout and Graphics:** Jennifer Creasey, Joyce Haughey, Corrie Niehaus

**Proofreaders:** John Greenough, Linda D. Morris

**Indexer:** Sharon Shock

---

**Publishing and Editorial for Technology Dummies**

    **Richard Swadley,** Vice President and Executive Group Publisher

    **Andy Cummings,** Vice President and Publisher

    **Mary Bednarek,** Executive Acquisitions Director

    **Mary C. Corder,** Editorial Director

**Publishing for Consumer Dummies**

    **Kathleen Nebenhaus,** Vice President and Executive Publisher

**Composition Services**

    **Debbie Stailey,** Director of Composition Services

# Contents at a Glance

# Table of Contents

· · · · · · · · · · · · · · · · · · · · · · · · · · · · · · · · · · · · ·

# Introduction

· · · · · · · · · · · · · · · · · · · · · · · · · · · · · · · · · · · · · · · · · · · · · · · · · · · · · · · · · · · · · · · · · · ·

*T*rying to target the new media customer these days is getting increasingly hard. Customers and clients are online, sharing and exchanging ideas on products and services. They seek information from reviews and comments on multiple websites. This shift has changed shopping from a solo exercise to a social experience and is the key element to the growth of social commerce.

In addition, the new media customer has a growing distrust of traditional advertising and marketing methods. In 2010, the Altimeter Group (`www.altimetergroup.com`) heralded an enterprise conference on the groundswell of social commerce:

> *It is not about you! It is not about the brand. It is about the collective wisdom of the community, who share insight from people that the buyer trusts. This is a marked change for a product-centric company that has built a living on push-based advertising about their brands. For now, it is not about your website, your fan page, or your sponsored communities. The shopper is a skeptic. They are the most likely to buy based on posts on third-party websites.*

Shoppers want to connect with the companies and people with which they do business. They want to feel important. They want their opinions to be respected and their feelings to be understood. They crave a buying experience that puts them in a place of influence. The power is shifting to the consumer. By using social media commerce effectively, you can bridge the gap between you and your customer while you build your bottom line.

## About This Book

So many tried-and-true methods have fallen by the wayside and the traditional ways to do business have been disrupted. What's a businessperson to do?

To hear the voice of your customer, you need to keep up with the rapid pace of change. Technology and social marketing are constantly evolving. Facebook, Twitter, LinkedIn, and YouTube are the undisputed leaders in online networking. Upstarts such as Google+, Pinterest, and So.cl are adding to the gaggle with new methods of engagement that allow you to make the most of the current communication trends. Joining in the conversation is your key to converting customers.

As businesses and professionals, we need to combine new technologies with traditional marketing to bring in sales. Technological touch points such as QR codes are an example. Although engagement through the use of these codes is off to a wobbly start, they have proved increasingly effective when used with direct mail and at point of sale.

Many businesses are underestimating the involvement and planning needed to properly utilize social media for commercial gain. Social media isn't just another outlet for marketing — it must be integrated into your company's culture. A successful strategy that is committed to connecting and engaging with your consumers increases your bottom line.

Customers value transparency and authenticity. Although it can be a challenge to separate your marketing message from your social content, finding your voice becomes second nature, and rising to the occasion pays off.

Social media is more than just setting up a Twitter feed and adding a Facebook like button to your website. You have to give the customer something — and someone — to like and follow. First, work on making your own site social and providing your customers with a channel to connect directly with you.

Integrating social media into your business plan may sound daunting, but I wrote *Social Media Commerce For Dummies* to show you how. In this book, you find the answers to some important questions as we explore the following topics:

- Defining your customers in new media and knowing where they hang out
- Connecting through social media and converting "friends" into loyal customers
- Bringing your website up-to-date by integrating social commerce engagement points
- Competing with the big brands
- Monitoring your reputation and catching criticism before it goes viral
- Enhancing your connection to the customer through e-mail marketing
- Adding new twists to traditional marketing practices

## How to Read This Book

Read this book in traditional fashion from beginning to end or feel free to read it as you would use a cookbook, jumping around from recipe to recipe (or chapter to chapter). Either way, be sure to keep the book handy to answer future questions as they come to you.

# *Foolish Assumptions*

I assume you realize that the social media trend is here for the long haul. (And if you're not yet convinced, check out Chapter 1.) Some of you might want to know how much time and effort are involved in jumping into the online conversation so you can make an informed decision about whether to give it a go. For those who have decided that it's time to use social media to benefit your business, I make some other assumptions:

✔ You have a business or are part of a professional organization.

✔ You enjoy the Internet and can find your way around.

✔ Some of your friends (or even you) are on Facebook. You know that this is an outlet for ads and promotions and you want to know how best to approach utilizing them.

✔ You've heard about Twitter and perhaps have even given it a whirl.

✔ You like the idea of getting feedback from your customers and finding out how best to increase their loyalty.

If you can say yes to most of my foolish assumptions, you're off and running! Take a few moments to read the following section to see how I've put this book together.

# *How This Book Is Organized*

Thanks to my editors, this book has five parts. Each chapter can stand on its own. That means you can read Chapter 12 after reading Chapter 8 and maybe skip Chapter 10 altogether — but I know you won't because that's where I discuss cashing in!

## *Part I: Prepping for Social Media Commerce*

Reviewing the data that shows why social media has taken such a large chunk of today's advertising dollar is a good place to start your investigation. In Part I, you consider the right place to position your business and how not to create a major faux pas at the outset. You also look at how best to invest your time and who you should trust to manage your outreach. I also provide valuable information on setting up a social media policy for employees who might represent your business online.

# Part II: Adapting Your Web Presence

You probably have a website for your business — if you don't, I suggest you get one right away. Part II shows you how to buff up that site for the twenty-first century by making it more engaging for your customers. I propose ways to add content that invites shares and comments. You'll also find out how to connect and create your social persona.

Your website is *your* home on the Internet, and your home page is your front door, where you welcome your customers. I show you how to install some free tools to make it easier to connect in real time through live chat — and have a dedicated (free) phone number for customer service interactions.

# Part III: Casting for and Catching Customers

In Part III, you hone in on your customer. You discover some good tools for identifying your customers and finding them in the social media realm. I also describe the strengths and weaknesses of different social media sites.

You also get tips about connecting on Twitter (yes, in 140 characters or less) and how to build a following. You discover a quick way to get into Facebook commerce with your own store and find out how to connect (and profit) with your customers through mobile.

Most of all, Part III gives you clues on how to monetize, even if you have no physical products to sell.

# Part IV: Supporting Your Social Media Commerce Efforts

In Part IV, you discover ways to streamline your existing customer service reach through online media and to diffuse issues before they become damaging. I address simple (and free) ways of monitoring your online reputation. This task isn't a big mystery and will take far less time than you think.

You also find out how to update your advertising, including how to start and reinvigorate an e-mail campaign, and how to build a valuable following online.

## Part V: The Part of Tens

In Part V, you get an immediate action list. I've condensed all the knowledge in the book into a 10-step program for online success. In addition, a tip sheet helps you get feedback on new business ideas through your online community.

New media has a language of its own, so I've also included a glossary. Feel free to refer to the glossary often as you peruse other parts of the book.

# Icons Used in This Book

All *For Dummies* books have cute little icons. I certainly wouldn't want to ruin your reading experience and leave them out. So I selected a few and used them sparingly throughout the book. Be sure to take heed when you see them.

If I need to interject something — okay, it's something I'm jumping up and down to tell you but it won't fit directly into the text — I indicate it by including a Tip icon. You'll know the text to follow will be right on target!

Do you really know people who tie string around their finger to remember something? Me neither, but this icon gives me the opportunity to give you a brief reminder. Think of it as a sticky note.

I like this picture of the bomb device that Wile E. Coyote slam-dunks in the cartoons. In that vein, if you don't heed the warning indicated by the small petard (hey, Shakespeare knew about old-fashioned bombs), you may end up "hoisted by your own petard," or made a victim of your own foolishness.

# Where to Go from Here

It's time to hunker down and delve into the book. Take this information and study it. The fun of building an engaging community online awaits you. I can't wait to hear your success stories if I meet you at a social media event or a book signing in your town.

My goal is to help you reach your goals. Feel free to visit my websites at www.reputationspecialist.com and www.coolebaytools.com or subscribe to my blog at mcollier.blogspot.com. For more about me (and to contact me), visit www.marshacollier.com (just click the Send Marsha an Email link). To contact me in less than 140 characters, you can find me on Twitter (@MarshaCollier) almost every day. Join me on Facebook, too, at www. facebook.com/MarshaCollierFanPage, where I share even more. (Perhaps I overshare?) I respond there too.

Please send me suggestions, additions, and comments. I want to hear from you and hope to update this book with your words of wisdom. (Humorous war stories are also gratefully accepted!) I truly appreciate your comments. Please know that I read every e-mail I get, but I can't always answer every one.

Occasionally, Wiley has updates to their technology books. If this book does have technical updates, they will be posted at

dummies.com/go/socialmediacommercecfdupdates

# Part I

# Prepping for Social Media Commerce

The 5th Wave       By Rich Tennant

# In this part . . .

In the moving target that is social media commerce, it's important to grasp the basics: the how's and why's. In Part I, you get up to speed on how social media can work for your business. Also, you find some tips on deciding how much time you need to spend online to achieve your goals.

# Chapter 1

# Social Media Commerce and Your Bottom Line

*T*echnologies change and, we hope, improve the way we do business, but the modes of transmission also change. What's new is old — and what's old is new.

Traditionally, news about a subject or product was broadcast through advertising, marketing, word-of-mouth, and even gossip. Broadcast media concentrated on manipulating customer emotions. The brands were king and often got away with calling the shots. Stores ran daily sales on one line of merchandise and then another to keep up with projected figures.

The public came to depend on promotions, and stores could sell little at a retail price. The continual fire sales lost their charm, and the practice dwindled. "You can fool some of the people some of the time." Many retailers weren't acting like "people" or respecting the customer.

Technology disrupted the way business was done and the way advertising was delivered. No longer is it considered a successful campaign to broadcast relentless sales and discounts to prospective customers. The public has tired of obvious manipulation.

Transparency in communication is the key to business now. Connecting with the customer through social networks brings business and brands into the day-to-day lives of the public. In this chapter, I provide a brief history of the transition and ideas on how you can make the shift to new media.

# Social Commerce Beginnings

Back in the 1700s, the town crier rang his bell and made proclamations in the town square. These criers were the sole means of communication with the populace, which was mostly illiterate. When literacy spread, people craved more information and the newspaper was born. Our nation's first daily newspaper, the *Pennsylvania Packet and Daily Advertiser* (see Figure 1-1), ran ads on the front page, giving those in a trade or with goods to sell a platform for marketing. The daily newspaper is one of the first examples of reaching customers by combining content with marketing.

Today, content-based marketing gets repeated in social media and increases word-of-mouth mentions; it's the best way to gather buzz about a product. It worked in the past and it does now.

Think back to the first days of television, whose sponsors crafted messages that would blend with the entertainment value (content) of the show. For example, Phillip Morris, the cigarette manufacturer that sponsored *I Love Lucy*, protected their brand to the extent that the word *lucky* was forbidden on the show so that the audience wasn't reminded of a competing brand, Lucky Strikes.

As advertising progressed through the years, marketing created catchwords that carried messages through word-of-mouth.

**Figure 1-1:**
Front and center on our country's first newspaper: Ads!

Person-to-person contact is a proven method to build sales. During the Great Depression, the Avon lady and her samples were welcomed into homes. With 25,000 representatives in the field, sales grew to $6.5 million in 1939, from just under $2.8 million in 1929. Trust, education (content) and personal contact built the sales network today to 6.4 million representatives in 100 countries. In the History section on the Avon website, they remark that long before Facebook, "It connected women, who were otherwise isolated and immersed in domestic life," in what the company calls "the original social network." Indeed it was.

In 1991, the World Wide Web was put online by Tim Berners-Lee, and forward-thinking commerce types saw a new opportunity. Jeff Bezos founded Amazon.com in 1994, and in the following year, Pierre Omidyar started a person-to-person marketplace called eBay. These early online sellers made a name for themselves by offering discount pricing and a vast array of merchandise, but they added a new twist: Their sites were also *social* networks. Buyers could comment, leave feedback, and post reviews of the items they purchased. Customer service took a new turn.

Thus began — for a few smart companies — social commerce.

# Defining Social Media, Social Business, and Social Commerce

Grab a cup of coffee. The new train of thinking you'll need to wrap your head around is all about being social. Commerce has always been propelled by people. Whether a business is serving the customer (B2C, business to consumer) or selling products and services to another business (B2B, business to business), making a sale always starts with an interaction. In today's business atmosphere, initial and ongoing contacts and interactions must build trust.

*Social* is the heart of commerce today. Dictionary-style definitions read this way:

- **Social media** refers to varied methods and web-based applications for online media that enable social interactions. These platforms are accessible to businesses and consumers through scalable publishing techniques via blogs and public sites. User-generated content is augmented by person-to-person interaction and conversation is encouraged. This online arena is the place where social business communication, networking, and social commerce are played out.

✔ **Social business** is revolutionizing the way companies function and generate value for all involved. This new trend toward internal communication and socially minded organizations transforms from the inside out. The transformation is propelled through relationships within and without the company. Social business connects the internal staff with external vendors and customers. It breaks down the organizational silos that stand in the way of intracompany communication, building mutual collaboration between all departments.

✔ **Social media commerce** is where the rubber meets the road, where the dollars are made. Social media commerce is the specific use of social media technology and networks to produce commerce, whether on the web or in bricks-and-mortar businesses.

Although the terms sound similar, they refer to three different ways for people (and business) to benefit from pubic exposure and transparency. All three are bound by the word *social*.

The following strategies can be accomplished through the social media conduit:

✔ Raise awareness of new products

✔ Teach customers how to care for your product

✔ Develop or sell new product lines, based on customer comments

✔ Adapt your business to match customer needs

✔ Promote seasonal bargains and marketing messages

✔ Deliver on your customer service promise

This list gives you just a few ideas. Throughout this book, you will find lots of suggestions to help you change your business into a much more trusted (and profitable) enterprise.

# *Making Money by Connecting with People*

Selling through social media isn't just about posting bargains on Facebook or Twitter. You must also build trust with today's customer. Social media engagement leads to a more personalized means of communication versus Tweeting deals and requesting Facebook likes.

Nielsen's latest Global Trust in Advertising report (see Figure 1-2) surveyed more than 28,000 Internet respondents in 56 countries. The report found that a whopping 92 percent of consumers around the world say they trust *earned media* (versus paid advertising) and social word of mouth (such as recommendations from friends and family) more than other forms of advertising.

| To what extent do you trust the following forms of advertising? | | |
|---|---|---|
| **Global Average** | Trust Completely/ Somewhat | Don't Trust Much/ At All |
| Recommendations from people I know | 92% | 8% |
| Consumer opinions posted online | 70% | 30% |
| Editorial content such as newspaper articles | 58% | 42% |
| Branded Websites | 58% | 42% |
| Emails I signed up for | 50% | 50% |
| Ads on TV | 47% | 53% |
| Brand sponsorships | 47% | 53% |
| Billboards and other outdoor advertising | 47% | 53% |
| Ads in newspapers | 46% | 54% |
| Ads on radio | 42% | 58% |
| Ads before movies | 41% | 59% |
| TV program product placements | 40% | 60% |
| Ads served in search engine results | 40% | 60% |
| Online video ads | 36% | 64% |
| Ads on social networks | 36% | 64% |
| Online banner ads | 33% | 67% |
| Display ads on mobile devices | 33% | 67% |
| Text ads on mobile phones | 29% | 71% |

**Figure 1-2:** Data from *Nielsen Global Trust in Advertising Survey* Q3, 2011.

Today, earned media spurs engagement through community versus paid media (advertising), which drives customers to make purchases. To make your message resound with customers, you need to take advantage of social network channels and interact with the community on your website. Buyers no longer trust traditional advertising.

Your website is the hub of your social media reach and should provide tools and features that build consistency and collaboration. (For more on building a more social platform, see Chapter 4.) If you let your customers know your company, their investment is not just in your products and service but also with you and your staff as extended friends.

Paul Chaney, author of *The Digital Handshake* (Wiley), recently wrapped up the philosophy this way:

> *Tactics aside, what is of greatest importance is that your social media engagement be marked by authenticity and transparency. People want to be told the truth. They want their interactions with you to be validated by a genuine personal response. And they want the acknowledgement that what they have to say matters.*

So the way business connects has changed. Social engagement requires transparency and targeting your words and advertising to the people who are interested in your brand and your message.

Targeting social ads to those who are friends, or friends of friends, makes a profound difference in the impact of your advertising. In another Nielsen study, advertising recall increased by 55 percent when an ad was targeted directly to a business's social network. Ads become more memorable when social content is referenced.

Content engagement (personalizing to the customer) entices customers to try your business for the first time. Continuing interaction keeps them coming back for more. This technique is demonstrated craftily in the portion of an e-mail from ShoeDazzle shown in Figure 1-3. The sales pitch in the e-mail is tied to and delivered during the month's horoscope. So as not to leave out those who are not of the Taurus persuasion, the e-mail lists engaging quotes for each sign of the zodiac.

Notice the bottom of the e-mail? ShoeDazzle doesn't write the traditional "Follow Us on Facebook." Instead, they tell their customers that they *love* to be social — and provide links so that the customer can meet and connect with the brand on social media sites.

**Figure 1-3:** The "social sweet spot" of Shoe-Dazzle's e-mail.

**GEMINI**
BE OPEN ABOUT YOUR NEEDS WITH SOMEONE SPECIAL THIS MONTH, WHETHER YOU NEED SPACE OR A FOOT MASSAGE.

**CANCER**
YOU'VE GOT WANDERLUST THIS MONTH, BUT TRY FINDING ADVENTURE CLOSER TO HOME (MAY WE SUGGEST GIRLS' NIGHT?).

**LEO**
SOME OF THE LESSONS YOU LEARNED FROM PAST LOVES MAY COME INTO PLAY THIS MONTH—CALL IT THE "EX" FACTOR.

**VIRGO**
MAY IS ALL ABOUT PARTNERSHIP FOR YOU, SO FIND SOME COMMON GROUND, SIT DOWN ON IT, AND HAVE A PICNIC.

**LIBRA**
THIS MONTH IS ABOUT FINDING YOUR COMFORT ZONE, WHETHER IT'S IN A PARTNERSHIP OR AN APARTMENT.

**SCORPIO**
MAY IS ALL ABOUT THOSE THREE LITTLE WORDS, SCORPIO, SO TELL SOMEONE YOU LOVE 'EM, WHETHER IT'S YOUR MAN OR YOUR MOM.

**SAGITTARIUS**
YOU MIGHT FEEL LIKE HIDING FROM RESPONSIBILITY THIS MONTH, BUT TAKE CARE OF BUSINESS…THEN GO OUT AND PLAY.

**CAPRICORN**
YOUR COMPASSION AND KINDNESS WILL MAKE A DIFFERENCE FOR SOMEONE THIS MONTH—YOU'LL EARN YOUR WINGS.

**AQUARIUS**
PAY IT FORWARD IN MAY, AQUARIUS. DO A GOOD DEED, AND THE GOOD WILL COME BACK YOUR WAY, INDEED!

**PISCES**
YOU'LL FEEL LIKE SUPERGIRL THIS MONTH, BUT BEFORE YOU RUN OUT AND SAVE THE WORLD, REMEMBER TO BRING A SWEATER.

**ARIES**
FEELING A LITTLE LOST THIS MONTH? FEAR NOT, YOU'LL FIND WHAT YOU'RE LOOKING FOR…AND A GREAT PAIR OF PUMPS.

we ♥ to network!

As a customer, I liked ShoeDazzle on Facebook, and now, when I go to the site, my entry page is personalized with my Facebook picture (see Figure 1-4). Smart, eh? What a great way to make the customer part of the brand.

By the way, I just bought a pair of shoes from them while writing this chapter. See? Reaching out in a personal way draws attention and really does work.

**Figure 1-4:** My personalized entry page on ShoeDazzle.

# Changing Communication through Technology

After people began trading on eBay and shopping for books on Amazon, the game changed. Tim Berners-Lee, the inventor of the World Wide Web (sorry, Al Gore) as we know it today, executed his initial proposal in 1989 and put the first website and server online at CERN in France in 1991. Even though the purpose of this early technology was to connect scientists, Berners-Lee saw the future:

> *The web is more a social creation than a technical one. I designed it for a social effect — to help people work together — and not as a technical toy. The ultimate goal of the web is to support and improve our weblike existence in the world. We clump into families, associations, and companies. We develop trust across the miles and distrust around the corner.*

Built to bring the world closer together, this new World Wide Web enabled trust between strangers, businesses, and customers.

In 1999, a ground-breaking book on the future impact of commerce and the Internet was published. *The Cluetrain Manifesto,* by Rick, Levine, Christopher Locke, Doc Searls, David Weinberger, et al (Basic Books) in its description of how interactions with customers was about to change in the newly connected marketplace, was a call to action for all businesses. The book was almost clairvoyant in its prediction that the Internet would enable commerce by "human to human" conversations, thereby radically transforming traditional business practices.

Social media commerce is a byproduct of this brave new world. In the new media (through social media), CEOs and janitors converse and have equal power to change the business atmosphere. Social media is the twenty-first-century way of spreading the word and connecting about a topic, product, professional, or brand. If the topic at hand happens to be related to a product you sell, you have an opportunity to piggyback your message with it and include your call to action.

## From word of mouth to 1s and 0s

Pioneers in communication and commerce built platforms that enabled engagement and person-to-person commerce. The following list gives you an idea of how quickly the world has turned digital:

- ✔ **1978: CBBS,** Computerized Bulletin Board System, came online to a few hobbyists over regular telephone lines through modem connections.

- ✔ **1980: CompuServe** became the first online service to offer real-time chat thought their CB Simulator program.

- ✔ **1995: GeoCities** was the first site to promote free personal home pages. Although most pages were pretty basic, the service gave regular people a place to stake their claim on the web.

- ✔ **1997: eBay** (previously Auctionweb), a person-to-person marketplace, introduced a feedback system in which customer and sellers could comment on their e-commerce transactions. eBay also instituted user boards so that eBay members could chat, share ideas, and discuss their sales.

- ✔ **1998: PayPal,** originally called x.com, was founded as a person-to-person payment service. PayPal fueled eBay and future e-commerce growth.

- ✔ **1999: Blogger,** the first free blogging service, opened. They were purchased by Google in 2003.

- ✔ **2002: Friendster,** the first official social network, was created. By 2008, they reached a peak of 115 million registered members worldwide.

- ✔ **2003: MySpace** was developed by some Friendster users, and implemented the latest technologies and higher bandwidth than previous platforms. They reached a peak of 75 million visitors per month in late 2008.

- **2003: LinkedIn,** the first business-skewed social networking site, began attracting professionals as a way to connect.

- **2004: Flickr,** a photo- and video-hosting site, initially had a chat room, which was shelved early on. Today, Flickr is owned by Yahoo! and will eventually replace Yahoo! Photos.

- **2004: Facebook** launched quietly to students of Harvard University. These students opened the site to 800 other colleges in 2005, and by 2006, the site was available to any person over the age of 13.

- **2005: YouTube** was created by three former PayPal employees as a site where users can upload, view, and share videos. It was sold to Google for $1.65 billion in 2006.

- **2006: Twitter,** the text-based social networking and microblogging service, was born. Comments, called *Tweets,* are limited to 140 characters. Today, Twitter users serve up more than 400 million Tweets per day.

- **2010: Pinterest,** a virtual pinboard for pinning and sharing web-based images, quotes, and all things visual that users find interesting, was created. Within a few months, it became one of the largest social networks on the web.

- **2011: Google+** opened as a social networking and identity service as an invitation-only beta. Within two weeks of its limited trial, the site reached 10 million users. By the end of 2011, it had 90 million users.

The digital landscape experiences transitions and progress continually. One aspect that will not change for a long time, however, is the ability to immediately and positively connect with customers.

# The end of the cold call

Traditionally, the process of making connections and making appointments took days, weeks, and months. In today's digital world, connections can be made on the fly. You can find suppliers by a LinkedIn search and hone in on customer bases by using social media tools.

Cold calls are no longer cold; they are warmed by information and data that was never before available. The amount of statistics about you, your business, and your industry stored in online databases makes your business dealings more transparent than ever before. Your personal reputation online adds into the equation and can potentially make or break a sale.

Products, as well, are no longer a mystery. Customers come fully armed with information on brands and models when they shop. Before the digital age, people went shopping during their lunch break. As e-commerce and high-speed connections grew, they squeezed a little time on their work computer for online shopping. Now, mobile technology fuels the online market.

More and more, consumers pick up their smartphones or tablets and conduct research before making a purchase. Customers get an instant and complete picture of a product's features through news and user-generated reviews. They can figure out which product or service they want — as well as where to find it. Consumers of all ages are embracing social content and mobile technologies. According to research by Nielsen, as of February 2012, nearly half of U.S. mobile subscribers owned smartphones (see Figure 1-5).

The 2011 holiday season was a turning point in e-commerce. A study from Google and IPSOS OTX found that of people who used smartphones for product research

- 46 percent went to a store to make their purchase

- 37 percent purchased online on a computer

- 41 percent purchased on a smartphone

- 19 percent visited a store to check out the product and then purchased online on a computer

- 18 percent visited a store to check out the product and then purchased online on a smartphone

- 8 percent visited the store first and then purchased on a smartphone

It's clear that consumers shop and make decisions not only from their computers but also from mobile devices. Your window of opportunity to grab customers and "wow" them narrows and you can no longer be guaranteed of their undivided attention.

**Figure 1-5:** In February 2012, 50 percent of U.S. mobile subscribers owned a smartphone. Smartphones trending up!

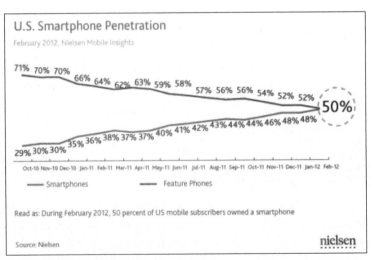

## Adding social media to the mix

A review of a venue, a comment about a business, a news story — words can go viral. When news breaks, it takes some time for the news media to confirm the details, but platforms such as Twitter and Facebook are immediately abuzz. The moment a news flash appears, the folks online go into broadcast mode and Tweet the results.

Although trust and persuasiveness carry strength in influencing participants in social media, perceptions, loud voices, and the number of human connections can bring staggering results in the spread of news:

✔ Within an hour of the 8.9 earthquake in Japan, the number of Tweets coming out of Japan alone surpassed 1,200 per minute (with the country's phone system disabled). Tweets in the United States shared news and translated Tweets from Japanese (using Google Translate) so that English-speaking readers could read the news as it happened.

✔ Suspicions of the topic of the presidential address leaked on Twitter at 9:46 p.m. At 10:24 p.m. Keith Urbahn (@Keithurbahn on Twitter), the former chief of staff to Donald Rumsfeld, Tweeted "So I'm told by a reputable person they have killed Osama Bin Laden. Hot damn." Within one minute, 80 people reposted the message. Within two minutes, over 300 reactions spread to the site.

✔ The dining-centered website, Eater.com, published a post with a picture that purportedly showed a receipt from a wealthy banker who dined at a restaurant. The image revealed a 1 percent tip along with a hand-written snarky note on the margin of the bill. The post went viral and was reported on CNN. Several days later, the restaurant produced the original bill — the post on the web had been Photoshopped.

Word spreads with lightening speed in social media, far faster than any public relations or marketing person you might employ. Our increasingly connected world has made the everyday person a broadcast news source.

# Creating Relationships with Your Customers

Gone are the days when businesses can say "We own our customer." The power today lies with the customer who, due to the Internet, has more options than ever before.

Doc Searls (coauthor of the *Cluetrain Manifesto*), in his new book, *The Intention Economy: When Customers Take Charge* (Harvard Business Press), says:

*Relationships between customers and vendors will be voluntary and genuine, with loyalty anchored in mutual respect and concern, rather than coercion. So, rather than "targeting," capturing," "acquiring," "managing," "locking in," and "owning" customers, as if they were slaves or cattle, vendors will earn the respect of customers who are now free to bring far more to the market's table than the old, vendor-based systems ever contemplated, much less allowed.*

# Social media commerce transaction . . . almost

An interesting example of how social media commerce works was posted on the web. A consumer saw a coat he liked on Tumblr and saved it on his Pinterest page. (More information on these platforms in Chapter 11.) He remembered seeing the coat's brand in Bergdorf Goodman while on a trip to New York.

Because the store was far from his home, he decided to post a query to Bergdorf Goodman's Facebook page. Within an hour, he received a reply, saying that the store was checking to see whether they carried the coat and asking what color he was interested in. A little more time

passed and another response was posted saying that they didn't carry that particular coat but the store would be glad to arrange a special order.

All this help — in less than a few hours. However, the customer never saw (or responded to) the Facebook messages, so Bergdorf's Twitter account (see the figure) made the effort to find him on Twitter as well. Bergdorf and the customer direct-messaged back and forth. Unfortunately, Bergdorf's pricing and the customer's budget were not in sync. Yet this sort of personal interaction will build a customer base — even for a small business.

In the twenty-first century, traditional and tried-and-true won't cut it with your customers.

It's time to think of your marketing message as just that — a message. Consumers have gradually become hip to the fact that a campaign of nonengagement is there only to sell them something. They have no way of knowing whether the proposed experience or purchase in a nonengagement campaign will enhance their lives.

One-on-one communication through social media enables the consumer to more easily make the transition from brand (or business) to commerce with human beings.

Social media even affects the way people look at ads. Product placements in film, TV, and even blogs catch the eye more than the in-your-face type of ad from days gone by.

Social ads, delivered through a social media site to those within a network, gather more attention too. Take a look at the numbers in Figure 1-6.

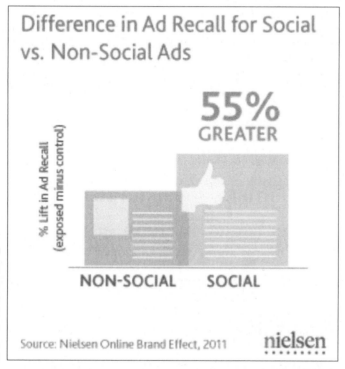

**Figure 1-6:** Difference in ad recall for social versus non-social ads.

Difference in Ad Recall for Social vs. Non-Social Ads

55% GREATER

% Lift in Ad Recall (exposed minus control)

NON-SOCIAL    SOCIAL

Source: Nielsen Online Brand Effect, 2011

*Source: Nielsen Online Brand Effect, 2011*

Every day, new data explodes on the web touting the values of social media. The following quick data bytes provide some eye-opening statistics:

- **90 percent of all purchases** are subject to social influence (*Wired Magazine* UK)

- **150 million people** engage with Facebook on external websites each month (Facebook, 2011)

- **1 million+ sites** have implemented Facebook's Social Layer (Techcrunch)

- **90 percent of consumers** trust recommendations from people they know (Nielsen)

- **$30 billion predicted revenues** for social commerce in 2015 (Booz & Company)

Don't think that what you've been doing so far in your business will become passé. If you've been successful in the past, and your strategies are still working for you, keep them up. The addition of social media to your marketing toolkit will only expand your customer base.

With the help of new media, you can discover new ways of doing just about everything relating to your business. Keep reading to find out more.

# Creating a Social Media Action Plan

So you've checked your customer demographics and decided to give social media commerce a try. Good first step. Remember, though, that success in social media commerce occurs meticulously step-by-step.

If you're thinking of using social media as an advertising channel, think again. In this new world of messages and engagement, old-school product messaging goes down in flames quickly.

With the understanding that you'll need to look at things in a slightly new way, here is the rest of your mission to enact your plan:

1. **Examine the various social media sites to understand the attitude of the denizens and how they connect.**

   Check out your competition and their interactions. By closely observing what they do, you'll get a good idea of what you can do — and perhaps do even better.

2. **Start slowly.**

   You might want to start with Twitter because it's a bit more forgiving than Facebook. The chance for disaster is less due to the brevity of messaging and the fast pace of Tweets.

3. **Visit my online list of big brands on Twitter (**`https://twitter.com/#!/MarshaCollier/brands-on-twitter`**).**

   Click the user names to see more Tweets. Be sure to check out the following examples of quality engagement:

   - @CEO_INGDIRECT, a stream from Peter Aceto, the CEO of INGDirect in Canada

   - @thinkgeek, a fun stream from thinkgeek.com, an online store for technophiles and geeks

   For more on engaging on Twitter, see Chapter 9.

4. **Decide whether your Twitter account (or accounts) should be in your business name.** If so, perhaps add another in your name. As the head of a business, your comments will add credibility to the stream. You might want to start with a personal stream and then branch out.

5. **Focus on some realistic objectives:**

   - *Generate leads:* Find people online who discovered your business and may benefit from (and purchase) your products or services.

   - *Answer questions and complaints online to improve customer service:* Many huge brands agree that social media is the new customer service. Chapter 13 discusses how customer service outreach succeeds in social media.

   - *Engage with customers:* Make old customers more loyal and entice new ones through communication and content. Perhaps Cyrano de Bergerac illustrates best how words and conversation can lead to love — or in your case, to new customers.

   - *Keep an eye on the competition:* Social media gives you the perfect anonymous platform to do just that. You can make a list of your competition's accounts (perhaps also businesses in your industry from other states) and check out what they are doing online.

   - *Identify new product ideas, services, or lines to carry:* Try *crowdsourcing*, a new-media phrase for using your online persona for research. You can run polls or simply ask questions to find new products or ideas that might enhance your bottom line.

   - *Increase traffic to your website and improve search engine rankings:* The purpose of social media commerce is to sell, and social media engagement helps you bring your newfound friends and followers to your website. Be sure to take some time and add some community and social content there as well. Part II gives you some great ideas on how to execute these plans for your audience.

   You can accomplish all these objectives easily — after you get in the trenches and begin to engage.

6. **Read this book.**

   You'll get a grasp of the technology and culture of the various social media sites.

7. **Prepare your company's governance model.**

   This model should include the guidelines and policies in Chapter 3, as well as procedures and educational resources (such as this book!).

8. **Meet with your employees to get their input.**

   Don't limit yourself to one meeting. Consider starting collaborative social media training with your employees. Work with them to refine your plans and evaluate your outreach as it unfolds. By sharing experiences, you will form a solid core for your plan.

9. **Gather the tools you want to use to make your company's online interaction and monitoring easier.**

   Check out Part IV for suggestions.

10. **Be prepared to measure your results.**

    Ultimately, your endeavors will build your client and customer base, which will result in a bigger bottom line. Be patient: The return on social media investment may not show up right away.

While monitoring your results, if one platform is giving you the oomph you need and another is not, put more focus on the performing one. Don't emphasize procuring large numbers of followers or fans; you want quality engagement.

Do not expect a massive increase in business a month from starting your outreach. Building a social community takes time, but the investment will be worth it. Loyal customers will also become your ambassadors and spread word of your brand, service, or business throughout their social communities and networks.

# Chapter 2

# Competing in the Social Media Realm

Competiton is a tough row to hoe, and an even tougher word to swallow. Don't you experience enough competition each day when you walk into work? Whatever your occupation, some person or company is out to scoop your clients or customers. Competition is part of what turns a business owner's hair gray.

Social media, however, is pretty much a level playing field. I say "pretty much" because the big boys hire high-powered agencies to handle their social media outreach. These big brands need big agencies to do what you, the small-business owner, can do every day.

You and your staff speak to your customers daily, so you innately understand social media. Bring your business personality and culture to the web by personalizing your website and social media interactions.

In this chapter, you find out why being small is better and why you should get past the learning curve for social media commerce as soon as possible. When your competition jumps onto social media, you'll have the value of these lessons and they'll be fumbling to get started.

# Big Advantages of a Small Business

As a small-business owner, you have enormous advantages over the big brands. Small firms can act more quickly than large ones. If the marketing team at a large company comes up with an idea, their proposal has to work its way through many layers of management, until someone at the top approves it or rejects it. A small business, on the other hand, can react quickly to new ideas.

Another aspect of large companies is that each department can become its own little fiefdom, or *silo*. Big businesses are often fraught with the "my department versus your department" culture, but small businesses have more of a "we're in this together to take care of the customer" attitude. Figure 2-1, from David Armano, executive vice president of Edelman Digital, shows how hard business has to work to create "team overlap," which is second nature to most small companies.

Entrepreneurs have the edge in another way. If they start a campaign on one social media network and then think that the campaign would work better on another platform, they can do a swift 180. Should an online promotion fail miserably, a change can happen almost immediately without permanent damage to a brand.

**Figure 2-1:**
Silos
encourage
defined
territories
versus
overlapping
responsibili-
ties.

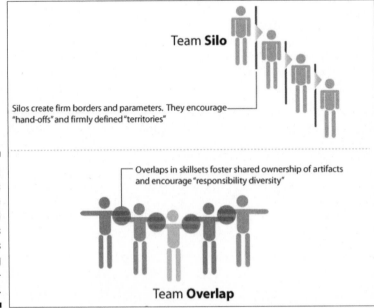

Team **Silo**

Silos create firm borders and parameters. They encourage "hand-offs" and firmly defined "territories"

Overlaps in skillsets foster shared ownership of artifacts and encourage "responsibility diversity"

Team **Overlap**

# There's no business like small business!

Don't be afraid or ashamed to admit that you are, indeed, a small-business owner. (Note that a small business isn't necessarily small. As defined by the Small Business Administration, a small business has fewer than 500 employees.) You're a risk taker, part of the crazy group of entrepreneurs that creates more than half of the non-farm, private GDP (gross domestic product) in the United States. Yes — more than *half*.

Need more proof as to the importance of small businesses? Small firms

✔ Represent 99.7 percent of all employer firms

✔ Employ just over half of all private sector employees

✔ Pay 44 percent of total U.S. private payroll

✔ Generated 64 percent of net new jobs over the past 15 years

✔ Hire 40 percent of high tech workers, such as scientists, engineers, and computer programmers

✔ Are 52 percent home-based and 2 percent franchises

✔ Made up 97.3 percent of all identified exporters and produced 30.2 percent of the known export value in 2007

✔ Produce 13 times more patents per employee than large patenting firms; these patents are twice as likely as large firm patents to be among the 1 percent most cited

(Source: U.S. Dept. of Commerce, Bureau of the Census and International Trade Administration; SBA Advocacy-funded research by Kathryn Kobe and CHI Research, Dept. of Labor, Bureau of Labor Statistics.)

Of the 5,369,068 U.S. firms that employ people, 99.7 percent have fewer than 500 employees and 78.8 percent have fewer than 10 employees. More recent data also suggests that very small firms — those with fewer than 10 employees — hire part-time employees at a rate almost twice that of very large firms (those with 1,000 or more employees).

Small-business owners can also reply to social media messages quickly, without having the messages pre-approved by a communications department. The allure of social media is that it happens in real-time. A spontaneous response, whether to breaking news or to comments, is far more effective than a scripted corporate missive.

Can you picture a major corporation hiring an agency and starting a social media campaign, only to have it end up in shambles? Big business can't possibly right commerce wrongs as quickly as you can. Social networking is your chance to shine.

# Examining Big-Business Mistakes

Learning from mistakes can be a humbling and sometimes expensive experience, unless the mistakes were made by someone else — preferably your competition. Many of us have been through the school of hard knocks when it comes to our businesses, and seeing someone else make the game-changing mistakes creates lessons that are so much sweeter.

Armchair quarterbacking can be fun, as long as the solution to the problem becomes a part of your stored knowledge. Following are a few short and expensive social media horror stories from personal brands:

- **Gilbert Gottfried:** A comedian and famous as the voice of the Aflac duck starting in 2005, Gottfried lost this lucrative job in March 2011 after posting a string of highly offensive Tweets, which he considered funny, about Japan's Tōhoku earthquake and tsunami. Figure 2-2 shows one of the least offensive quotes.

  Aflac takes natural disasters seriously — plus, the insurance company does 75 percent of its business in Japan. In Aflac's public firing announcement, Michael Zuna, senior VP and chief marketing officer, wrote that "Gilbert's recent comments about the crisis in Japan were lacking in humor and certainly do not represent the thoughts and feelings of anyone at Aflac. There is no place for anything but compassion and concern during these difficult times."

- **Mark Cuban:** The billionaire and Dallas Mavericks owner was fined several times by the NBA for using Twitter to publicly criticize officials during and after basketball games. He was fined $25,000 in 2009 and $75,000 in 2012. (ESPN reports that Cuban has been fined more than $1 million for his criticism of officials during his career.)

  His response to the NBA in 2009 was snarky. But in February 2012, he managed to turn his faux pas around by matching his fine with a charitable donation, as shown in Figure 2-3.

**Figure 2-2:** Even after publicly apologizing, Gottfried lost his long-standing job over Tweets like this.

@RealGilbert
Gilbert Gottfried

My Japanese doctor advised me to stay healthy I need 50 million gallons of water a day.

12 Mar via Twitter for iPhone ☆ Favorite ⅄ Retweet ↩ Reply

**Figure 2-3:** Marc Cuban pulled out a nice save by donating to charity.

Daniel Post-Senning, great grandson of Emily Post, was quoted in SmartMoney after the Cuban situation: "Public Tweets are a public and permanent record. . . . You're accountable for what you do on Twitter just as if you put up a sign in the main street of your town."

✔ **Connor Riley:** A 22-year-old pursuing a master's degree in information management and systems at University of California, Berkeley, Riley interviewed and was accepted for a position at Cisco Systems. Great, right? But Connor chose to assume her Twitter account was a private affair and Tweeted publicly: "Cisco just offered me a job! Now I have to weigh the utility of a fatty paycheck against the daily commute to San Jose and hating the work."

Cisco (founded in 1994) is a huge player in technology; they design, manufacture, and sell networking equipment. Their employees are also on Twitter. Shortly after Riley's Tweet, Cisco employee Tim Levad responded with the Tweet shown in Figure 2-4 — and Cisco retracted their job offer.

If you think 140 character comments (Tweets) made on Twitter can breeze by unnoticed, think again. Both Google and Microsoft's Bing integrate social data (also from Facebook) into their search results. In addition, since March 2006, the Library of Congress has been permanently archiving all public Tweets on Twitter. After you post, you can't take it back — and that post may return to haunt you or your business.

**Figure 2-4:** Cisco is clearly versed in the web.

@theconnor Who is the hiring manager. I'm sure they would love to know that you will hate the work. We here at Cisco are versed in the web.

timmylevad
Tim Levad

Make it difficult for you or someone who posts for your company to accidentally send a post from the wrong social media account. Keep your personal Facebook, Twitter, and Google+ accounts on one app or platform and the business side on another. This setup makes posting a little more inconvenient but can save you from embarrassing mix-ups.

In this section, I provide true stories that will illustrate some pitfalls of hiring someone to Tweet for your business.

## A Motor City kerfuffle

Traffic can be a challenge for the best of us. People often use their smartphones to make voice-to-Tweet comments about the crummy traffic they have to deal with daily. Every major city has its challenges when driving, and Detroit, home of America's automobile manufacturers, is no exception.

During a particularly tough drive to work one day, an employee of New Media Strategies (the social media agency for Chrysler) dropped the f-bomb in a Tweet, which is captured in Figure 2-5. I'm sure he thought he was Tweeting from his personal account — but he wasn't. He was Tweeting from the official @ChryslerAutos brand account.

The Tweet was deleted as soon as it was discovered, but not before it was reTweeted by many others. You can still see one of the reTweets here: `http://twitter.com/tverma29/status/45483012326031360`. (The Internet has a good memory.)

The Chrysler account bounced back with an apology, assuming their account had been compromised (a fairly safe assumption on first blush). But after a swift investigation, they learned the truth. The agency staffer lost his job, and Chrysler ended their contract with the agency.

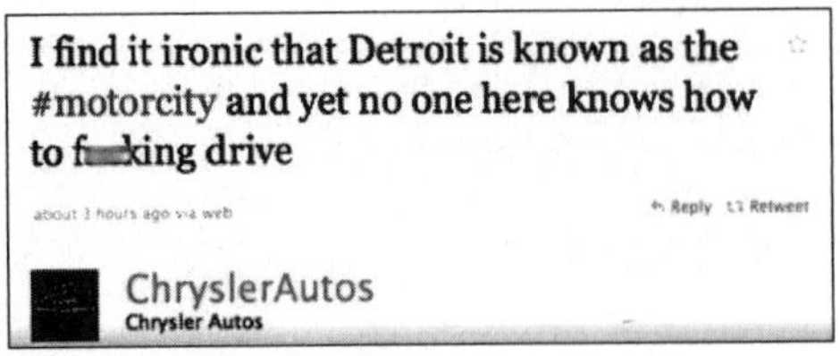

**Figure 2-5:**
Building a brand in social media rarely includes using the f-bomb.

> I find it ironic that Detroit is known as the #motorcity and yet no one here knows how to f▬king drive
>
> about 1 hours ago via web                          ← Reply  ⇄ Retweet
>
> **ChryslerAutos**
> Chrysler Autos

By 3 p.m. that day, Chrysler posted a blog entry stating that the employee who sent out the vulgar Tweet had been terminated (`http://blog.chryslerllc.com/blog.do?id=1337&p=entry`). They also wrote an apology: "Chrysler Group and its brands do not tolerate inappropriate language or behavior, and apologize to anyone who may have been offended by this communication."

The lesson to be learned: Keep your private accounts separate from your personal accounts.

The way a mis-Tweet is handled publicly can go a long way in a positive or a negative direction for a brand's reputation. A creative response can turn a gaffe into a blessing.

## Red Cross disaster recovery

Late one February night in 2011, a slip of the finger sent a mis-Tweet from the American Red Cross Twitter account. As shown in Figure 2-6, someone named Ryan was doing it right with some beer. Within a half hour, Wendy Harman, director of social strategy, was awoken from her sleep and was on the case.

An hour later, the Tweet was deleted and replaced with self-deprecating humor and an endearing Tweet that diffused the situation:

> *We've deleted the rogue Tweet but rest assured the Red Cross is sober and we've confiscated the keys.*

**Figure 2-6:** #getting-slizzered with the Red Cross.

However, enough people had seen the Tweet that #gettngslizzered became a trending topic on Twitter. Dogfish Head Brewery (the brand of beer mentioned in the Tweet) started reTweeting, asking for donations to the Red Cross.

The next day, the Red Cross posted the following to their blog `http://redcrosschat.org/2011/02/16/twitter-faux-pas`:

> *While we're a 130-year-old humanitarian organization, we're also made of up human beings. Thanks for not only getting that but for turning our faux pas into something good.*

## Revitalizing a brand with social media

When you think of Old Spice, what do you think of? Grandpa? Childhood Father's Day gifts from Walgreens? Pretty much. In 2010, Procter & Gamble went full out and did something about the brand's image. During the Super Bowl, they began "The Man Your Man Could Smell Like" ad campaign, featuring actor and former NFL practice squad wide receiver Isaiah Mustafa.

The commercial (`www.youtube.com/watch?v=owGykVbfgUE` ) was posted to YouTube in February with the comment line: "We're not saying this body wash will make your man smell like a romantic millionaire jet fighter pilot, but we are insinuating it." As of today, the video has garnered over 42 million views.

In June 2009, Old Spice joined Twitter and began to build followers based on the popularity of the Super Bowl ad. On July 12, 2010, a single post from Old Spice tempted their audience (see the figure). Waiting in the wings, Old Spice's marketing agency, Wieden + Kennedy, had a team of marketers, copywriters, techies, and social media specialists at the ready in a studio in Portland. For three days, they invited users to interact with the Old Spice Guy on various social networks and tracked responses. The comebacks were sent not only to web celebrities but also to everyday people who had previously commented on social platforms and showed an affinity for the brand.

Fans responded with comments and homemade videos, and the team answered with comments and videos. In the following three days, the team filmed 185 30-second videos in real time; responding to mentions of @OldSpice from high-profile social media influencers, including the one pictured here to my friend, Jim Alden (@TechFrog on Twitter).

The videos were filled with non sequiturs delivered by Mustafa standing in his shower. His offbeat, cool-dude persona, peppered with carefully scripted responses, made each video more engaging than the one before. Allowing the team complete freedom to write marketing content in real-time was considered a brave move by Procter & Gamble.

At the end of the campaign, the "Old Spice Man" thanked everyone and said goodbye in a video (`www.youtube.com/watch?v=nFDqvKtPgZo`.) In three days, Old Spice had attained 1.8 billion campaign impressions. According to *PRWeek,* Old Spice sales increased 107 percent over the previous month.

Although this type of campaign is beyond the realm of most small businesses, scaling down the idea might just work.

The lesson to be learned: Not every brand is lucky enough to have some-one like Wendy Harman to handle their social media. Your social media responses need to be posted by someone invested in her job and your busi-ness. Immediate response with a mea culpa shows you're human, and humor can make an impropriety endearing.

# Studying Success Stories

Small business, big business — eventually all businesses will be affected by social media. That's the result of the world becoming "social" on the web.

Many small businesses and professionals are successful right now. The best don't hire outside companies to write their posts and handle their online per-sona. Instead, they build their bottom line personally.

With or without huge budgets, business *can* make a mark and engage with cus-tomers online. Get started now and own your space in the future. In this sec-tion, I show you a few outstanding examples of professional-grade outreach.

Run a search on Google for the businesses described in this section. Then run a search on your competition. You'll see that successful companies have a full first page of search results from their web, e-commerce, and social media connections.

# Finding out who has Klout

Want to find the leaders and the laggards? The Klout site measures the influence and engagement levels of those in the social media arena. Each persona or brand is assigned a Klout score, which changes daily. Since 2008, Klout has been measuring online accounts in many platforms on social media. From their site:

> *The Klout Score measures influence based on your ability to drive action. Every time you create content or engage you influence others. The Klout Score uses data from social networks in order to measure:*

✔ *True Reach: How many people you influence*

✔ *Amplification: How much you influence them*

✔ *Network Impact: The influence of your network*

A Klout score measures influence on a scale of 1 to 100. Over 100 million people are followed by Klout, which analyzes more than 2.7 billion pieces of content and connections daily.

Go to http://klout.com and, in the search box at the top of the page, type a topic that relates to your business. For example, in Figure 2-7, I've searched *customer service.* By searching a topic (food, restaurants, medicine, lawyers — you get the picture), you can find the top influencers. Study these accounts and see what they are doing right in social media. Embrace their best practices and make them your own.

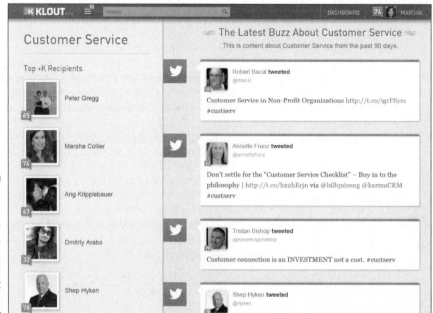

**Figure 2-7:**
A topic search on Klout shows the online leaders in that industry.

# Social media reach for professionals

When talking to degreed professionals about the importance of social media in their marketing plan, I get the same response I received from shopping center marketing managers in the mid-90s. They can't fathom that such tactics are for them.

Granted, marketing a professional's services takes a certain amount of delicacy. Wrong moves in new media can switch your image from professional to huckster. For example, lawyers are in business to uphold the law and defend their clients. In social media, their attitude and intelligence must shine.

Yet people do go online to find degreed professionals in almost every field. They search for online posts regarding their particular situations (divorce, skin rashes, sore gums), and professionals who post online often snag their business.

 You can connect with a customer or a client on many platforms, but professionals especially should have a website as the hub for client outreach. Any additional social media outreach should direct the potential customer to your website, the nucleus of your information. Trust, concern, and content (again) are pivotal to building your online (and offline) following.

A remarkable example of a professional site is `www.rosen.com`, from Rosen Law Firm (the largest divorce firm in North Carolina). Rosen Law Firm opened in 1990 and has had a website since 1994. Lee Rosen, the firm's founder — and social media maven — had not only a vibrant website for the firm but also a personal presence for the brand on YouTube (over 1.3 million views since 2008), Twitter (@LeeRosen, with over 18K followers), Facebook, LinkedIn, Google+, and legal blogs (at `http://divorcediscourse.com/` and `www.stayhappilymarried.com`).

A visit to their website, shown in Figure 2-8, opens with the opportunity to hear some personal, uplifting words from Lee Rosen. In a friendly manner, he expresses concern for and encouragement to the viewer. He guides visitors to the different areas of the site and invites people to post questions to the forums. Even if you don't watch the video, a scroll down the home page reveals the many ways that prospective clients can engage with the firm. The site has no hard sell, only comforting and accurate legal information.

Rosen Law has covered almost every base possible on their website, with links to the following:

✔ **Divorce article library:** Prospective clients can come here to pore over the well-indexed information on the state's divorce laws. Hundreds of topics are discussed with authority.

✔ **Life stories:** This page links to personal divorce case studies, where real clients tell their stories through words and video.

**Figure 2-8:**
Rosen Law
Firm has
won many
awards for
online legal
service
innovations.

✔ **North Carolina divorce forums:** Three lively forums on emotional, legal, and parenting issues are moderated by Rosen Law Firm attorneys, for the benefit of visitors to the site. To post, users must register on the site.

✔ **Divorce talk radio:** Rosen attorneys host a live weekly call-in podcast at 11 a.m. EST every Wednesday to discuss the numerous fine points of separation, divorce, and coping. The shows are archived on the site by category.

✔ **Stay happily married:** This link goes to the sister site, www.stayhappily married.com, where visitors can get advice on how to beat the odds. The site is filled with information from counselors as well as links to other websites with advice.

✔ **Do-it-yourself divorce instructions and forms:** Rosen provides step-by-step instructions, should someone want to do a divorce on their own, along with all requisite forms and sample agreements.

✔ **Lawyer locator:** Find a list of lawyers for clients out of the Rosen Law firm area.

✔ **Apps:** The site contains an easy-to-use North Carolina alimony and child support calculator. Rosen Law Firm also has the child support calculator available on the iTunes store as an iPhone app.

Yes, there's more: FAQs and even a divorce legal fee calculator. The Rosen Law Firm presence on Facebook, shown in Figure 2-9, links to their blog posts, podcasts, and the main website for more information.

# Growing a base for an online retailer

Whether you're an online or a bricks-and-mortar retailer, your web presence can make a big difference in your gross sales. But having a store on the web presents a unique challenge. If you put up an e-commerce site without doing the proper work, no one will show up. Websites have to get some traction through online interactions and quality content before they bring in some coin, and social media is the fastest way to begin your monetization on the web.

Just as we can learn from the mistakes of others, we can learn from their successes. Next up is the story of someone I met in my early days writing about eBay. Their online business is one of the top e-tailers in their category.

In 1999, businessman Gordon Becker was selling coins on eBay as a hobby. He also had a love of fine watches and had collected far too many. His wife, Carolyn, suggested that he sell some watches on eBay, thinking that the customer demographics for rare coins and fine timepieces were similar.

By 2003, sales got so big on eBay that they started the Beckertime.com website. Combined eBay and website sales in 2005 soared to $4.5 million. Gordon passed away that year and Matthew continued in the footsteps of his father (and best friend). "Nothing makes me happier than to continue his tradition and think that he'd be so proud for keeping our customers happy and making money, and for all the right reasons."

Today, their website (www.beckertime.com) is the hub for Internet sales, as shown in Figure 2-10. As one of only ten diamond-level Powersellers (eBay's highest level seller designation), they are the largest provider of pre-owned Rolex watches on eBay, with a monthly sales volume of more than $1,000,000. They have an 11-year positive feedback rating of 99.9%.

Aside from selling items (and offering repair services) on the site, they provide educational information on Rolex, how-to articles, links to related content, and a glossary. Their site offers a three-day money back guarantee, no questions asked: "We do business the way karma says you should do business."

Their pages also stress their policy: "If you ever want to trade in your Beckertime Rolex for an upgraded model, a newer model, or just a different one, you can exchange your watch and receive the full price of what you paid towards the purchase of another pre-owned Rolex."

Beckertime has a broad social media outreach to Rolex fans:

- ✔ **YouTube:** Beckertime, to date, has 10 instructional videos on how to wind, set, and take care of various Rolex watches.
- ✔ **Blog:** The blog is the hub for articles that feed out to the web. Every few days, a new post appears on various Rolex models, how to spot authenticity, how a Rolex works, and more.

**Figure 2-10:** Beckertime runs discounts for those who follow them in social media.

✔ **Facebook:** People love to connect on Facebook, and Beckertime's page is full of interesting posts. People post Rolex questions and Matthew answers swiftly and sincerely. As you can see in Figure 2-11, their Facebook page has links to their other social media platforms.

✔ **Google+:** The Google+ presence links to posts from their blogs. Although interaction isn't as brisk at this time, being on Google+ is a worthwhile investment in the future.

✔ **Pinterest:** Beckertime has an almost encyclopedic volume of photos of the many variations and styles of Rolex watches. They see lots of participation on Pinterest, with likes and repins.

✔ **Newsletter:** Don't consider e-mail old school. Beckertime still gets sign-ups for their e-mail newsletter.

Beckertime continues to increase their business, looking to join any new media platform that will help get the word out.

**Figure 2-11:** Facebook links everything together.

# Burgers with a little humor on the side

Many businesses cover two ends of the spectrum. I believe that Joe Sorge, owner of five restaurants in the Milwaukee area, covers an entire rainbow. His main Twitter stream, @JoeSorge, is personal and engaging. Here are two of his Tweets: "seems like 1/2 my stream during business hours is made up of 'list' blog posts" and in his next Tweet: "The other half is restaurant food porn. *head2desk* :) #mybad." (*Food porn* is the new media phrase for pictures or descriptions of incredible edibles — more social media jargon is defined in the Glossary). Joe is a funny guy, and he's funny enough to support multiple Twitter accounts.

Joe's company, Hospitality Democracy, has other active accounts on Twitter to represent his restaurants. Following is a list of his Twitter accounts and his brief description of the restaurants:

✔ **@AJBombers**: Fun! w/ a side of Pnuts, Burgers, & Beer. Milwaukee's best cheeseburger! See the figure for AJBOMBERS fun Twitter feed.

✔ **@SwigMilwaukee**: Milwaukee's small plate pioneer! Now in the 3rd Ward with lunch and entrees too. We love wine

✔ **@Water_Buffalo**: Milwaukee's home for comfort food and riverfront dining!

✔ **@SmokeShack**: Barbeque, Barbecue or BBQ? Now Open in Milwaukee's Historic 3rd Ward. Get here early! We sell out.

✔ **@ZaffirosPizza**: Famous for its thin-crust pizza, Italian dishes and neighborhood bar atmosphere.

# The "Bagel that won the West" goes worldwide

If you own a local business with one or a few locations, you might think, "Why bother with the Internet?" Well, wouldn't some extra profit be a good idea? You'd be surprised how social media can bring in new customers — and perhaps help you sell your products online.

In this section, you read about an example of the American dream: a family business that's been successful for more than 65 years. Today, they are boosting sales through social media and their website.

David Ustin, the son of an immigrant, started working at a New York bakery at a very young age. One day, he overheard a union representative say that California had no good bagels. His entrepreneurial spirit took over, and he, two business partners, and his wife opened Western Bagel, the first bagel bakery in Los Angeles, in 1947. At their grand opening, they sold 4,773 dozen bagels, totaling $1,145.90!

The business moved in 1958 and they began a wholesale route, serving local restaurants and delis. They moved again in 1993 to a new factory, nearly doubling their production capacity. David's son, Steve, who worked with his father during high school and college, bought out his father's surviving partner and is now president of the company. Today, Western Bagel has ten restaurants in Los Angeles, plus the old bakery in the valley. Steve Ustin has been true to the family's entrepreneurial dream.

In early 2010, I stopped by the bakery and saw the sign shown in Figure 2-12. Perhaps Steve's son, Brad, established the company's Facebook and Twitter accounts. Their restaurant locations also feature creative signage inviting customers to join them on the social media sites.

On their Facebook page (shown in Figure 2-13), which has close to 7,000 likes, they regularly post bagel lore, news, luscious photos of their specialties, and luncheon deals. Customers can ask questions about their items, such as when the green bagels celebrating St. Patrick's Day will be available. Comments about their stores and restaurants are posted almost daily.

You can also find fans reviewing and complimenting their restaurants on Yelp (trending 5 stars). Western Bagel also has a presence on foursquare — one location alone has close to 700 check-ins to date! (See Chapter 8 for more on these platforms).

**Figure 2-12:**
Possibly
the biggest
sign I've
ever seen
promoting
social media
outreach!

**Figure 2-13:**
The
Western
Bagel
Facebook
page gets a
lot of traffic
from bagel
lovers.

Western Bagel has also enabled their website for e-commerce, as shown in
Figure 2-14. So if you'd like to try one of the "Bagels that won the West," visit
their website at www.westernbagel.com and order some!

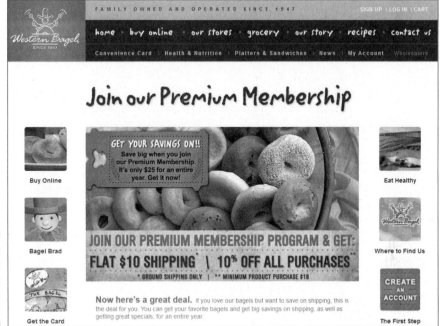

**Figure 2-14:**
Delicious
bagels can
be shipped
to you.

Western Bagel has certainly embraced the best of the twentieth and twenty-first centuries.

## Stellar Twitter accounts

As you've probably figured out, I'm a big believer in learning from studying others. I pay attention to quality outreach on all platforms. In this section, I describe two Twitter accounts worth watching. Observing their quality and different styles is worth more than a moment's glance. They both represent huge businesses, yet both are customer-service driven:

✔ **Kathy Ireland:** An example of a brilliant entrepreneur is @kathyireland on Twitter (see Figure 2-15). Yes, the stunning *Sports Illustrated* swimsuit model turned multibillion dollar entrepreneur, author, and head of Kathy Ireland Worldwide, is on social media. License Global Magazine named Kathy Ireland Worldwide the 28th most powerfully licensed brand, and Fairchild Publications listed Kathy Ireland as one of the 50 most influential people in fashion.

Her companies maintain blogs and Facebook pages, and she personally Tweets almost every day. An early adopter (and smart marketer), Ms. Ireland joined Twitter in October of 2008, according to http://www.whendidyoujointwitter.com/. The woman who took the time to be a key speaker for the American Israel Public Affairs Committee (AIPAC) conference, with such luminaries as President Shimon Peres and President Barack Obama, chats with real people — discussing real issues.

Few people know how to build a brand better than Kathy. Follow her lead. Read her Twitter stream and see how she does it.

✔ **American Airlines:** Your business is probably not as big as American Airlines, but you can learn some lessons from them. They maintain a page on Facebook, post photos on flickr, have videos on YouTube, and run an active Twitter account. People from every corner of the planet Tweet about flight delays, lost baggage, and any other complaint a flyer these days might have (see Figure 2-16).

@AmericanAir on Twitter answers as many Tweets as they can, averaging 33 per day. (They helped find my tablet when I left it on a flight, and directed me to a changed gate when I was late.)

**Figure 2-15:**
Kathy
Ireland
started on
Twitter in
2008.

**Figure 2-16:**
@American-
Air often
takes it
on the
chin with
a cheery
response.

# Finding the Time to Initiate Social Media Commerce

Now that you've read about these stellar examples, are you thinking that social media will take up too much of your day? You probably have barely enough time to finish everything you need to do now, right? I feel your pain. My own social media outreach takes a portion of my already full day. However, my business has grown due to social media. I sell more online than I did before there were platforms to get my name and my product out.

## Hiring help

If you find that you simply don't have the time for social media outreach, you may have to hire someone.

Many people claim to be experts in the social media realm, so be careful when you hire someone. Look for the following:

- **Their personal social media stream:** If they aren't active on one of the major sites, don't waste your time interviewing them. Social media is a walk-the-walk type of business. If you don't do it, you don't understand it.

- **Work examples:** They should be proud to provide examples of the work they've performed for their clients.

- **References:** Call their current and former clients and find out if they had a satisfactory working relationship.

- **Level of maturity:** Someone must have life experiences to fully understand the consequences of Tweeting for a business.

- **Communication skills:** For social media execution, one needs to fully understand the meaning of innuendoes and the art of communication. Getting the point across requires top-notch writing skills.

- **Pricing:** Know their prices and the level of service for those prices up front. On the low end, the person might Tweet five times a day for you and respond to those who Tweet back. On the high end, he might put together a Facebook page design and manage your Facebook responses. Additional platforms add to the costs.

Plenty of qualified, experienced social media freelancers and companies are available. I put together a directory and posted it on my website at www. reputationspecialist.com.

The person you hire should at the minimum have a good grasp of your business and ideally be an expert in your field of endeavor. For example, if my business were in the automotive field, I'd seek out Gary May of Los Angeles (on Twitter @imacsweb). He has 19 years of business development in the bicycle and automotive industries, and his company is highly respected as a leader in the automotive social media scene.

## Doing your own social media

Participating in social media is not such a chore. After you get into the swing, you'll look forward to connecting with your customers. Tweeting or posting doesn't have to be a daily task — until you enjoy it, at which point it may become a habit. For example, every day while drinking my morning coffee, I respond to Tweets.

Throughout this book, I mention various sites to which you can connect. Many can send an e-mail notification (or an SMS to your phone) when you have a comment that needs to be moderated or answered. This way, you'll be able to stay on top of responses.

In addition, phone and computer apps can automate posts. Chapter 16 gives you a tour of popular applications that can schedule your posting on more than one platform — all at once.

Social media is the key to twenty-first century commerce. The examples in this chapter, I hope, will inspire you to do something similar for your business.

# Chapter 3

# Creating a Social Media Policy

*In This Chapter*

▶ Shaping media guidelines for your employees

▶ Determining the topics to include in your policies

*W*hen entering the world of new media, the critical starting point is to develop social media policies and guidelines that govern employee behavior on the social web. Consider the web as an open ear to anything and everything you choose to post publicly — comments, news, and advertising included. All posts give a clue to your opinions and business direction, so be sure to select your words carefully.

Common sense (which we all know isn't always so common when dealing on the Internet) comes into play when executing your outreach. Very little on the Internet disappears, so we live and die by every word we place on the web. This may sound a bit dire, but as my father said, "Never put anything in writing that you wouldn't want to appear on the front page of the *New York Times.*"

As of March 2012, 76 percent of companies do not have a clearly defined social media policy. In this chapter, I help you to begin forming yours.

## Twelve Guiding Words

Someone whose opinion I respect, Farris Timimi, M.D (Mayo Clinic cardiologist and medical director of Mayo Clinic's Center for Social Media, @FarrisTimimi), cuts through long-winded policies and sums social media rules into 12 words to guide you:

> *Don't lie, don't pry*
>
> *Don't cheat, can't delete*
>
> *Don't steal, don't reveal*

The Mayo Clinic's Friday Faux Pas blog (yes, even the Mayo Clinic is in social media), at `http://socialmedia.mayoclinic.org/category/friday-faux-pas/`, is an ongoing reminder of how social media posts can go horribly wrong. A sample blog post is shown in Figure 3-1.

**Figure 3-1:**
The Mayo Clinic's Friday Faux Pas of social media.

# Determining Employee Guidelines

It seems perfectly plausible that a large percentage of the people you hire will be personally participating in social media in some form. Their emotional (and legal) investment in your company may not be at the top of their minds when it comes to their Facebook, Twitter, or other online postings.

Off-handed comments, unauthorized deals, and personal mentions about your company can put your business and even your customers at risk. One rogue post can unravel years of hard work and reputation building.

## $50,000 fine for leaving out a few small details

Spirit Airlines was fined $50,000 by the U.S. Department of Transportation for not clearly disclosing the full price in a 2011 promotion. As part of their campaign, Spirit posted Tweets on Twitter about $9 one-way tickets from Los Angeles to Las Vegas. Sounds like a great deal, right? What they didn't say was that including taxes and fees, the $9 fares were $35 each way. Additionally, to qualify for the $9 fare, customers had to sign up for Spirit's "$9 fare club" for an annual fee of $59.95. Don't forget the examples in Chapter 2 if you start to feel cocky and Tweet before you think.

Facebook and Twitter are not the only platforms where gaffes occur. You need to clearly outline all media connections, including LinkedIn and YouTube, in your social media guidelines. Your employees may also participate in video sharing, photo sharing, blogs (their own or commenting on others), podcasts, wikis, online communities, and "private" groups, such as those on Facebook. Figure 3-2 shows the vast outreach your employees may have.

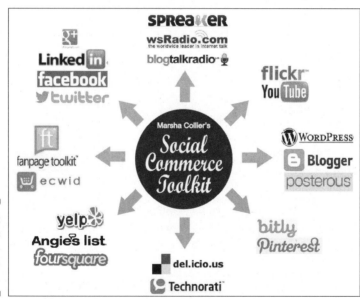

**Figure 3-2:** Platforms that disseminate new media.

Everyone you employ is a reflection of your company. Whether or not they put a disclaimer in their personal online biography ("All my Tweets are my own" or "Opinions and thoughts are mine"), customers, friends and other employees might know that they work for you.

Before jumping on the terror bandwagon about what your employees might post, consider the benefits of having your business mentioned on a world-wide platform. The point of being on new media is that you can spread the word in a positive way.

Hiring employees who understand your company culture — those who have a group spirit and are not self-focused — is the first step toward not only positive social media mentions but also a productive work environment. Employees who can back your ideas and embellish with their own experience are invested in your success and reputation online.

Be sure to keep confidential information confidential. Employees should never be able to share metrics, internal communications, and performance data about your company.

When it comes to employee governance, try to keep it light. My publisher, John Wiley & Sons, posted employee social media guidelines that promote experimentation with engaging their audiences through social networks. The company trusts that their employees understand the ramifications of partici-pating in social media.

Consider the following employee guidelines in your company social media policy:

- ✔ It is best not to participate in personal attacks, foul language, disparag-ing comments, harassment, or topics of a flammable nature. In reality, comments such as these never lend to any form of credibility.

- ✔ Speak respectfully about the company and our current, past, and poten-tial employees. What one says reflect back on all those involved.

- ✔ Before posting photos of or tagging fellow employees, clients, vendors, and business partners, be sure to ask their permission.

- ✔ Always identify yourself as an employee when referring to our business or services.

- ✔ If you see a customer service issue involving your company, alert the appropriate person within the organization so he can respond immediately.

✔ Unless you are given explicit permission, please do not speak on behalf of the company or represent that you do.

✔ Your personal sites should remain personal in nature and should not be used to share work-related information.

On my website, I list links to online versions of policies from major corporations, which should give you further ideas for your own governance plan.

# Establishing Clear Company Guidelines

Your organization's social network outreach is best handled by a single person (or a single department in a larger company). In this way, you avoid duplication and the generation of opposing ideas.

If you feel that the nature of your business means certain topics are verboten, state such topics clearly. Outline your expectations for social engagement and provide examples of what is and is not acceptable. The point of social connections with your customers is commerce, so it makes plain sense not to do anything to alienate the reader or commenter. (Your online reputation and perception are where social commerce is so intrinsically tied to customer service.)

Chapter 7 gives you a good idea of the type of posts that will engage your audience. When crafting the items you post, remember that certain pictures and articles appeal to different groups, so the demographics of your customer should guide you. For example, if your customer base is less than 30 years old, news stories quoted from the AARP website might not resonate. If your customer base reflects all age groups, you will need to pepper your posts with ideas that appeal to a broad range of customers.

New York–based Lisa Merriam is a brand consultant who has made a career of helping companies build and manage brands. On her blog (`http://merriam associates.com`), she shares the following "basic points to cover" in your social media policy:

✔ **Make sure people know they are personally responsible for what they write.** After something has been said, it can't be unsaid, and there is no telling who will see what is written. Everyone should think twice before hitting the Share button.

✔ **Be real.** Don't create a fake persona or a faceless corporate presence. Use your real name and identify your relationship with the brand.

✔ **Think about your audience.** You will be talking to clients, future clients, employees, bosses, suppliers, competitors — everybody. Be careful not to alienate them. Ray Catena Lexus, a New York area car dealer, likes the Mets on his Facebook page — how do Yankee fans feel?

✔ **Stay away from religion, politics, and sex.** Good advice for polite company at a dinner party is also good advice for using social media. Be especially careful when thinking of voicing a negative opinion about anything — and never badmouth the competition.

✔ **Don't get defensive.** Your company may come under criticism. Resist the urge to fight back. Be polite to detractors and use the opportunity to present additional information and resources. Don't call people names or denigrate their thinking.

✔ **Don't misuse copyrighted material.** Be sure to provide attribution for any material you share. Never post confidential material.

✔ **Be helpful, bring value, be amusing.** Don't just blare out commercial messages and public relations fluff. If you get a reputation for being a walking, talking commercial, you'll be considered a spammer and will be tuned out — often rudely.

When training employees on the fine points of social media, be sure to include these important points.

In June 2012, the National Labor Relations Board (NLRB) protected social media under the category of "concerted activities":

> *Company policies on social media are usually adopted in order to inform employees of the company's position on use of the company name or logo in social media posts, to prohibit dissemination of confidential business information of the company, and to prohibit employees from presenting their personal views as those of the company. While these are all legitimate concerns, and prohibiting this conduct does not violate the National Labor Relations Act, many employers have wrestled with stating these legitimate policies specifically enough that they could not be broadly construed as chilling employees' rights to use social media to communicate with co-workers about workplace conditions.*

This discussion lends credibility to an important dialogue of the employer/employee relationship and the Fourth Amendment. I suggest that you visit the NLRB website (`www.nlrb.gov`) and search for *social media* to learn about further developments.

# Part II
# Adapting Your Web Presence

The 5th Wave                    By Rich Tennant

"Here's an idea. Why don't you start a social
network for doofuses who think they know
how to set a broken leg, but don't."

# In this part . . .

*I*t's time to figure out how to make your website engaging. You'll want to make it both a place where customers visit for real, sharable information as well as a hub for your social media outreach. Find out which pages can be added to the site — and shared on social networks — to help build an engaged community. You also discover how participating in the 411 in review sites can boost your bottom line.

# Chapter 4

# Passive Engagement: Creating a Social Persona through Your Website

● ● ● ● ● ● ● ● ● ● ● ● ● ● ● ● ● ● ● ● ● ● ● ● ● ● ● ● ● ● ● ● ● ● ● ● ● ● ● ● ● ● ●

*In This Chapter*

▶ Planning and hosting your website

▶ Attracting customers

▶ Starting a blog

● ● ● ● ● ● ● ● ● ● ● ● ● ● ● ● ● ● ● ● ● ● ● ● ● ● ● ● ● ● ● ● ● ● ● ● ● ● ● ● ● ● ●

*P*ossibly the last place you can imagine you might get social with your customers is on your business website. You might initially feel that a site is unnecessary because your business is local or because you are a service professional (such as a doctor, a lawyer, or an accountant). Au contraire.

Your company website is on the web for a reason (no, not because everyone else has one). It is there for you to connect with your current customers or clients — and attract future customers. For those reasons alone, a website generates revenue for you when it's presented in a social format, with the customer in mind.

Read this chapter for ideas on refreshing the look of your company website and for adding value. Social commerce changes happen quickly on the web, and you want to be sure not to miss the latest tool that will draw customers to your site.

# Getting Started with the Basics

A website is an essential tool for sharing information and promoting your products or services. You don't need to hire a fancy consultant to put together your site; you need someone who understands you and your business. That person should help you set up the technical part of your site. The content should reflect your business and your company culture.

Why are you in business? Part of building confidence (and revenue) from your web outreach is convincing visitors that your business is valuable. Persuading others that you take your business seriously will go a long way to bringing them in as customers.

Your business is your passion, right? The other day, I spoke to two small-business owners. One is a sprinkler repairman and the other is a coin dealer. I got the same message from both: They care about their business. They were passionate about doing their job with the utmost care and respecting their customers.

Most people want to do business with those who enjoy their work. When planning your site, your company culture has to come across the moment the home page loads.

## Planning your site

Before you set up your website or improve an existing site, set aside some time for introspection. Consider the following:

- **Purpose:** What is the purpose of your business? You may think the answer is obvious, but it might not be obvious to a site visitor. Your site needs to reflect you (as the business owner), your company, and the industry you serve. What is the message you want to get across to your client?

- **Focus:** What is the main focus of your site? Will your website be an online hub for a bricks-and-mortar business? Will you be selling a product? (Chapters 10 and 11 provide ideas of what you can sell — no matter what business you're in). When people land on your site, they need to know at a glance what you're all about. The tone and design of your site tells the visitor who you are.

  Take a look at the two restaurant landing pages shown in Figures 4-1 and 4-2. Although both sites are in the same business, you can identify at a glance their different focus.

**Figure 4-1:**
The Daily Grill in Los Angeles stresses healthy eating.

**Figure 4-2:**
AJ Bombers tantalizes the cheeseburger vice!

✔ **Time:** How much time will you or one of your staff devote to the site after it's up and running? Do you want a site that's self-working? Perhaps you prefer something that promotes but does not have to be updated weekly? You can achieve that goal with a few catchy tools, as you discover in the next few sections.

✔ **Customers:** Who will visit your site? Yes, you hope prospective customers visit, but who are they? Do you know the demographics of your customer base? Your site needs to appeal to the widest demographic possible, while giving a nod to your core customers. (In Chapter 8, I describe some free tools that can give you ideas for positioning your website's reach.)

After you answer these questions, it's time to look for a place to host your site.

## Hosting your site

When building a website, one of the first things you'll have to decide is where to host your site. An online search for web hosting will net you hundreds, perhaps thousands, of results. Carefully consider which company should host your site. If all goes well, you'll be married to this company for a long time. For beginners, look for a web host that includes a web design tool and templates. A few good examples are Network Solutions, Web.com, and GoDaddy.com. The learning curve is usually gentle, and the best companies have quality tech support.

Think about the features you may want from your web host. Decide whether you will need the following:

✔ **Upgradability:** You will probably start with a beginner plan, so be sure your web host offers an upgrade. Your site may develop and become more popular than you can fathom (for now).

✔ **FTP:** File Transfer Protocol (FTP) enables you to upload and download files and images from your website hosting account. FTP is not compatible with many of the do-it-yourself web publishing tools.

✔ **HTML5:** Whether you know what HTML5 is now, know that you'll want to be able to use this tool in the future. Make sure that your host will be able to accommodate HTML5 (now or in the near future).

✔ **E-mail addresses:** You may want to have business e-mails that include your domain name, such as mcollier@coolebaytools.com. You may also want to have e-mail addresses for your billing or customer service departments. Not all web hosts offer custom e-mail boxes.

✔ **Disk space:** If you want to upload audio or video files for visitors to use (rather than linking to them on, say, YouTube), you'll need a lot of disk space.

✔ **Bandwidth:** Bandwidth (similar to a smartphone data plan) is the amount of traffic your website receives. If you have many visitors to your site, you'll use more bandwidth. Additional bandwidth is often included as a site upgrade, and many sites offer unlimited bandwidth.

Pricing isn't the only thing to look at when selecting a web host. Customer service is pivotal whether you are a beginner or an advanced user. When checking out the company's customer service, make sure they are available 24/7 because you may want to work on your site during off hours.

Hosting is important, but design is the face of your business. Templates can make the initial design easy. When you want to expand, however, I recommend not going the do-it-yourself route. Find someone whose aesthetics fit your style — and whose price fits your budget — to work with you to design the site.

Whether or not you hire someone, make sure there is an easy way for you to update the site yourself. Updating a website can be as easy as using a word-processing program. Calling a web designer every time you want to make a minor change can become burdensome — and expensive.

Some people prefer to hire a company that dives in and manages *everything* in one big package: website, e-commerce, and social media outreach. The results are generally less than inspiring, even if you pay big bucks. No one knows your business like you do. Make sure that the person handling your web outreach understands your business and core values, or find someone on your staff to oversee and approve what appears on the web under your name. Your website is a reflection of you and your business.

## Putting together the pieces

Many companies look for an economical solution and put their sites together themselves. With an expert company, and the suggestions I give you in this chapter, you should be on the web swiftly.

Whether you hire someone to design your website or are planning to do it yourself, all websites should have the following basic pages:

✔ **Home page:** Your home page is the first face of your company the website visitor sees. Make the home page crisp, clean, and easy to read. Welcome your customers and let them know — at first contact — how important they are to you and your business.

Be sure to have clickable links to lead your customers to the rest of the pages in the site. Even a simple site, like the one in Figure 4-3, can get the point across while linking to related pages.

Your website visitors will have different levels of reading ability. Keep your wording simple (unless you're selling to or wanting to connect only with rocket scientists or enterprise-level business). Take a tip from the way we write in the *For Dummies* series.

✓ **Products/Services:** If you have products or services to sell, start with a page that lists them individually. At least provide a short synopsis of the items and include a link to other pages on your site.

✓ **About page:** Who are you? When was your company founded? (Here's where your mission statement comes in.) What do you do that sets you apart from others in your field? In addition to your About page, include a link to the Meet the Staff page and more. Figure 4-4 is a stunning About page from a landscape company.

✓ **Meet the Staff page:** Your key employees (or partners) have a vested interest in your company. You hired them because they do a great job and have a passion for their work. List them on the Meet the Staff page. (If you want to include resumes, add a link to another page.) Give your site visitors a reason to trust that your staff will do a great job.

**Figure 4-3:** im@cs consulting tells their story quickly.

For example, Zappos.com is serious about their business but takes a humorous approach on their web pages. Photos and short descriptions of each department link from the main Meet the Zappos Family page. For example, Figure 4-5 shows the Zappos.com IT (information technology) staff along with a funny, casual description.

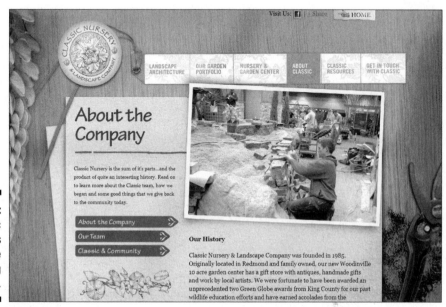

**Figure 4-4:**
Classic Nursery's About page is inviting and homey.

**Figure 4-5:**
The Zappos IT team looks like a fun bunch of people!

On the Meet Your Staff page, show that your company consists of real people. Include photos of you and your staff (even if the staff consists of family members). People love to see the people with whom they do business. If you'd like to give your site a warm, fuzzy feeling, toss in a picture of your office pet or family dog.

Don't use overly posed images with you and your staff in suits. That type of photo looks like it should be framed and hanging on the wall of the local Chamber of Commerce — in 1980. Also, don't use overly made-up photos taken at a glamour studio.

If you visit the Zappos website (`www.zappos.com`), click the About link at the bottom of the page and then click the Meet Our Monkeys link. Figure 4-6 shows their head monkey, CEO Tony Hsieh, in a casual pose.

Show friends and colleagues the pictures you plan to use (or post them on your site and send me the link). If your friends don't smile when they look at the photos, they probably don't portray you or your company. Be you, be real.

✔ **Privacy policy:** Your privacy policy is a statement that discloses the ways your website gathers, uses, discloses, and manages a customer's or client's data. Several state and federal laws require a website privacy statement. Your policy can be so complex that it covers an entire page or as simple as the following: *Your privacy is important to us. Any information collected on this site will not be sold or shared with third parties.*

**Figure 4-6:** CEO Tony Hsieh sporting a Zappos tattoo on his shaved head.

Most businesses are safe using this simple example. But if you intend to share or use the data gathered on your site from subscribers or clients (such as e-mail addresses) in any way, you are bound (legally as well as morally) to disclose what and how you share.

Because legal ramifications are involved in online privacy issues, I recommend going to Iubenda, at `www.iubenda.com/en`. On this site, shown in Figure 4-7, you can generate a privacy policy for an existing website in three steps. Legal skills are unnecessary. Your privacy policy is hosted on the web (in the cloud) and is embedded into your website using a small amount of code. Iubenda offers a simple policy for free; their Pro version covers more complex legalities and is available for a monthly fee.

✔ **FAQs page:** In Chapter 5, I go over the types of information you should include on your FAQs (frequently asked questions) page. This page is an immediate customer service shortcut that can save you and your staff precious time on the phone. Your soon-to-be, as well as current, customers and clients will appreciate this page.

✔ **Contact page:** The Contact page is second only to your home page in importance! If you want to generate business, make it easy for customers and clients to contact you. At a bare minimum, give the world your phone number and e-mail address. If you have a walk-in location, put a map to your business on this page.

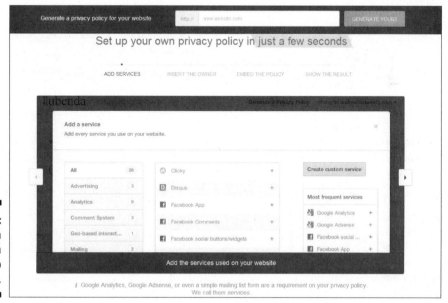

**Figure 4-7:**
Use Iubenda
to build a
policy step
by step.

A customer may want to ask you a question that is not covered on your site. Include a place (perhaps a page) to help the customer begin the interaction. You web hosting company may have a free tool that you can use to set up a contact form, so why not give them a call first?

✔ **Sitemap:** How many times have you been to a site and not been able to find a specific piece of information that you know should be there? The sitemap (see Figure 4-8) is an often overlooked but important page that lists every live page on the site. A link to it is generally found at the bottom of the home page.

A sitemap is also important because web spiders from search engines use this page to index your site. A thorough sitemap can help your search engine rankings.

✔ **Social media links:** Throughout this book, you'll see that social media is the tie that binds your social commerce. In Part IV, I show you all the places you need to be (and how to use them), but joining a social media site is pointless if your customers don't know you have a page there! Figure 4-9 shows representative logo icons for various social media sites. Link these to your social media account pages.

Add a custom bar to the bottom of your website that will not only link to your social media accounts but also allow your customers to interact with you, as shown in Figure 4-10. After you set up all your social media connections, visit www.wibiya.com to customize your toolbar.

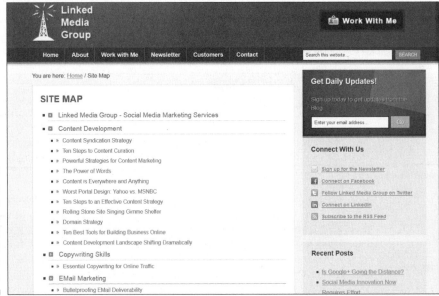

**Figure 4-8:**
This sitemap
is on the
Linked
Media
Group home
page.

**Figure 4-9:**
Include
social media
icons on
your site so
customers
can find
you.

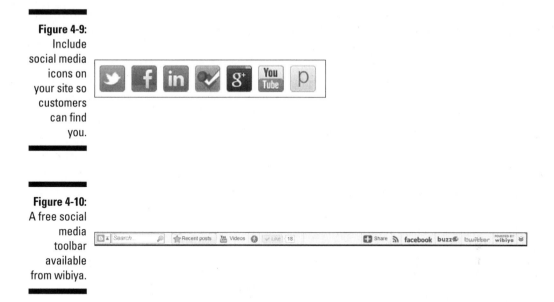

**Figure 4-10:**
A free social
media
toolbar
available
from wibiya.

The previous list contains the bare minimum for a basic website. After you have these pages in place, you should think about adding the bells and whistles that give people a reason to visit your site. For details on those additions, see the remaining chapters in Part II.

# Getting, Engaging, and Keeping Customers

Business follows a path: Find the customer, engage them, sell products, and keep the relationship going. Even service businesses have the opportunity to sell products that complement their profession these days. Bricks-and-mortar and online sellers also need to follow the attraction/engagement cycle. All businesses can benefit from the networking tips in this book.

Your job is to get the customer to your website. Why should people visit your website? How do they get there? The simple answer is that people performed a search in Google and your name came up, right? But how do you get listed on the first page of Google search results? Content.

Several things come into play in the engagement cycle, but the most important is viewable content. You can choose to add a blog to your website (see the "Blogging for Your Business" section, later in the chapter) or you can place industry-related content on your site to engage your viewer's interest. Both approaches turn your viewers into readers. Give them a reason to visit your site — and buy from you. Here are a few ideas on elements to add to build your audience.

## Adding industry information

Today's customers want to be educated consumers. The sites they visit more than once are those with good content that teaches them about services or products they are interested in buying. No one knows your business better than you, right? So here's your chance to shine.

Your content can come in many forms. Blogs are discussed in the next chapter but take ongoing effort on your part. Other content can consist of posting pictures and videos and sharing articles from other sites (with permission).

See how you might apply the following suggestions to your own website:

✔ **Glossary of terms:** Does your industry have its own lingo? Let your visitor in on the secrets by publishing a glossary, like the one shown in Figure 4-11.

**Figure 4-11:**
A glossary of watch and fine jewelry terms from Beckertime.

✔ **Product care information:** Does your product require certain care? Is certain ongoing maintenance needed? If you're in a service industry, there may be recommendations for upkeep. These topics are perfect to write about.

✔ **Apps:** Does a smartphone app compliment your business? If not, you might find someone who can put one together for you. The attorneys at Rosen.com (see Chapter 2) added child support and alimony calculators on their website, and the calculators are available also for iPhone and Android. You might make an informational app, game, or mini-version of a white paper you've produced. For example, I have a mini-version of my *eBay For Dummies* book as an app.

✔ **Podcasts:** You might think that there isn't much to talk about in your industry, but you'd be surprised. You can host question-and-answer podcasts or just talk about a subject; on your website, include a link code for visitors to click and listen.

Several sites offer podcast services. I recommend Spreaker.com (`www.spreaker.com`), which offers a basic service for free. They host your podcast content on their site and provide a simple widget you can use to make the podcasts available on your website as well.

✔ **Videos:** Products often need demonstration. A video that provides technical support for your products or services can be valuable as well. Most companies host their videos on YouTube and embed or link to the videos from their own sites. For example, Dish Network hosts their how-to and product announcement videos at `www.youtube.com/Dish`. In Chapter 7, you find out how to set up and post a video online and make it a vital part of your social commerce.

United Linens (a family-owned linen service in Bartlesville, Oklahoma) produced a series of videos that show viewers how to create the fancy napkin folds you see at grand events (see Figure 4-12). These videos have become popular and have built their brand through online buzz.

✔ **News feeds:** Install a news feed with industry news on your site. A news feed will automatically populate with stories that match your selected topic. Generally, your web host provider will have a tool to enable this feature.

✔ **Business history:** People who want to buy your product might also be interested in information about how your industry started (or how your business came about).

United Linen Napkin Folding: Ice Cream Cone Fold

unitedlinen    Subscribe    155 videos

Like    + Add to    Share

3,981

Uploaded by unitedlinen on Jun 17, 2009

#8 in our series on napkin-folding. In this segment we show you how to turn a
linen napkin into an Ice Cream Cone.
For this and other napkin folding videos, see United Linen's channel on
YouTube
http://www.youtube.com/user/unitedlinen
Become a fan of United Linen on Facebook
http://www.facebook.com/unitedlinen
Follow United Linen on Twitter

4 likes, 0 dislikes

**Figure 4-12:**
A United
Linen video
on how to
fold a napkin.

## Selling and linking to products

If you have a site based on e-commerce, you must install a shopping cart to
sell your products. Your web host should have an application that can integrate a shopping cart into your site. Accepting payment online has become a
standard practice. If you don't have your own online payment system set up,
you can arrange for payment through PayPal.com.

If you don't sell products but others sell products (or books) that might
be of interest to your clients or website visitors, you can become an affiliate. A popular affiliate program is the one from Amazon (see Figure 4-13). In
Chapter 11, I show you the best practices for setting up a minishop on your
site unobtrusively.

With a simple sign up, you can sell Amazon products to your visitors and
make a commission on the sale. You select the products you want to sell, and
Amazon provides you with a tracking code to put on your website. The code
enables customers to click a text link or product picture and buy the product
on Amazon.

**Figure 4-13:**
The Amazon
Associates
program
gives you a
commission
on sales.

# Blogging for Your Business

When you feel you're ready to take the next step and do something beyond a website, you can develop a blog to connect with customers. Blogs provide a place for your company to enhance its message as well as to respond to readers' comments. A *blog* (from *web log*) can be a commentary, as in a journal, or a description of events.

The Technorati 2011 State of the Blogosphere cited some important figures about entrepreneur bloggers:

> *13% of the blogosphere is characterized as entrepreneurs, or individuals blogging for a company or organization they own. 84% of these bloggers blog primarily about the industry they work in, with 46% blogging about business and 40% about technology. 76% blog to share expertise; 70% blog to gain professional recognition; and 68% to attract new clients for their business.*

Sound about right to you? If this sounds like a good idea, a blog may be for you — or your business.

## Deciding whether to blog

When considering whether to blog, start by searching for blogs in your industry and see what others are doing. You might become inspired.

---

# Getting recipes (and advice) from an expert blogger and liquor store owner

One of my favorite small-business experts (and coauthor of *Small Town Rules*) is Becky McCray. She also writes an occasional blog post for her liquor store at www.allensretail.com. This retail store's blog is filled with interesting facts and tips that are geared toward her local audience. She hosts the site with Google's Blogger. The figure shows one of my favorite posts; engaging content can be just about anything that has to do with your business.

She offered the following advice for small business blogs: "Write down every basic question a customer asks you. Start today, and do this for two weeks. If you end up with a long list of questions you can answer, you have enough material to start a blog." Combine those questions with information about your products, and you'll have the start of your own commercial blog.

Becky adds, "The one BIG secret to making it work? Focus on what the customers want to know, not what you want to tell them about your business."

## Allen's Retail Liquor Store

Alva, Oklahoma's Source for Wine - Spirits - Beer

*Welcome to Allen's Liquor Store! Making it easier to find and buy from the best selection of wine, liquor and beer in Alva, Oklahoma.*

Oklahoma State Law prevents us from shipping orders or delivering. Thanks for understanding.

**THURSDAY, JUNE 30, 2011**

### How to spike punch with 190 proof grain alcohol

Making some trash can punch or cowboy kool aid? Here's how much Everclear or 190 proof alcohol to add to reach your target, or at least get close.

For 1 Gallon of punch:

- to get 3%-4%: add one half of a 200ml bottle of Everclear
- for 5%-6%: add 200 ml
- 8%-10%: 375 ml

**OUR LOCATION**

Allen's Retail Liquors
916 Oklahoma Blvd.
Alva, Oklahoma 73717
580-327-0290
allensretail@gmail.com

Google maps

**WE ARE OPEN**

Some people view a blog as a low-cost alternative to a website, but that position is simply not the case. Instead, if you want a blog in addition to your website, make sure your blog is linked to several times from within your company site.

To blog successfully, you must

✔ Enjoy writing — or at the very least, enjoy researching the web for tidbits on your industry to share

✔ Have a good command of the English language and grammar

✔ Schedule a time to produce your blog and be prepared to post at least once a week

Your company's blogger should be you, a respected employee, or a family member. If you won't be blogging yourself, you must be comfortable that the blogger's message reflects what you would say yourself.

## Blogging successfully

After you've established a well-run, quality website, a blog can improve the site's organic search rankings. (*Organic ranking* is based on the content of your site and how relevant your site is to search terms.) A blog may also allow you to brand yourself as an expert in your industry. According to a report released by eMarketer, the number of companies planning to use blogs along with their website for marketing will increase from 34 to 43 percent in 2012.

Running a business blog gives you a leg up on your big-business competition. Before their posts can appear online, they must be checked — sometimes by several departments. You can move faster and make changes on the fly.

More than 156,000,000 blogs are on the Internet, read by approximately 400,000,000 people worldwide — a lot of blogs, and a lot of people spending time online. Follow these guidelines to make your blog different from the rest:

✔ **Provide quality content:** Your customers need to visit your blog and actually read it for it to be a valuable resource for your business and worth your time. Countless blogs receive just a few hits a day; if your customers are busy, a marketing-oriented blog may be the last place they want to visit. The goal is to engage reader's interest, so write about topics that you enjoy and that your readers will find interesting. You might want to hone the focus to a niche of broader-interest topics. Bottom line: Have a plan and an objective to focus on before you start writing your blog topics.

Find which posts on your blog attract the most reads by monitoring with a free service such as Feedburner.com. By using Feedburner, you'll be able to see which posts get the most views (and by whom), thereby enabling you to tailor future posts to that particular area of interest.

Do you think your customer doesn't have time to read a lengthy blog? Keep your posts short!

✔ **Post current customer service issues:** Are your shipments being delayed by a snowstorm or floods? Did an employee or a customer discover a problem with a product? In your blog, tell your customers about these matters — and provide a solution.

✔ **Answer comments:** If your readers post comments on your blog, be sure to respond. Every comment — negative and positive — should be addressed. Don't let anything remain on the blog unanswered for days.

✔ **Be transparent:** As the owner of your business, you are a reflection of your company. Always speak from your own point of view. Be available, honest, understanding. And don't fake positive comments on the blog.

✔ **Get personal:** Add a little personal information to the narrative. Your blog allows you to put a face and personality to your business online. People like to know with whom they do business, so share a little. Talk about your family, growing up, or what happened in the office yesterday. Personal posts are most successful when you tie elements of your life to your business.

## Making blogging easy with free tools

The digerati have an ongoing disagreement about which online platform is best for your blog. To decide for yourself, visit the sites listed in this section, kick some tires, and see which seat feels good to you.

The blog arena has two major players. Here are their basic statistics:

✔ **Blogspot** is a free hosting site owned by Google. They hosted 275 million blogs in 2009 and an estimated billion plus in 2012. Statistics on most Google products are hard to find, but statistics on your blog are readily available to the blog owner. The Blogspot blog publishing service is Blogger.

✔ **WordPress** is a free hosting site with many for-fee upgrades and widgets. This cross-platform content management system (CMS) software is available from WordPress.org and can be used on almost any web host. WordPress.com currently hosts about 35 million blogs and the WordPress CMS runs on 60 million blogs on other hosts.

From personal experience, I can say that Blogger is easy to use and intuitive. They do not offer the plethora of widgets (small apps that add features) that WordPress does because the bulk of what you need is already included. WordPress also has widgets to improve search optimization — but Blogger is a Google service, and until Google is no longer the leading search engine, I don't think that search engine optimization (SEO) is a worry.

A few other popular blogging options follow:

- ✔ **Tumblr** hosts 58 million blogs, although it was originally a micro blog site. Tumblr is like a social media network unto its own. Those with blogs on Tumblr follow other blogs and the site lets you know when the accounts you follow last posted. Tumblr also supplies easy-to-find statistics. It's free and has templates. Some big brands are using it.

- ✔ **Posterous** was recently acquired by Twitter and is the youngest platform of the bunch, debuting in 2008. They host about 23 million blogs, or Posterous spaces. I like their browser add-on that makes sharing stories or infographics from other sites easy.

I have two Blogspot blogs: my personal blog at `http://mcollier.blog spot.com` and a blog for one of my books at `http://theultimate onlinecustomerserviceguide.blogspot.com` (see Figure 4-14). I never got around to buying a custom URL address for the second blog. Instead, I use a URL shortener, which changes the URL to an easy-to-remember `http://bit.ly/custsrv`.

**Figure 4-14:**
This blog promotes one of my books.

I also have a Posterous site at `http://marshacollier.posterous.com/` that I use because of the convenience of the browser add-on. Posterous also has an option that lets me repost to my personal Blogspot site when I want to share.

Check out each site and see which works for you — note that you can easily customize most blog templates. In addition, find out what platforms others are using.

# Chapter 5

# Active Engagement: Connecting Directly with Your Customers

*A*fter you have your website up and running, you should periodically evaluate it to make sure you're giving your customers enough information to make a clear business decision. People make decisions by reading, perusing, and basically getting a "feel" from your website.

In this chapter, I show you how to have fun while making your customers feel closer to your business and making your website a lot more engaging.

## Romancing the Customer

You may find it a challenge to portray your business on the web. To make the process easier, think of your website like your home or business. The physical appearance of your store or office says a lot about you.

How annoyed are you when you sit in a waiting room only to find year-old magazines and worn furniture? Did it make you feel positive about the professional you were waiting to see? In a retail store, what story does dusty merchandise and unkempt shelves tell you? The situation is similar with a website.

Consider the design of your own website: How accessible are you to your customers? Are you giving your audience access to information and descriptions of services, or are you merely saying where you are and what you sell and then asking for an order?

Gone are the days when you could say "Here I am. Here's what I do. Now do business with me." Twenty-first-century social media commerce works on trust and requires a little romancing of your prospective client.

The Edelman Trust Barometer (a measure of online credibility) states that 77 percent of people refused to buy products or services from a company they distrusted.

If all you do is put up a website, promote your business with search engine optimization, and wait for the money to roll in, you're not providing any sort of service to your customers. (And, no, accepting PayPal payments for online sales don't count.)

# Understanding How Service Affects Sales

In a 2010 study, STELLAService (a company that measures online customer experience) focused on customer service and its affect on sales. They found that the value of great customer service in the U.S. economy is a staggering $267.8 billion per year. This figure was calculated based on the average "spend" per person per year with each type of company. Table 5-1 shows the premium consumers are willing to spend on a product or service if they know they will receive great customer service.

| Table 5-1 | The Value of Great Customer Service | | |
|---|---|---|---|
| Consumer Category | Average Spend per Person per Year | Average Extra Value Consumers Are Prepared to Pay | Estimated Total Value of Great Customer Service ($m) |
| Internet service provider | $649.34 | 11.2% | $17,978 |
| Hotel | $546.71 | 11.0% | $14,834 |
| Consumer products | $1,361.84 | 10.9% | $36,593 |
| Online retail | $653.29 | 10.7% | $17,267 |
| Healthcare | $1,047.04 | 10.6% | $27,338 |

| Consumer Category | Average Spend per Person per Year | Average Extra Value Consumers Are Prepared to Pay | Estimated Total Value of Great Customer Service ($m) |
|---|---|---|---|
| Wireless carrier | $854.61 | 10.2% | $21,543 |
| Insurance | $1,307.57 | 9.7% | $31,410 |
| Financial services | $640.46 | 9.7% | $15,346 |
| Cable and satellite TV | $911.84 | 9.7% | $21,815 |
| Travel and transportation | $929.61 | 9.5% | $21,825 |
| Landline carrier | $549.67 | 8.8% | $11,922 |
| Utilities | $573.87 | 8.6% | $12,251 |
| Government agencies | $463.82 | 7.7% | $8,837 |
| Paid subscriptions | $472.70 | 7.6% | $8,887 |
| Total | $10,962.36 | | $267,846 |

Note: Consumer spending is highest (more than $1,000 per year) in healthcare, consumer products, and insurance. As a result, the value of great customer service is estimated to be higher for these categories.

The 2012 Global Customer Service Barometer from American Express (United States findings) supported the STELLAService result that found customers willing to spend more for good service. Respondents in the American Express study reported the following:

✔ 66 percent said they would spend an average of 13 percent more with a company that provides excellent customer service — matching the results in 2011 and up from 9 percent more in 2010.

✔ When asked the question "Why would you be willing to spend more with a company that provides excellent customer service?" 35 percent felt that companies who provide excellent service have *earned* their business.

✔ 25 percent were willing to spend more with a company they believe placed a high value on excellent customer service.

✔ 18 percent felt that "excellent service is worth spending more."

✔ 41 percent were willing to spend more with a small business versus a large company when both provided excellent customer service. *Another plus for small business!*

Examining the Online Retail category in the STELLAService study (shown in Figure 5-1), the leading factor in determining great customer service was speed of delivery. Ease of access to information on a website came in second.

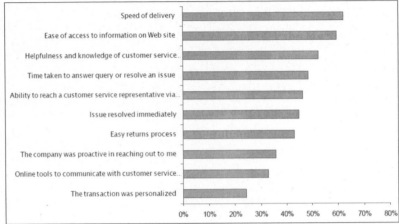

**Figure 5-1:**
Leading
factors
for great
customer
service.

Two findings were surprising. When shopping on sites with great customer service, more than 80 percent of consumers expected a reply to their e-mails within 1 hour and more than 30 percent expected their phone call to be connected to a live representative in less than 30 seconds.

As far as preferred channels for customer service, the American Express study found that customers prefer getting answers to simple inquiries through a company website or e-mail.

Now that you have the data, I hope you will believe me when I say that giving good customer service

- ✔ Attracts customers
- ✔ Builds customer loyalty
- ✔ Allows you to charge more for your products or service

If you're going to do business online, deliver customer service through information on your website. By doing so, your customers will know that they can connect when they need to reach you.

Gone is the 9-to-5 workday — the web is open 24/7. The more information you give your customers on your site, the less often they need to call you with questions.

# *Educating Your Customers through FAQs*

The FAQ (frequently asked questions) page on your website should answer your customer's questions about the process of dealing with your company. When writing the information on your FAQ page, use an accessible, conversational tone. Stay away from jargon and language that sounds good but doesn't say anything concrete. Be direct and use terms with which your audience is familiar.

When writing my book, *The Ultimate Online Customer Service Guide: How to Connect with Your Customer to Sell More*, I spoke to Paul Hopkins (@future-customer on Twitter), previously head of Customer Experience at easyJet, a United Kingdom–based airline that books 98 percent of its fares online. He used a simple Get Satisfaction solution (more on community customer service platforms in Chapter 13) on the FAQ page, which displays a clickable listing of FAQs and a keyword search to the airline's online solution database.

Paul had the following tips to share:

> When writing FAQs, write the content, then halve it — then halve it again. It may seem rather direct, but [most] people don't have time to read lots of text. Since I have used this approach, self-serve rates and customer satisfaction related to the helpfulness of FAQs have gone up. Also, ensure that the customer service team — not the web content team — manages the FAQs.
>
> Use web chat on FAQs; [since it's a place where] people would usually send an e-mail, this will reduce your volume of e-mails. It is also stops e-mail ping-pong, as the first e-mail is cheap and the second is expensive, [because] the agent has to read all previous content and then write the same answer in another way.

FAQ pages don't have a lot of requirements, but here are some guidelines to help you:

- ✔ Curate questions from e-mails, customer notes, and discussions with employees. Take time to put together a list of any possible question that can be asked about your business, practice, or store.
- ✔ Write answers thoroughly, in a conversational style.
- ✔ Organize questions by category (such as services, product information, ordering, shipping) in bold headlines or bullet points or both.
- ✔ Place the most important questions at the top of the page.

✔ **Make your design systematic.** Put related topics next to each other so that they flow.

✔ **When an answer is more than a paragraph long, make the link go to a separate page.**

Make sure the customer service or FAQ link is easy to find on your home page. What's the point of having a FAQ section if your visitors can't find it?

Figure 5-2 shows the FAQ page from 37signals (visit `http://help.37 signals.com/basecamp`). The information is easy to read and flows logically from one topic to the next.

If your company caters to a more whimsical type of customer, take a look at the customer service page from ThinkGeek, at `www.thinkgeek.com/help/`, shown in Figure 5-3.

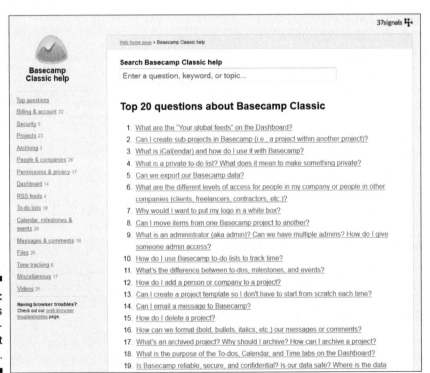

**Figure 5-2:**
37signals top 20 questions about Basecamp.

**Figure 5-3:**
Timmy the monkey is a charming icon for customer service, don't you think?

# Connecting with Your Customers through Web Chat

In the 2011 Avaya Consumer Preference Report, the preferred mode of contact for customer service matters was the telephone. (In other studies, such as the 2012 American Express study, telephone was preferred only for complex issues.) The second choice for communication was e-mail, followed by web self-service (such as FAQs) and then web chat.

In a live web chat, customers ask their questions or describe their issues and you or your employee provide immediate, specific answers. Web chat is a flexible (and swift) way to handle simple customer issues that come up — after customers have read your FAQs. This form of contact can be handled by someone in your office or through a mobile device or a smartphone.

As society becomes mobile (smartphone subscribers topped the 100-million mark in January 2012) and tablets become commonplace (70 million now, with a projected 133.5 million by 2015), more and more web visitors want a way to get swift and direct answers to their questions.

## Grabbing visitors quickly with SnapEngage

If you'd like to reach out to people who visit your site through web chat, check out an elegant yet flexible and easy-to-use app called SnapEngage. The web-based platform allows you to add an immediate contact action to blogs, websites, and your Facebook business page.

You can sign up for a free 15-day trial on their website at `http://snap engage.com`. I installed the app on my blog in less than five minutes by placing a snippet of supplied code in the HTML footer of my layout. The app appears as a Help tab on the left side of the page (see Figure 5-4). The process was just as easy on my website.

You (or your employee) can log in to SnapEngage's online web client (see the visitor side view in Figure 5-5) to handle any incoming chat requests. If you plan to be mobile, you can answer chats through Google Talk or the Skype mobile app on your smartphone.

**Figure 5-4:** This Help tab enables visitors to ask me a question, directly from my blog.

**Figure 5-5:**
Your pro-
spective
customer
can chat
with you
directly.

After you chat with the visitor, you can provide further information. For example, by entering a single shortcut command, you can automatically redirect the visitor to another page on your site to explain a service or demonstrate a product. Because I get inquiries about my books, I set up keywords that direct visitors to my books on Amazon (see Figure 5-6), incorporating my affiliate code. (In Chapter 11, I show you how to set up an Amazon Associates account.)

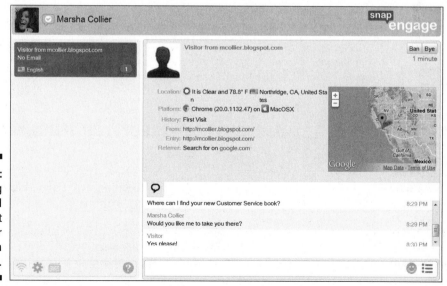

**Figure 5-6:**
By inputting
a keyword, I
can redirect
the visitor
to a chosen
page.

If you're not available to chat (on any mode of communication — you do get to sleep) and someone clicks the Contact tab, a window opens suggesting that the visitor send you a message through e-mail.

You can also add a "Chat with us" icon to your Facebook page to invite visitors to chat. Granted, someone could contact you by using Facebook chat, but when you are contacted through a platform-personalized button, the visitor gets a far more personal interface, as shown in Figure 5-7.

**Figure 5-7:**
The Facebook fan page client side is more engaging than Facebook's chat.

A transcript of chats can be sent to your e-mail address for follow-up. SnapEngage offers a host of other options and configurations. I recommend you visit their website for more information.

## *Setting up a customer service number through Google Voice*

I use Google Voice as my professional call solution every day. It integrates into Google Mail and all my other Google applications.

After you sign up for Voice service through your Google account, you can select a new phone number within almost any area code or any city. You can choose to keep this number private or put it on your business cards, e-mail signature, and more. The beauty of this number is that it can be configured to forward calls to any of the phone numbers you choose to register in the system, such as your mobile, office, store, or home phone.

For customer service, Google Voice has website widgets that can forward calls to any of your numbers or directly to a prerecorded voicemail message that you've prepared for your customers. Figure 5-8 shows you the easy configuration.

**Figure 5-8:**
Add Google Voice to your website for customer support.

The features of Google Voice are robust:

- ✔ You can assign custom voicemail greetings for different incoming phone numbers and use features such as call merging and free domestic calls.

- ✔ International calling is available at highly reduced rates. I can call a landline in the United Kingdom for 2 cents a minute. (For Google Voice International rates, visit www.google.com/voice/rates.)

- ✔ Your voicemail is stored in the cloud on the Google Voice site, where you can access it from any web browser or phone.

✔ Google Voice can send you an e-mail message with the transcribed text of your voicemail. You can also receive a text message (SMS) with the transcription of the message.

✔ From the web interface, you can send a text message via SMS to any mobile phone or other Google Voice number.

✔ You can return calls from your mobile or place calls displaying your Google Voice number in caller ID.

Google Voice apps that enable you to make calls from your tablet via Wi-Fi or make international calls on your smartphone at Google's reduced rates are available from your phone provider's online app store.

## Making free calls with Skype

Skype is an alternative to Google Voice for placing and receiving calls. You can use Skype to place free calls from computer to computer and, for a small fee, to forward incoming calls to your landline or cell phone.

When you sign up for a Skype account, you have the option of capturing code for using buttons on your website. The buttons, shown in Figure 5-9 (available at `www.skype.com/intl/en-us/tell-a-friend/get-a-skype-button`), are easy to customize and can be installed anywhere on your site. After you install the code for the button on your web pages, all your customer needs to do is click, and Skype rings you at your computer and allows you to talk live.

In addition, a button can show your availability on Skype: Call Me, Skype Me, Online but Not Available, Offline, or I'm Away. Keep in mind that there's no reason to ever be "away." For a tiny fee, Skype forwards all queries to your landline or mobile. If you're really not available, whoever is trying to reach you can also leave a voicemail.

Your customers can contact you through their computer microphone and speakers to yours at no cost to you. You can also opt to have Skype forward incoming calls to your home or cell phone when you're away.

 Providing that extra level of customer service through person-to-person, live-voice interaction can save many a sale and gives you the opportunity to negotiate, add a personal touch to transactions, or up-sell. For example, if customers are making a large purchase, offer them discounts or sale prices on related items. (The operators at Victoria's Secret do this very successfully.)

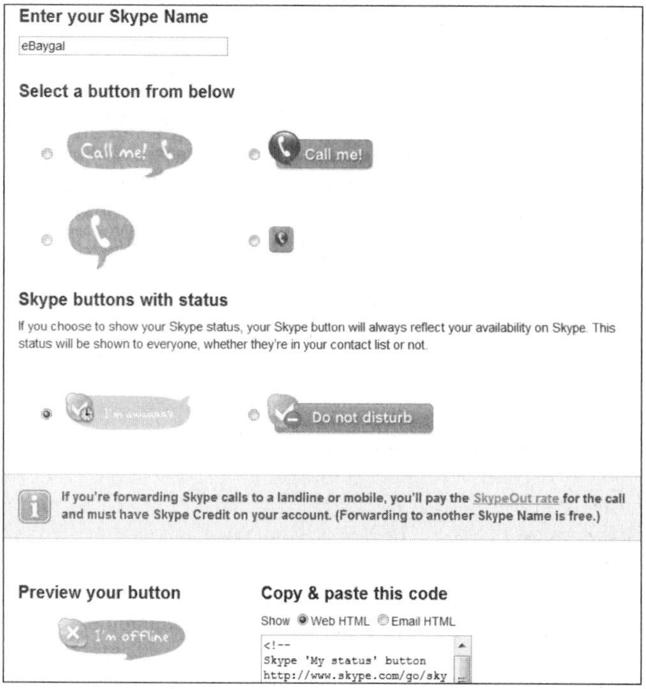

**Enter your Skype Name**

eBaygal

**Select a button from below**

**Skype buttons with status**

If you choose to show your Skype status, your Skype button will always reflect your availability on Skype. This status will be shown to everyone, whether they're in your contact list or not.

Do not disturb

If you're forwarding Skype calls to a landline or mobile, you'll pay the SkypeOut rate for the call and must have Skype Credit on your account. (Forwarding to another Skype Name is free.)

**Preview your button**

I'm offline

**Copy & paste this code**

Show ● Web HTML ○ Email HTML

```
<!--
Skype 'My status' button
http://www.skype.com/go/sky
```

**Figure 5-9:**
Select the button you want on your site.

With all of today's technology, there's no excuse for failing to connect online to your customers.

# Chapter 6

# Claiming Your Space on Review Sites

*W*ord of mouth (or WOM, as it is called in ad circles) has been the most relied-upon form of business promotion since the beginning of commerce. Deceptive ad practices force consumers to be wary of what they hear and read in adverting, so a recommendation from a trusted friend generally trumps paid promotions. Getting a reference to dependable service professionals is treated as sharing trade secrets — from friend to friend or colleague to colleague, over the phone and in person.

At the turn of the previous century, WOM was even more prevalent. To protect businesses from spurious rumors, the Better Business Bureau system was founded in 1912. Their goal was to vet businesses and to promote legitimate ones while protecting consumers from mistruths and idle gossip. Today, they are still in business and on the web at `www.bbb.org`.

Now, with new media, the consumer has many more options (and websites to visit) to get reviews and information from their peers. User-generated content on almost any business or service is publicly available for all to peruse. In this chapter, I show you how this trend developed and what you should know in today's world to defend your business reputation.

# Amazon and eBay Lead the Way

In 1995, Amazon.com allowed buyers to write their own book reviews. This spurred a retail-driven, customer-generated online community that is credited towards helping the site succeed. Today, the Internet viewer generally heeds Amazon's ratings (see Figure 6-1) when making purchasing decisions. In addition, an April 2012 Harvard Business School study of Amazon book ratings found correlations between Amazon user ratings and expert ratings.

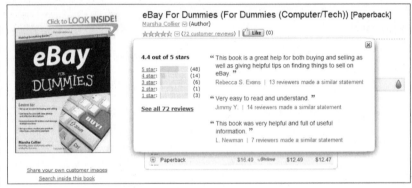

**Figure 6-1:** When a product gets enough reviews on Amazon, the consensus is generally spot on.

Within a year of Amazon's founding, someone else had an idea for a community-based commerce site. This time, rather than selling to customers, the customers were the sellers on the site. eBay, the first person-to-person online marketplace, was born. In February 1996, Pierre Omidyar, founder of the burgeoning eBay marketplace, posted a startling memo on the site, announcing a new feedback system in which both buyers and sellers could rate every transaction in which they participated on the site:

*Now, we have an open forum. Use it. Make your complaints in the open. Better yet, give your praise in the open. Let everyone know what a joy it was to deal with someone. Above all, conduct yourself in a professional manner. Deal with others the way you would have them deal with you. Remember that you are usually dealing with individuals, just like yourself. Subject to making mistakes. Well-meaning, but wrong on occasion. That's just human.*

The Internet tipped the scales of power from highly regarded, paid reviewers to the hands of "real people." The same kind of trust that is based on word of mouth is now available to everyone on the Internet. The new acronym is OWOM (online word of mouth).

# Understanding the Effects of Peer-to-Peer Reviews

SearchEngineLand.com — a news and information site covering aspects of search engines and search marketing led by journalist Danny Sullivan — produced their second Local Consumer Review Survey in 2012. To better understand how Internet reviews sway the customer, the study measured consumer trust and appreciation of online reviews. Approximately 72 percent of consumers surveyed said that they trust online reviews as much as personal recommendations. Also, 65 percent of consumers (versus 58 percent in 2010) read 2–10 reviews before they feel they could trust a business.

The survey also asked, "How do online customer reviews influence your decision to use/select a local business?" Figure 6-2 shows the results, compared to responses received in their 2010 study.

**Figure 6-2:** More than half of all consumers are more likely to use a local business if it has positive reviews.

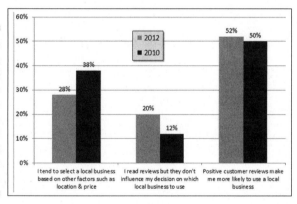

Online word-of-mouth data specializes in just about any profession, product, business, or store. For example, more than 30 sites compile opinions on medical professionals alone. The leaders are Angie's List, RateMDs.com, HealthGrades.com, and Vitals.com.

If these facts don't convince you, think about how many people you know who use a smartphone. Do they look at them for directions and addresses? You bet they do. (Chapter 12 tells you more about location-based services and their popularity.) However, those people not only look up directions but also read reviews associated with the businesses they search.

Almost every business has a page on many of the most visited review sites — whether or not they have set up the page themselves. These pages are put up for all to see without permission. Visitors can post comments, and you can't erase their positive or negative words. Sites with reviews are the basis for today's new media transparency.

To paint the most positive picture of your business, you need to go to these sites and claim your page. After you've been verified as the owner of the business, you might be able to do the following (depending on the site):

✔ Respond to reviews, usually directly on the site but often through site-sponsored e-mails

✔ Update your company's contact information, hours of operation, and details

✔ Upload photos of your current products, menus, or services

Some sites also let you purchase advertising, which gives you extra benefits. You'll be able to promote specials and seasonal deals for readers of the site, and you may even be able to run ads on your competition's page.

When someone searches your business on the web, the pages with the most mentions of your name appear first. The person goes to these sites to find out how your business rates. The fact that your business appears on sites such as Google+ Local makes your participation in social networks all the more important. (Read the section on Google+ Local later in this chapter.) Your activity on your own website, blog, and other online presences fills up the first page of a Google search quickly. These efforts are the best tool to foil review sites when you have been slammed unfairly by bad reviews.

Internet claims abound that if you buy advertising, you have some vague sort of control over the order in which reviews appear on your page. If you've been in business long enough, you may have heard of this practice, perhaps in reference to the Better Business Bureau. The rumor goes that after you become a member, they "help" you clean up your reputation on the site.

I have no experience to say with authority that any of this goes on. You will have to rely on your spidey sense and listen carefully to any sales pitches you receive regarding review sites. However, Yelp prevailed in a class-action lawsuit that accused them of manipulating reviews by asking businesses to pay in exchange for removing negative reviews. Jeremy Stoppelman, Yelp CEO, wrote the following in a company blog post:

*At Yelp, our mission is to connect people with great local businesses. Part of that work is to protect consumers and businesses from unreliable reviews. Another part of that work is helping small businesses understand how customer reviews work online and how they can help amplify and improve the reputation they've earned offline. We will continue to focus our efforts on both.*

To monitor a single page on a site that mentions your business, you may want to set an RSS syndication feed to let you know when additions have been made to the page. Although individual review websites do not offer this service, you can set up an RSS feed for your newsreader by going to `http://page2rss.com/` and typing the URL of the page in. Sweet. In Chapter 14, I show you the best ways to monitor your business name on sites and blogs across the web.

# Three Review Sites to Watch

The top three review sites are Yelp, Angie's List, and Google Local. Although other valuable review sites are available, these are the most popular. In this section, you can get a feel of how they work.

## Yelp

Although Yelp started by listing and allowing users to post restaurant reviews, the site has expanded to cover all sorts of retail businesses (and professionals) in their local consumer-generated reviews. People regularly go to the site for person-to-person recommendations. In the first quarter of 2012, Yelp quoted a reach of 71 million visitors per month and listed a startling 27 million reviews. During the same time period, their mobile app was used by approximately 6.3 million unique devices.

People check Yelp loyally and regularly to select places to visit. True to the site's roots, the two most popular categories are restaurants and retail shopping.

Yelp.com currently offers business reviews in most major cities in the United States and is expanding rapidly. When you visit Yelp for the first time, you may be surprised to see that your business is probably already on the site; Yelp gets its listing information from many sources.

When someone chooses to review your business listing, she can leave a commentary-style review and post a rating of one to five stars. The rating at the top of the page reflects an average of the ratings your business has received from each person's review.

### *Setting up an account*

Yelp can help you build exposure for your company, monitor public opinion of how you're doing, and facilitate research as to what your local community wants from an organization like yours. To set up a free business account, visit `http://biz.yelp.com/support`.

The basic account enables you to do the following:

- ✔ **Communicate with your customers:** Yelp allows you to answer your customers privately or on the public page for your business, for all to see. Because engaging customers is what the online world is all about, a personal message (as well as responses to some on the public page) to each reviewer will go a long way toward building your transparency and loyalty.

- ✔ **Set up a profile page:** Take note that this profile page is about your business and requires you to include all pertinent information. Yelp's administration page for company owners gives you a ton of choices for sharing your business information with your customers. Be precise and honest, so that prospective customers will know exactly what to expect when they walk in your door, whether bricks-and-mortar or digital. Be sure to mention anything that makes your business special — any information that might convert a website browser to a regular, paying customer. Be sure to keep the information you provide up to date.

- ✔ **Get access to Yelp metrics:** Track how users are engaging with your listing on the site. A graph of user views tracks traffic to your Yelp page from mobile devices so you can see from where people query your business. You also can view the number of mobile *check-ins* (when customers use the app to report that they're at your place of business), calls to your business from the site, requests for directions to your location, photos uploaded, clicks from Yelp to your site, and more.

- ✔ **Add extras to your profile:** You might include photos, a detailed business description, updated information, a company history, or a list of your specialties.

- ✔ **Receive review alerts:** When your business page is updated with a new post, Yelp sends you an e-mail alert so you don't have to check your page every day.

- ✔ **Offer special discounts to Yelp users:** These discounts should be valuable enough to persuade someone to come to your business. Direct these discounts specifically at Yelp users.

- ✔ **Announce upcoming events**: Yelp gives you 140 characters to announce a company-sponsored event. Use your marketing skills here to craft an appealing title. Make your statement read like a tabloid newspaper headline and be sure to include a shortened URL to link to a page where users can access further information.

The site sends out a weekly e-mail newsletter to its users as a local edition. After you set up a business page, the posts you provide — announcements, discounts, or in-store events — may just land you a personal space in the Yelp newsletter. In addition, your paid advertising discounts may pop up on other local profile pages, as in the AJ Bombers listing shown in Figure 6-3.

**Figure 6-3:** AJ Bombers reviews are so positive that they may outweigh any competitors' ads posted on their Yelp page.

Should your business offer a Wi-Fi connection to your customers, it's a smart idea to place a tent card on the table that mentions your Yelp business URL along with your other social network affiliations.

### Advertising on Yelp

Advertising on Yelp costs between $300 and $1,000 per month — consider the advertising an entrée to a premium account. Your ads appear at the top of the list when users perform a search related to your business. Your ads are also positioned on pages of nearby businesses. Note that competitors' ads will *not* be placed on your listing page.

# Angie's List

If you don't already know about AngiesList.com, you should — especially if you offer a service or have a professional business. Angie's List, shown in Figure 6-4, is a subscription-only regional aggregator of consumer reviews of local service providers. Subscription prices are based on where you live (in over 186 markets).

**Figure 6-4:**
Founder
Angie Hicks
greets
visitors on
the home
page.

Different than Yelp, Angie's List centers on "high cost of failure" services, those that would be expensive for the consumer to fix if projects or services don't end up as planned.

Customers influence one another more than companies do. Angie's List recognizes this trend by providing an open forum for registered users (real people) to recommend — or warn others about — plumbers, roofers, gardeners, handymen, doctors, and more. Angie's List believes in accountability and provides ways for businesses and consumers to work out issues.

With an estimated 1.2 million consumer members, Angie's List reports receiving approximately 40,000 new consumer reviews on service companies each month in more than 500 categories. The site does not allow the posting of anonymous reviews because it expects its members to "take responsibility for their words."

Reviews are more structured on Angie's List than on Yelp because it uses a standard format that consumers must follow. Angie's List also averages the reports to give them a letter grade of A through F.

Your business can receive reviews on Angie's List whether or not you register at the site. However, registering allows you to interact with customers who may post complaints about your business. Their Company Connect department can help you respond to reviewers and acts as a liaison between customers and contractors. If your business receives a complaint on the site and you don't respond, you might be put in the "Penalty Box," for all consumers in your area to see.

To register your business at the site, visit `http://business.angieslist.com`.You'll also be allowed to customize your profile and access business tools.

## New in town: Google+ Local meets Zagat

Get found on Google free of charge! Because 97 percent of consumers search for local businesses online, and Google is the top search engine, guess where they go? Google Places is gone and Google+ Local has taken over for a Zagat-infused search that shows up at the top of the page, in the number one spot.

Google+ Local reveals recommendations based on previous reviews and Zagat ratings. If you're a member of Google+ and on the site, you will also see recommendations from those in your circles. In Figure 6-5, I clicked the Local tab and local recommendations from my personal circles appeared.

Whether a search for a business name is made from Google, Google Maps, Google Local, or Google Mobile, the business listing also shows up on Google+ Local. All types of bricks-and-mortar businesses are listed. For example, I searched for and found listings for an endocrinologist, a sprinkler repair person, and a plumber in my city.

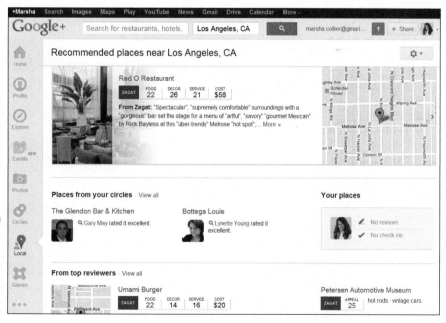

**Figure 6-5:**
Google+
Local view
from my
account.

All ratings are based on the Zagat 30-point system. Individual user scores are based on a 0 to 3 point scale:

3: Excellent

2: Very good

1: Good

0: Poor to fair

Averaged scores, as in the Zagat system, are calculated on a 30-point scale based on user reviews:

26–30: Extraordinary to perfection

21–25: Very good to excellent

16–20: Good to very good

11–15: Fair to good

0–10: Poor to fair

A search for a specific business within a city resembles a Yelp search, but the data is more thorough. For example, Figure 6-6 shows the listing for my favorite deli, which Zagat rated number one in Los Angeles.

**Figure 6-6:** A well-rounded description in the Google+ Local listings.

Each local business listing is based on information that Google gleans from many places, including the Yellow Pages. To make the most of your listing, add photos and update your address and hours.

Adding your local business listing is free, and Google doesn't accept payment to include particular listings or sites in search results. To claim you page and have access to the free goodies (or insert your page if there isn't one), go to www.google.com/local/add/businessCenter.

Google Places is free, but you can support your page with advertising from Google AdWords.

After you claim your page and beef it up and more people begin to visit, you get access to seriously good statistics that show how users interact with your listing, so you can add or remove information to make it better. You'll be able to see the following:

✔ **Impressions:** The number of times your listing has been displayed during a search on Google, Google Maps, and Google Mobile

✔ **Source:** What people clicked when they visited your listing

✔ **Activity:** All impressions as well as viewers' actions when they click links in your listing

✔ **Searches:** The Google searches that returned your business as a result

✔ **Driving directions:** The geographic location from which the request for driving directions came

Even more statistics are available, so I wouldn't wait. The online review sites are places where you need your listing to be crystal clear and accurate.

# Handling Positive and Negative Reviews

If you receive a bad review from an online community member, deal with the issue immediately. First, take a deep breath and rein in your emotions. Sit down quietly and read the review closely. You may find some honesty that you hadn't previously considered. You may even find a distinct flaw in the way you do business. These realizations don't feel good but *will* help you solve the problem.

If necessary, investigate the issue with your staff. After you get over the initial insult, contact the reviewer and offer to make things right. Some customers can't be placated — the best you can do with this type of person is to connect and show that you care. Other times, though, when you work toward a resolution, a negative attitude takes a 180-degree turn and the person turns into a loyal customer and perhaps a vocal defender and promoter.

The more you see your customers as real people with families and problems like yours, the more you will take pleasure in making them happy online.

# Chapter 7

# Knowing Where to Share Your Content

*In This Chapter*

▶ Creating posts on Facebook and Twitter

▶ Uploading a YouTube video

▶ Developing a podcast

▶ Sharing photos

*Q*uality websites or blogs constructed with interesting text, images, video, or audio content, will hold the visitor's attention. The same is true for your connections on social networks. With all the quality subject matter free to read on the Internet, few people spend time on a site or page without substance. You must provide good content and share something that will catch a visitor's eye.

If you don't love or don't have the time to write, you might be more comfortable making a video. A video doesn't have to be any fancier than sitting in front of your computer's webcam. (Later in the chapter, I give you tips on how to make your video clips look more professional.) If you're not one for being filmed (I'm often in that category), a podcast might suit you just fine. Remember that you have options when it comes to posting.

In this chapter, I advise you on where to find and share opinions, articles, and visual and audio content. After you get your online program rolling, visit Chapter 16 for specific apps that help streamline your network posts as well as refine your online style.

# *Posting on Facebook and Twitter*

Part of building a community on social media is establishing a presence on social networks. Think about what would happen if you opened a business but didn't let anyone know it was there. Websites are like that too. Building your name and your brand via posts and engagement opens your circle of connections — and customers.

Your website visitors increase when people on social networks want to know more about you and your business. Of course, the act of typing your website address in the About You area of your personal and business pages on Facebook (and in your Twitter bio) is appropriate. But getting someone to click and visit the site from social media networks requires that you make regular interactive updates.

Facebook requires a personal touch to maintain an audience. You *can* get a bunch of people to like your page with a promotion or sweepstakes, but they may never return if you don't provide intriguing updates. To find out which Facebook posts resonate with your audience, you can use Insights data.

If your business Facebook page is new, Insight data is not available. Your page must receive at least 30 likes before Insights will generate data.

Your Facebook business Insights page displays data on how many people interact with your page over a 28-day span. Figure 7-1 shows metrics from the Reach tab of the Insights page. The online user interface displays about 500 posts below the graph. Be sure to check these metrics at least once a month. Tips on ways to apply this data to advertising appear in Chapter 15.

By clicking Reach in the Page Posts section of your Insights overview, you can sort by most popular posts first.

From personal research (IMHO the most reliable) and information from others, posts provide a window to the people behind the company are the most appreciated ones on Facebook. However, the social web moves at the speed of light, so your fans may prefer other types of posts. After you begin to post, check your own data and see what attracts comments. (In Chapter 8, I help you decipher the data from Facebook Insights.)

After analyzing nearly 300 content posts, Omnicom's OMD found that the average shelf life of a Facebook post is about 18 hours. I find that my posts start hearing crickets after about three hours. Facebook's EdgeRank algorithm filters posts from a user's news feed when engagement peters out.

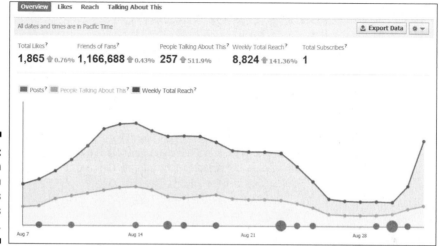

**Figure 7-1:**
The Reach
tab in
Insights
shows visits
to the page.

Tweets are consumed as Twitter users log on and off the site each day. The
average lifespan of a Tweet is less than two minutes (see Figure 7-2 for some
stats). Users generally view Twitter in real-time versus the delayed and
EdgeRank-filtered Facebook news feed. Most people on Twitter do not read
all of a person's Tweets — although those with only a few followers may scan
all Tweets for the day when they sign in or even go back further in history.

Twitter users are more data- and technology-driven than Facebook users,
so know that educational and news posts tend to garner more clicks.
Conversation is also king on Twitter, so jump in when you see one that
interests you. (Talking to strangers about a common interest is what makes
Twitter interesting.) Because Twitter is not as visual as Facebook, you've got
to make your Tweets as engaging as possible.

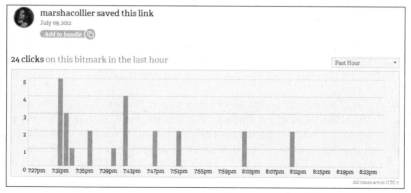

**Figure 7-2:**
Although
this Tweet
lasted 40
minutes,
it petered
out quickly
(measure
by bitly).

# Posting Videos on YouTube

YouTube, which is the best choice to host videos that you post on your website or blog, can bring a new audience to your business and help build your brand on the web. Videos are growing in popularity as a way to give more visual clues to your marketing message. One video can be viewed — delivering your message — thousands of times.

Also, when videos (and images) are titled correctly, they often organically appear on first-page search results when searches are performed for the keywords in the title. Forrester found that videos were 50 times more likely to appear on first-page results than text-based posts. (The fact that Google owns YouTube might have something to do with this.)

To engage those who want to read and perhaps print information, make sure to accompany video posts with text that explains the topic and invites the viewer to watch the video.

Think about how you could engage your customer with video. If you're in real estate, for example, show tours of homes. A baker could demonstrate how products are made, a vintner could show how grapes are cultivated, and a doctor could demonstrate a particular procedure to make it less frightening.

Here are a few more ideas:

- ✔ **Take the viewers behind the scenes of your business.** You will be surprised at how many people are interested in the "how" of what you do.

- ✔ **Ask and answer questions.** I have a few YouTube videos in which I filmed people (with their permission) at a conference asking me questions. People view these videos on a regular basis for tips on how to run an eBay business.

- ✔ **Review products.** If a new technology relates to your business, talk about it in an interesting way to draw in views.

- ✔ **Educate customers on your business.** Do people have questions about what you do or how you do it? A heart-to-heart chat on a video goes a long way to show you're human. You can also build trust because a prospective client can look you in the eye.

- ✔ **Provide tech support.** Demonstrate how to perform various tasks with your product or service. Thousands of small businesses are embedding demonstration videos on their websites, such as United Linen's napkin-folding videos (mentioned in Chapter 4).

Keep your video short! Videos that get the most views are less than three minutes long (two minutes is even better). Blame it on today's short attention span, but longer videos rarely get watched all the way through. Better to make a series of short videos than one long *Lord of the Rings*.

My faith in YouTube as a commerce platform has many examples. Here are a couple of success stories from people I know and respect.

John Lawson from 3rdPowerOutlet, an eBay and online seller, purchased a large lot of bandanas. In the process of selling them, he found that customers didn't know how to fold them. If customers didn't know how to make the bandanas look cool, why would they buy them? His solution was to post a video that demonstrated how to fold a bandana (see Figure 7-3). To date, the video (posted in 2007) has accumulated more than 230,000 views!

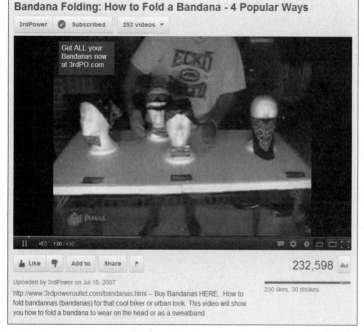

**Figure 7-3:**
John Lawson demonstrates bandana folding.

This video is cruder than many of the professional videos you see on the web, but it is still working for 3rdPowerOutlet. He has sold tens of thousands of these babies.

eBay seller Curt Buthman put together a package of Pico projectors but found that people had no idea of their value, so he demonstrated how it all worked. When there's money invested and product to move, make a video! In less than 9 months, his amateur video had more than 52,000 views (see Figure 7-4). Unfortunately, Curt's source dried up and he no longer stocks the package as a regular item. Hard lesson learned.

**Pico Micro Projector Home theater**

CurtButhmanTV ✓ Subscribed | 14 videos ▾

2:06 / 6:58

👍 Like | 👎 | Add to | Share | ⚑ | 38,666

Uploaded by CurtButhmanTV on Nov 8, 2011
Complete Portable Pico Micro Projector Home Theater System!
The Best you can get and all put together for you. Includes Pico Laser (Focus
FREE) Projector, Philips External Powered Speaker (subwoofer available),
Gorilla Tripod & Philips.
Please contact me at: Curt@BeSociable.Me

18 likes, 3 dislikes

**Figure 7-4:**
Curt
Buthman
had a dozen
units to
sell —
he could
have sold
thousands!

Another benefit of posting on YouTube is the statistics you get about your audience. Figure 7-5 shows one month's traffic to Curt's video. Very few of the views — 17 — came from an external website (no doubt his blog). The rest of the views demonstrate clearly what they mean by "going viral."

To make videos for your own business, your budget can be as small (or as large) as you want. If your business needs to reflect fine production values, you may have to increase your budget. Here are the basics to get you started:

- ✔ **Camera:** A camera that shoots in HD is best, although your files will be larger. If you're just starting out, check the online reviews and get a get a low-cost (less than $100) digital video camera. Or if you really want to save money and already have a smartphone that shoots video, use that for your YouTube videos.

- ✔ **Tripod:** An inexpensive tripod can hold your camera while filming. I have a full-size one and a table model and use both regularly.

- ✔ **Webcam:** If you'll be shooting your videos from your desk, get a good-quality webcam. Your computer may have come with a camera and (as evidenced by a few of my YouTube videos), it's usually not a great one. Get an HD webcam and mount it on your monitor.

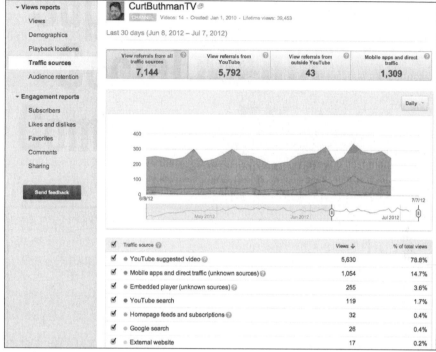

**Figure 7-5:**
YouTube
Analytics
provide
metrics
about your
audience
and views.

- ✔ **Microphone:** A microphone makes a big difference when it comes to sound quality. You can choose from hundreds of types of microphones that connect to your computer via USB. I use a Plantronics Blackwire 435 headset — it's almost invisible if I drape the wire behind my back.

- ✔ **Lighting:** Overhead office lighting does not flatter anyone. If you're filming in an office, try using additional side lighting to avoid unflattering shadows on your face.

- ✔ **Software:** Basic video editors are bundled with both Microsoft and Apple operating systems. In Figure 7-6, I'm using a Windows product to edit a short video. I can add fades, titles, and fancy effects and still finish the job quickly.

- ✔ **Practice:** Study an outline of what you want to say before going on camera. If necessary, print some cheat sheets and stick them on the wall, where they will work like a teleprompter. Don't be concerned if you have a few retakes.

When filming a video, do you best and move on. Going down a rat hole with take after take will frustrate your efforts. Just do it, post it, and embed it on your blog. Mention your blog in a Tweet and on Facebook.

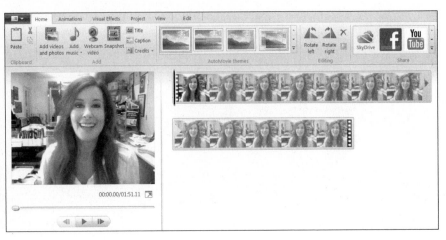

**Figure 7-6:**
You can
upload
videos to
popular
social media
sites
directly from
Windows
Live Movie
Maker.

# Developing Your Own Podcasts

I'm a big fan of radio, always have been. My books have been adapted to Audible audio books — people don't always have time to read but they can listen and learn while they drive a car, work out at the gym, or sit on the beach. A great deal of information is consumed via audio these days.

When talk radio turns into a multimedia digital file that is available for download for the Internet, it becomes a *podcast*. You don't have to be at a computer to listen; every smartphone can download and play podcasts by using an app such as iTunes (for iOS) or Google Listen (for Android).

I have broadcast *Computer and Technology Radio* with Marc Cohen on traditional AM radio as well as for podcast (in addition to *Marc and Marsha* on iTunes, at `http://itunes.apple.com/us/podcast/computer-technology-radio/id481915367`. Our show has opened up a whole new audience with whom I interact on Twitter during the live broadcast.

You can currently listen live on the wsRadio app or on the Internet. Our show is also archived and can be replayed when listeners go to the wsRadio site and is also uploaded to iTunes (see Figure 7-7). We reach tens of thousands of listeners all over the world.

Would your customers benefit from your podcasts? Rosen Law's Divorce Talk Radio (mentioned in Chapter 2) produces weekly podcasts on divorce issues that target his audience (`http://radio.rosen.com/`). Could you talk for 20 minutes about a particular topic weekly or bimonthly to embed in your website or host on a podcast service?

**Figure 7-7:**
My home
on iTunes
with Marc
Cohen.

All you need to get started is a microphone, but I suggest you also use head-phones to avoid feedback. Better microphones do make a difference! If you get serious, you might add some low-cost, professional-quality software such as SAM Broadcaster for a real radio station feel.

Do not use your Internet ISP to host your podcasts. Instead, hire a company that specializes in podcasts and their particular needs.

Following are a couple of reliable podcast hosts that have offerings in varied areas.

## Spreaker.com

A newcomer to the Internet radio scene, Spreaker (shown in Figure 7-8) is shaking things up. The platform allows you to host and broadcast a live Internet radio show from their online platform at your desktop or on their mobile app for an Android, iPhone, or iPad devices. Spreaker apps have an online mixer and an intuitive interface.

You can stream your show live and record it for embedding on any website. The podcast is also archived on your show's home page on the Spreaker site. You can prerecord shows, but note that a live broadcast enables you to inter-act with your audience in a chat room, on a social media network, or through Skype call-ins.

**Figure 7-8:**
Spreaker
hosts your
podcasts
and enables
you to
stream live.

In addition to its ease of use, Spreaker provides high-quality audio, streaming on 128 kilobits stereo (64K each for the right and left channels). Most other sites stream at 32 kilobits.

When deciding on a podcast provider, be sure to listen to multiple samples of existing shows on various platforms (computer, smartphone, and tablet). Be sure that the sound you hear is the sound you want to represent your business.

You can also download broadcasts as MP3 files and use iTunes-compatible RSS feeds to syndicate your podcast anywhere in the world. A statistics page enables you to see information on your podcasts and listeners calculated every hour.

Spreaker.com offers a free plan that you can use forever. If you catch the podcasting bug, however, I recommend that you upgrade to their broadcaster account, which is $199 a year.

## Liberated Syndication

Liberated Syndication (shown in Figure 7-9), which is known as libsyn, was the original pioneer of the system to host and publish podcasts in 2004. In 2010, libsyn was the largest podcast network, with more than 1.6 billion downloads and more than 15,000 podcasts.

**Figure 7-9:**
The libsyn
home page
points you
to many
options.

With libsyn, you do not live-stream your podcast. Instead, you record your show (they have experienced tech support) and then they host it. Further, they help you with managing, distributing, and monetizing your content.

All hosting plans (including the basic plan) provide the following:

✔ Media hosting for audio and video

✔ Your own webpage for your show

✔ An iTunes-compatible RSS feed for your podcast

✔ Flash and HTML5 video and audio player

They developed their own flash player, which can be configured and cus-tomized for audio and video podcasts, to embed on your website. Thanks to HTML 5, the podcast also works on mobile devices.

You can subscribe to include an app for your podcast, which helps you increase your audience. Your app could also enable monetization by running ads from Wizzard Media's advertising platform. Visit their site at `http://libsyn.com` for plans and pricing.

Start with the libsyn $5-a-month plan to see whether you like being a podcast host.

# Sharing Your Photos

How many photographs do you take with your phone each day? I bet some of them would be great to share on your website and in social media. Photos make a web page pop (see the sample in my log post in Figure 7-10) and are proven to attract more eyes to your updates.

Most smartphones allow you to upload photos directly to your Facebook account, but photos uploaded to Facebook are not sharable elsewhere (without bringing the viewer back to Facebook). Instead, try Google+ Picasa or Yahoo! Flickr when uploading and storing your photos. Either platform makes it easy to post images to promote your business.

Monday, June 07, 2010

## 25 years of Corvette Love: 1985 to 2010

When I was growing up, I'd see Corvette's on TV and in the movies - all the cool guys had them. It was my very first dream car. One day, I saw a picture of a gold corvette. That's gold, not light bronze or dark bronze, but sparkling gold. The tri-coat paint job made that car sparkle.

So, when my business became successful in 1985, I sought out my gold Corvette. I finally found one, one of only 1,411 made that year. So I coughed up the deposit and made it mine.

I had previously driven a stunning Pontiac Trans Am -with a hood scoop but no screaming chicken decal - and then a bright red two seater Pontiac Fiero (a fuel-efficient sporty commuter car). Both cars were amazing, but they were no Corvette.

What you probably didn't know about me, is that I wrote and photographed Auto Racing for several years. I've covered all the major venues in the US and love the sounds and smells of those mechanical wonders. I bought the Corvette and proudly brought my Vette to NASCAR and NHRA events. Even got to drive it several times on the old Riverside International Raceway. I loved that car - and still do. She's sitting in my garage today with about 45K original, one-owner fun miles.

So when General Motors asked me if I'd like to try out the 2010 Grand Sport Convertible Corvette, I jumped at the chance.

The engine is based on the legendary small block V8 that's been around for 45 years. I was amazed at how technology has improved it's power in the last 25. The car's premise is the same; a sexy low, road hugging sportscar. But technology took the 1985 "Tuned Port Injection" 350cc small block engine (through improved displacement) from the old 230 hp to 430 hp on the 2010. Accelerating at a quiet stop light is a fun experience. In 1985 0-60 mph took 5.7 seconds and today the improved version reaches 60 in 3.9.

**Figure 7-10:** In my review of the new Corvette, I included photos from my smartphone.

Flickr is one of the top choices because it lets you embed on your blog or site without sending the visitor back to Flickr. By not hosting the actual picture on the page, an embedded photo speeds up your site's page load time. In addition, you can create a link to your page post within the description on Flickr. In this way, those who see the image on Flickr may just click through to your site.

By posting pictures to one of these platforms in your business name, you benefit from increased search engine indexing. If you have a personal Flickr account, you can brand a set of albums in your business name within your personal collections. All major search engines consider these sites to be a major component in the social ranking aspects of searches.

I have a Flicker Pro account for the photos I have selectively uploaded to the site. I also have a Google+ account (which incorporates Picasa) for photos taken on my mobile phone.

When posting business photos in a personal account folder, be sure to mention your business name in the title of the image.

These sites do not store the photos on your computer. If photos are uploaded from a device other than your computer, you can (as the owner of the pictures) download them. (You can also give others rights to use your pictures.)

## Using others photos from Flickr

When posting on the web to enliven your updates, you might want to use a specific image but have no time to shoot the image yourself. Many photographers allow others to use their work on blogs or for other commercial uses.

To find images that you can use at no cost, follow these steps:

1. **Visit Flickr by typing** www.flickr.com **in your browser.**

2. **Sign in with your Flickr or Yahoo! ID.**

   You can also sign in with a Google ID or a Facebook ID.

3. **In the Flickr search box, type the name of the item for which you are searching. Click Search.**

   You will retrieve hundreds of photos matching your query.

4. **Click the Advanced Search link, which appears to the right of the search box.**

   At the bottom of the resulting page is an option to find photos with a Creative Commons license.

5. **Select the Only Search with Creative Commons option, and then select the Find Content to Use Commercially option. Click Search.**

6. **On the search results page, find a photo that interests you, and then click that photo.**

7. **Click the license, which appears to the right of the photo.**

   The Creative Commons license appears, as shown in Figure 7-11, outlining the legal rights for photo usage (generally you have to credit the photographer).

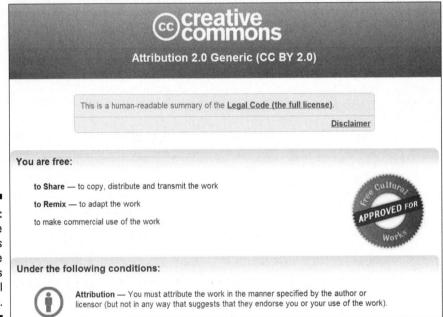

**Figure 7-11:**
A Creative Commons license that allows commercial sharing.

8. **If the terms look good, click the Share menu to see your options for downloading, sharing, and embedding, as shown in Figure 7-12.**

If you find nothing in the free photos, you can find photos that can be licensed for as little as $20:

1. **Perform your search as in the preceding Steps 1–3.**

2. **On the initial search results page, note the text to the right of the thumbnails regarding photos licensed by Getty Images. In that text block, find and click Flickr Members.**

   You arrive at a page with photos that are available for use.

**Figure 7-12:**
Flickr gives you various options for using the image.

3. **Next to the search selection box, click the Royalty Free option.**

   This option limits the search to images for which you do not have to pay ongoing rights.

4. **Find a photo that interests you and click it.**

5. **To the right of the image, click View Pricing in the pop-up window.**

   You see the charges associated with using the image.

6. **If the price is right, click Add to Cart in the pop-up window.**

7. **To pay for and download the image, following the on-screen instructions.**

Not every picture you have needs to be shared. On Google+, Picasa, Picasa Web, and Flickr, you can choose to make uploaded photos (such as those from your smartphone or mobile device) private or visible to only people you select.

## Storing and editing in Google+ and Picasa

A simple method for using (and improving) photos you want to upload is available through Google and Picasa's web albums. Picasa is versatile in that it has a great web interface and you can download their free photo organization program (available at http://picasa.google.com/).

After you install Picasa, it will find every photo on your computer and help you organize them into albums. You may also choose to automatically upload photos on your computer to Picasa storage.

Keep photos used for your business (whether for blogs or just to share) and personal images in separate albums.

After Picasa indexes your photos, it scans for facial recognition, and displays a folder of all faces it finds in the photos. You will be able to tag photos with the names of the people in your images. This feature is handy if you're taking pictures of employees for your blog or web page.

Picasa includes a free photo editor that enables you to perform most basic photo corrections, including retouching. If you want to add fancy effects, use the online Picasa Creative Kit. Creative Kit also allows you to edit in side-by-side mode so you can compare the results of your edit.

Google+ has a built-in photo editor that allows you to double-click any mobile upload and perform most edits necessary to make your image web-ready (see Figure 7-13).

**Figure 7-13:**
In Google+ photos, click Edit Photo to display a basic editor.

Because I am a Google+ member and use an Android phone, photos I take on my phone upload automatically to my private space on Google+. No photos become public until I choose to share them. From Google+, I can edit, download, and share any photo I take with my smartphone.

# Part III
# Casting for and Catching Customers

The 5th Wave          By Rich Tennant

@RICHTENNANT

"He saw your laptop and wants to know if he can check Facebook."

# In this part . . .

You have to find your customers before you can connect with them. This part provides solid tips to help you find where your customers hang out online and engage them to join in with your business. You discover how to monetize in areas that may be new to you. I also show you how to connect on mobile networks and how to generate revenue from your newfound followers.

# Chapter 8

# Finding Your Customer on the Social Web

As any business owner knows, market research is a big deal. When you first started your business, you no doubt studied the area in which you planned to operate. For bricks-and-mortar retailers or professionals, considerations such as foot traffic, ease of customer access, future population growth, and demographics all come into play.

Running an Internet business can be more complex. In the early days of e-commerce, the basic assumptions were that customers had a computer and were online. You knew where customers lived only by seeing the addresses to which merchandise was shipped. An online seller had to have a canny understanding of what products their customers might want, and placing ads was a hit-or-miss proposition.

Today, sellers must consider each social network as if it were its own country, having its own particular demographic. Luckily, new tools can help you understand and find your customer on the web. In this chapter, I show you some simplified ways to get data with little or no financial drain.

## Simplifying the Data Machine

Marketing data is considered the holy grail of information. As business owners, we often think to ourselves, "If I only knew exactly who makes up my market and how to reach them, my business would surely be incredibly successful."

True. If you were selling and marketing gloves for left-handed goat milkers, it would behoove you to send your message to the areas where they hang out — in real life and on the web. Although I've selected a particularly unique demographic subset, a simple Google search (shown in Figure 8-1 took 1.64 seconds to return 135,000 sites where I might connect with such a customer.

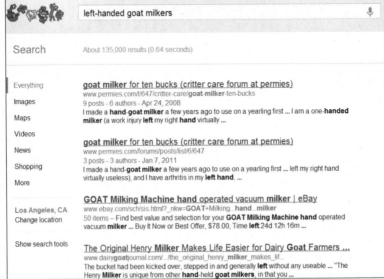

**Figure 8-1:** Certainly I can find people to buy my product in this group.

There you go. I just performed the most lightweight marketing research possible.

Each day, more and more data appears and is readily available to us on the Internet. We can study, refine, pinpoint — until we drive ourselves crazy. In weekly chats with customer service executives and aficionados on Twitter, I often hear remarks that as business people we "have too much data and exercise too little judgment" when making business decisions. It's easy to slide into the trap of making wrong conclusions based on overly detailed analyses.

As an entrepreneur, you have to straddle a delicate line between being too data driven and making purely visceral decisions (trusting your gut). When deliberating too long on marketing decisions due to a wealth of statistics, you tend to make less accurate judgments than those who trust their instincts. Balance validated data with your valuable gut instinct.

A recent blog post on this very subject by customer strategist Mitch Lieberman, vice president of market strategy at Sword Ciboodle (@mjayliebs on Twitter), came up with some valuable points on the subject:

*Something as valuable as data is not a problem; it is a powerful and valuable asset.*

*Help people to understand data; encourage them to be educated skeptics.*

*Gut instincts are not bad; just keep things in perspective, right place right time.*

*Start using data to better understand your customers!*

Taking all this into consideration, look for some simple ways of reaching your target customers on the web.

# Understanding Your Customer Demographics

Who is your customer? As a professional or a business owner who is on the premises every day, I suspect you have a pretty good idea with whom you transact business. Eyeballing your customers at the register is a simple way to profile for your Internet outreach.

If you'd like to expand your customer base in your local area, you might look to recent demographic data. Note I said "recent." Most data that you find is based on the United States census. (Be sure to check which year's census is quoted when you look up something.) However, the problem with using census data is that it is updated at the start of each decade. If the census is more than five years old, the data may have changed drastically.

Different generational cohorts — such as baby boomers, Gen Y, and Gen X — visit diverse sites and have specific preferences as to how they chose to interact on the web. Studying the peculiarities of each demographic segment helps you come closer to understanding their online preferences. By seeing what makes the various generations tick, you'll be better at positioning your social media outreach.

Find your customers on their own turf. With a little luck, these locations are the same places that best suit your own personality, company culture, and outreach style.

People make blanket statements regarding buying patterns and activities based on a population's stage in life. As an entrepreneur, your experiences with customers of various generations may shoot holes in these categorizations. But when you need a baseline, commonly accepted generational standards can be used to define demographic groups and classify them by age and the mores of their contemporaries.

In my book, *The Ultimate Online Customer Service Guide: How to Connect with Your Customers to Sell More!* (Wiley), I give an in-depth analysis of the various generational cohorts. (You might find that book a worthwhile companion to this one.)

The Pew Research Center (a nonpartisan "fact-tank") first surveyed users about the general role of the Internet in people's lives in March 2000. The Pew Internet & American Life Project continues to regularly track Internet users. A portion of their survey studies the demographics of Internet users 18 and older. Table 8-1 outlines the interesting results of their August 2012 survey.

| Table 8-1 | Demographics of Internet Users |
|---|---|
| | *Internet Users* |
| All adults | 85% |
| Men | 85% |
| Women | 85% |
| Race/ethnicity | |
| White, non-Hispanic | 86% |
| Black, non-Hispanic | 86% |
| Hispanic (English- and Spanish-speaking) | 80% |
| *Age* | |
| 18–29 | 96% |
| 30–49 | 93% |
| 50–64 | 85% |
| 65+ | 58% |
| *Household income* | |
| Less than $30,000/yr | 75% |
| $30,000–$49,999 | 90% |
| $50,000–$74,999 | 93% |
| $75,000+ | 99% |
| *Educational attainment* | |
| No high school diploma | 61% |
| High school grad | 80% |
| Some college | 94% |
| College + | 97% |

*Source: The Pew Research Center's Internet & American Life Project's February Tracking Survey conducted July 16–August 2, 2012. N=2,253 adults age 18 and older, including 900 interviews conducted by cell phone. Interviews were conducted in English and Spanish.* `http://pewinternet.org/Trend-Data-(Adults)/Whos-Online.aspx`, *accessed on August 24, 2012.*

In the following sections, I provide a few suggestions for gleaning local demographic data.

## Wolfram\Alpha

Wolfram\Alpha, at www.wolframalpha.com, is the pixie-dust behind iPhone's Siri, the vocal knowledge navigator. It's available for use on your website or as a mobile app for iOS, Android, Nook, and Kindle Fire devices. The program aggregates information from all over the web and curates 10+ trillion pieces of data from primary sources with continuous updating. You get a quantitative answer to your query, not opinions or reviews. Called a "computational knowledge engine" by its developers, Wolfram\Alpha is concerned only with facts and figures. Its mission is to unify the sum of human knowledge (a heady goal for a program).

For example, I typed *ZIP CODE 91325 demographics* in the text box on the Wolfram\Alpha website. I then clicked the Age and Gender button, and got the results shown in Figure 8-2.

**Figure 8-2:** Demographics by ZIP code from Wolfram\Alpha.

Data is continually being updated, often in real time. The types of data available are almost unlimited, from demographic data to the nutrients in an avocado. Don't forget this valuable site.

## Zillow

Zillow is famous for its up-to-date real estate valuations at www.zillow.com. In addition to giving values for homes, Zillow also gives you solid demographic data for most cities.

Here's how your find demographic data for your business location on Zillow:

1. **On the site's home page, type the city and the state abbreviation, and then click the magnifying glass to the right of the data field.**

   In my example shown in Figure 8-3, I typed *Los Angeles CA*.

2. **At the top of the resulting page, select Demographics from the drop-down Local Info menu.**

   You see the demographics for the metro area. If you're searching a small city or rural area, all the information will be here.

**Figure 8-3:**
Local info demographics from Zillow.

3. **If you're searching a metropolitan city, with neighborhoods, narrow your search by clicking one of the links on the left side of the page to view data for the various communities.**

Further down the page, you can find other data, including median household income, median age, and average household size. You'll also find unique sociological categories in the Who Lives Here and the What's Unique About the People sections (if available for the region), as shown in Figure 8-4.

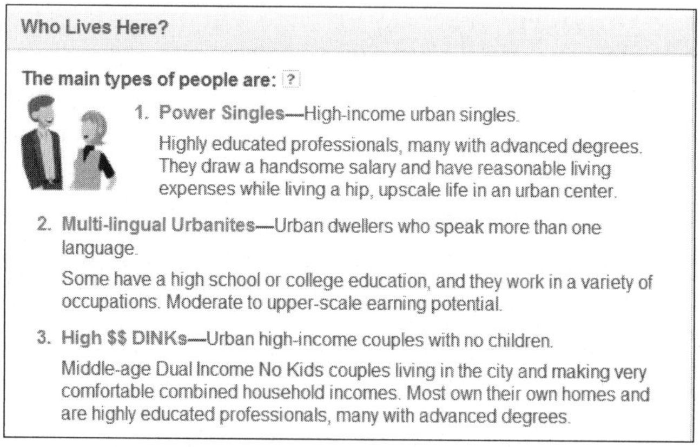

**Who Lives Here?**

The main types of people are: ?

1. **Power Singles**—High-income urban singles.

   Highly educated professionals, many with advanced degrees. They draw a handsome salary and have reasonable living expenses while living a hip, upscale life in an urban center.

2. **Multi-lingual Urbanites**—Urban dwellers who speak more than one language.

   Some have a high school or college education, and they work in a variety of occupations. Moderate to upper-scale earning potential.

3. **High $$ DINKs**—Urban high-income couples with no children.

   Middle-age Dual Income No Kids couples living in the city and making very comfortable combined household incomes. Most own their own homes and are highly educated professionals, many with advanced degrees.

**Figure 8-4:**
Sociological subsets, by community.

Now that you've narrowed your customer demographics data, it's time to find where your customers hang out on the web.

# Using Free Tools to Find Customers Online

Large organizations pay big money to consultants and agencies with access to huge amounts of information so they can crunch the numbers and apply the data to their business model. You probably don't have a budget set aside for specialists, so make the most of data available for free on the web.

If you're on the Internet, you are part of the digital human power grid of social data. It's no secret that websites know more about you than you probably wish they did. Everywhere we go, we leave a trail, exposing our likes and dislikes. Websites gather the data from the digital ecosystem and publish the information in easy-to-understand charts.

Following are the most popular social networks where people hang out:

- ✔ **Facebook** (7 billion visits per month): The site was founded in 2004 as a service for Harvard students to connect with each other online. Then the site was opened to anyone who was interested. A recent statistic quoted 901 million monthly active users. Statistics show that 42 percent of the U.S. population visits the site to connect via posts and photos with friends and family online.

- ✔ **Twitter** (182.2 million visits per month): The first microblogging service, Twitter allows members to send and read posts, or Tweets, of up to 140 characters in length. Early in 2012, they reported 140 million users generating 340 million Tweets and 1.6 billion searches a day. Twitter should see 250 million active users by the end of 2012.

   People follow others on Twitter who have similar tastes or interesting information to share, everything from the weather to politics. Even President Obama has a Twitter feed (@BarackObama).

- ✔ **Google+** (150 million active users): This site is based on social sharing of news, photos and data. Google+ is an identity service because the platform is built on people using their real names, as they use on a multitude of other Google platforms. (If you don't use your real name, your profile might be closed down and you may lose access to Google products.) People use circles on Google+ to organize their online friends for sharing, so posts may appear to only a selected group of friends. Hangouts facilitate group video chats for up to 10 people on the site.

- ✔ **LinkedIn** (98 million visits per month): The site was launched in 2003 as a professional networking site. You use LinkedIn's social network to build a contact list of people you have worked with in the past, through which you make new business contacts.

   Membership is gated. Contact with any professional requires a preexisting business relationship or an introduction. Many use this site to hire employees and contractors; members post their work histories and resumes to their pages.

- ✔ **MySpace** (31 million visits per month): MySpace was the first website deigned for social interaction. At its height, in 2006, it surpassed Google as the most visited site in the United States. With the advent of other, more organized networks, MySpace experienced a rapid decline. Figures released by Comscore suggest that they lost 10 million users just between January and February of 2011.

- ✔ **foursquare** (3 million check-ins per day): The original location-based social network, foursquare was founded in 2009 for use with mobile devices. Users check in at businesses and venues through mobile apps, often with comments and photos, and are awarded badges based on multiple check-ins. (Astronaut Douglas Wheelock unlocked the NASA Explorer badge by checking into foursquare from the International Space Station.) Mayorship of a business is awarded to the user with the most check-ins at a specific location.

Businesses may offer deals to those who check in and often provide bonuses to the mayor (such as a free order of French fries). American Express allows card members to merge their foursquare accounts with their credit cards, offering them discounts at preselected locations.

✔ **Pinterest** (34 million unique users): New on the social scene (launched in March 2010), Pinterest allows users to share photos, quotes, and videos in a pinboard-style format. (If you have a refrigerator with a lot of stuff on it, you'll quickly get the gist.) Pinterest's mission is to "connect everyone in the world through the 'things' they find interesting."

✔ **Angie's List** (1.5 million subscribers): As a way to capture word-of-mouth wisdom, Angie's List collects approximately 40,000 reviews each month solely from subscribers. The list is a paid subscriber model and prices are based on the geographic area that it serves. The site reviews businesses in the service industry, health care, and auto care.

Each company on the list has its own page and is rated by members who have used the services of that business. Reviews are based on price, quality, responsiveness, punctuality, and professionalism, with businesses rated from A to F.

✔ **Yelp** (54 million visits per month): In 2004, Yelp started a local search network that quickly turned into a popular user-review-based social networking site. Businesses can be searched by community, city, state, and ZIP code (for example, *Chinese restaurant in 91325*). After a search is run, users can select a business and go to that business's own page, where customers post reviews, comments, and photos.

I researched all these sites on Google Ad Planner, which provides free, directly measured traffic and audience composition reports. My results are shown in Table 8-2.

**Table 8-2    Age Distribution on Major Social Network Sites**

| Age Group | < 18 | 18–24 | 25–34 | 35–44 | 45–54 | 55–54 | 65+ |
|---|---|---|---|---|---|---|---|
| Internet Average | 18% | 13% | 17% | 19% | 17% | 10% | 6% |
| Facebook | 14% | 9% | 22% | 24% | 22% | 6% | 2% |

*(continued)*

### Table 8-2 *(continued)*

| Age Group | < 18 | 18–24 | 25–34 | 35–44 | 45–54 | 55–54 | 65+ |
|---|---|---|---|---|---|---|---|
| Twitter | 13% | 12% | 24% | 26% | 18% | 5% | 2% |
| Angie's List | 2% | 3% | 14% | 28% | 31% | 15% | 7% |
| Yelp | 3% | 6% | 22% | 29% | 27% | 10% | 4% |
| four-square | 6% | 9% | 27% | 30% | 21% | 6% | 2% |
| MySpace | 10% | 16% | 22% | 23% | 21% | 5% | 2% |
| LinkedIn | 4% | 5% | 24% | 30% | 25% | 9% | 3% |
| Pinterest (74% female) | 4% | 7% | 29% | 26% | 24% | 8% | 3% |
| Google+ (U.S.) | ? | 45.3% | 23.7% | 11.6% | 6.5% | 12.9% (and over) | ? |

*Source: Google Ad Planner and Plus Demographics*

The data in Table 8-2 fluctuates from month to month. However, the numbers clearly indicate that social media is not just for the young:

- ✔ 55 percent of Twitter users are 35 or older.
- ✔ 63 percent of Pinterest users are 35 or older.
- ✔ 65 percent of Facebook users are 35 or older.
- ✔ 79 percent of LinkedIn users are 35 or older.

## Baby boomers shake up the statistics

As recently as September 2010, a study by Wedbush Securities suggested that Facebook engagement with brands and businesses might not interest users over age 55. In that age group, only about 25 percent of Facebook's oldest users had liked a brand on the site, compared with 60 percent of those aged 18–34.

A post from eMarketer.com told the rest of the story: *"By November 2010, over-55s had begun to close the gap, however, and by April 2011, nearly half were connecting with brands. Engagement had also risen among 18- to 34-year-olds as well as the 35-to-54 age group over the period. Overall, 59% of adult Facebook users had "liked" a brand as of April, up from 47% the previous September. Uptake among the oldest users appears to have been a major factor in this rise."*

When studying the numbers, take into account the growing numbers of baby boomers who have the money for technology, have a desire to learn new things, and are coming online at a rapid pace. According to an AARP (Washington state) report, 70 percent of online Washingtonians age 45+ have at least one social networking account, and more than 50 percent joined within the last two years. Facebook, LinkedIn, and online communities related to hobbies or personal interests are the most popular social networking sites.

From the same report, 56 percent of those 45 and over say they have a Facebook account, and older adults are flocking to the site in increasing numbers. According to the report, respondents age 65+ are the fastest growing age group in Washington state joining Facebook. The most common reasons given among all respondents for using Facebook are keeping in touch with friends (86 percent) and extended family members (78 percent) and connecting with people from their past (67 percent).

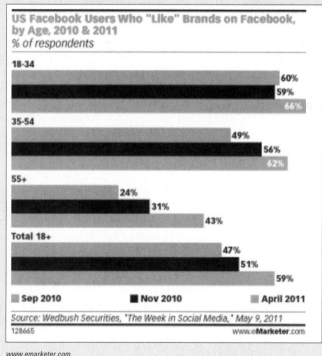

**US Facebook Users Who "Like" Brands on Facebook, by Age, 2010 & 2011**
*% of respondents*

**18-34**
- 60%
- 59%
- 66%

**35-54**
- 49%
- 56%
- 62%

**55+**
- 24%
- 31%
- 43%

**Total 18+**
- 47%
- 51%
- 59%

■ Sep 2010  ■ Nov 2010  ■ April 2011

*Source: Wedbush Securities, "The Week in Social Media," May 9, 2011*
128665                                                                www.eMarketer.com

www.emarketer.com

An interesting trend fueling social networks is that consumers are reaching out to a brand's customer service representatives online. This practice is gaining traction both on Twitter and Facebook and broadening their user base.

## Searching the competition through Alexa

If you're online, you can bet your competition is as well, as are their employees. When researching the competition, don't forget to check out their key employees by searching for them on Google to see if they are on Facebook, Twitter, and other social sites. Be sure to seek out and follow industry colleagues as well. Many an opportunity is mentioned via news bytes on social media sites and missed completely because it wasn't posted on the company main account.

A great way to personally check in on the competition is through LinkedIn. com. If you know your competition personally, invite them to connect with you on the site. After they are a connection, you can click the company name in their Experience area, which displays everyone on LinkedIn from that company, whether you're connected to them or not. How far you chose to take this investigation is up to you!

I'm sure if your competition has a website, they will be working hard to bring visitors there. Website monitoring is where Alexa.com comes in. Alexa is a subsidiary of Amazon.com and provides traffic data, global rankings, and other information on thousands of websites. Alexa states that 6 million people visit the website monthly. Alexa also chronicles the history of the web through www.waybackmachine.org, where you can see visual snapshots of almost every site since its inception on the web.

Sites are ranked on tracking information from users of the Alexa browser toolbar (or the Alexa Chrome extension). The data is aggregated based on the last three months' of browsing behavior. (Note that the data represents only a sample of Internet users, so it's not as accurate in ranking less-trafficked sites.) In Figure 8-5, for example, I looked up the popular blog of my friend, Chris Brogan.

For a small to medium-sized business site, you will see the following data (the most visited sites reflect more data):

  ✔ **Global rank:** Ranking based on page views and visitors from the entire world during the last three months.

  ✔ **Rank in *headquartered country*:** Ranking based on page views and visitors from the website's home country during the last three months.

**Figure 8-5:**
The Alexa
user base
ranks a blog.

✔ **Reputation:** Number of sites that linked the visitor to the site (updated monthly). Clicking here gives you a list of sites that may be related to your industry.

✔ **Traffic stats:** Unless the site is in the top one hundred thousand, you will not see stats. Note the subtabs that appear in the Traffic Stats tab (see Figure 8-6). Just below the chart area, you can type the names of four other website URLs. The stats for those sites appear on the chart, so you can compare your competitors.

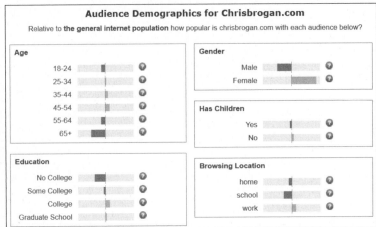

**Figure 8-6:**
Alexa's
audience
demograph-
ics for
Chris's blog.

If you agree to install the Alexa toolbar on your browser, you'll have access to advanced demographics and search analytics data that identifies search keywords and indicates which keywords drive the most traffic to your site. You can use these metrics to plan a pay-per-click (PPC) marketing campaign to drive visitors to your site through Google AdWords.

Regularly compare your website to your competition's websites, noting who they are reaching and the keywords that drove people to their sites.

## Checking out your website data through Google Analytics

Google Analytics (www.google.com/analytics) is a free service that generates detailed statistics about your website's visitors to help you plan your online marketing. Analytics is the most widely used service on the web, with a total of 10 million users, of which 57 percent are listed in the top 10,000 sites. Google offers a premium version for a fee, but most businesses are happy with the free basic version. You can use this tool right away to study the people who visit your site.

Analytics provides a huge breadth of data. You learn how people found your site, from where they found it, how they viewed it, and more. Figure 8-7 shows you the summary page of a site of mine that I rarely publicize on the web.

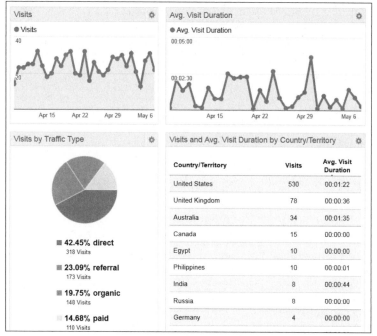

Figure 8-7:
Google
Analytics
overview
page.

From the Google Analytics data, you learn which parts of your site are reaching the most people and which items they find the best. A few of the statistics you can measure are

- **Demographics:** The language spoken by and the location of your visitors.

- **Behavior:** Whether your visitors are new or returning to the site, how often they return, how recently they visited, and the time they spent on your pages.

- **Technology:** Which browser and operating system your visitors used, as well as their Internet service provider.

- **Sources:** Where your visitors are coming from as well as whether they typed your URL directly or were referred from another site.

- **Search:** Which search engine, if any, your visitors used to find you and the keywords they entered.

- **Social analytics:** Which of your social media sites draw people in? Figure 8-8 shows a sample of traffic data from social networks.

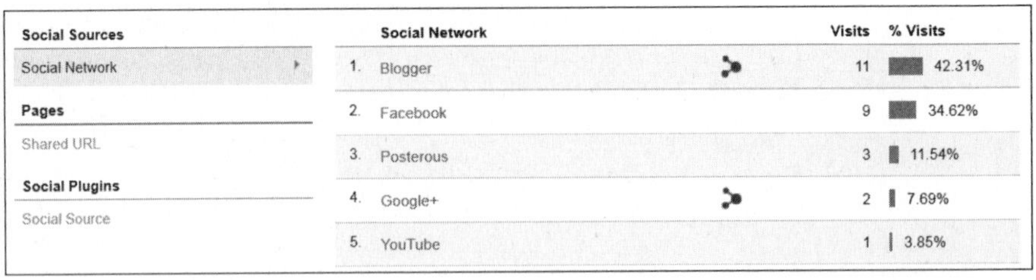

**Figure 8-8:**
A portion of
the Social
Network
referrals
for the site
from Google
Analytics.

| Social Sources | | Social Network | | Visits | % Visits |
|---|---|---|---|---|---|
| Social Network ▶ | | 1. Blogger | ✁ | 11 | 42.31% |
| **Pages** | | 2. Facebook | | 9 | 34.62% |
| Shared URL | | 3. Posterous | | 3 | 11.54% |
| **Social Plugins** | | 4. Google+ | ✁ | 2 | 7.69% |
| Social Source | | 5. YouTube | | 1 | 3.85% |

✔ **Content**: Which pages draw the most attention, the pages your visitors read, and the time they spent on each.

See which type of content resonates most with your site visitors. Then build more of that type of content to attract new and repeat visitors.

✔ **Conversions:** Transaction data on items you sell from your site.

To learn the ins and outs of Google Analytics, as well as find in-depth info on web statistics, I recommend *Social Media Metrics For Dummies* by Leslie Poston (Wiley).

## Getting insights from your Facebook business page

One of the benefits of having a Facebook business page is being able to access statistical information on your fans. To hone in on that data, you can use Facebook Insights.

Open your fan or business page and click the Insights link. A summary of your posts appears, as shown in Figure 8-9, with statistical information on the levels of social engagement you received on each.

The following metrics on the overall performance of your page are displayed:

✔ **Total Likes:** The total number of people who have stopped by and have clicked Like on your page. (In other words, they became a fan.)

✔ **Friends of Fans:** The number of your fans multiplied by the number of their unique Facebook friends. This number is your current possible total reach. If a fan shares a post from your page on their page, their friends will see it. The more the merrier, eh?

✔ **People Talking about This:** The number of unique (not repeat) visitors who posted about your page in the last seven days. These visitors may have liked, mentioned, commented on, or shared one of your posts. They may also have tagged you or your business in a photo or recommended your business.

✔ **Weekly Total Reach:** The total number of unique visitors to your Facebook fan or business page in the past seven days.

The Total Likes and the People Talking about This numbers can be seen by anyone who visits your page and give them a clue as to the vibrancy of your fan interactions.

By going over this data, you can find out the types of posts that appeal to your readers (the sort of posts you should post more often) and those that don't. To extract even more insight, click the numbers in each column.

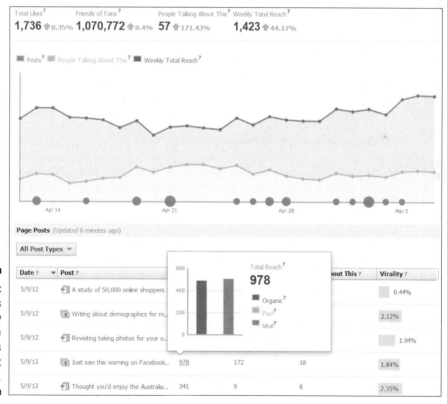

**Figure 8-9:**
The Insights overview page updates almost immediately.

If you sort your post according to most popular (Reach) by clicking at the top of the column, you see the dates of the post. Then click the date, and you see the time of day of the post. This information helps determine which days and times are best for connecting with your audience.

You'll also get some interesting demographic data on your fans, who interacts on your page, and who your message is reaching. Age and gender (based on the data your fans entered when they filled out their Facebook profiles) are represented as a percentage. You can also determine where your fans are from and their native language.

In Figure 8-10, I've lined up three sets of age data. Compare the total number of fans of your page with who has interacted on your page in the past seven days.

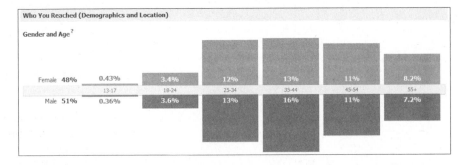

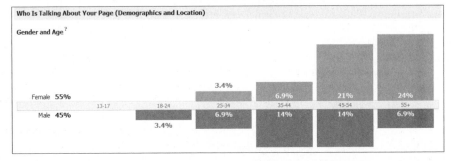

**Figure 8-10:** Comparing age brackets to see who is connecting on your page.

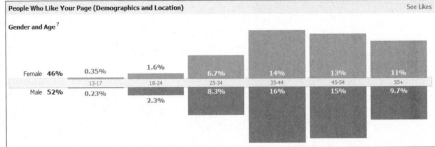

Insights provides a huge amount of information. Now that you know where to find it, I'm sure you'll click and dig deeper.

# Big Online Numbers Don't Mean Dollars

If your online goal is to conclude a sale to your social media friends and fans, you'll have to give these folks a cold, hard look. Some believe that more is better. But more what? You need to focus on people who, at the end of the day, may purchase something from you directly or through your website.

Facebook Insights, Google Analytics, and other tools help you decide if you're playing in the right ballpark. If your message isn't being received by the right people, you're wasting time and money in social media.

 Content is indeed king and your levels of engagement are what will draw attention to your brand. Quality content means publishing information that you think your followers, fans, or subscribers want to read — not what *you* want them to read. If you don't work your social media accounts, they cannot possibly work for you.

Connecting is even more relevant when it comes to Twitter, where members seem to make hobbies of gaining tens of thousands of followers. Many of those on the site rarely Tweet, but they get a thrill out of gaining more and more followers. Following accounts like those are a waste of time, and in the end hurt your trust and credibility on the site. Conversely, having a high number of followers does not mean that you are influential on the site.

The Edelman Trust Barometer, `http://trust.edelman.com/`, is an annual study on building trust through business and relationships globally. It has had a monster effect empowering businesses by providing the data to understand how to connect with customers with a high level of credibility.

The Edelman Barometer states that 77 percent of people refused to buy products or services from a company they distrusted.

> *"It is trust that makes someone act – for this reason alone, having a high trust score is considered by many to be more important than any other category. Trust can be measured by the number of times someone is happy to associate what you have said through them – in other words, how often you are reTweeted."*

You can search your Twitter account (or the competitions) to see how your Tweets resound on Twitter. To measure Twitter trust levels (and more), visit `http://tweetlevel.edelman.com`. Figure 8-11 shows the results of my account.

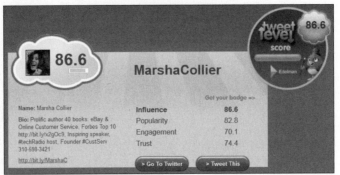

**Figure 8-11:**
Checking
these sta-
tistics can
help you
stay on
track.

In Chapter 9, I give you the lowdown on connecting with your prospective customers via Twitter. In this chapter, I am talking about numbers and demographics.

## Ranking your followers on Twitter

After your Twitter account is up and running (using the suggestions I give you in Chapter 9), wouldn't it be nice to have similar demographic information on the people who follow you back on Twitter?

If the type of person following you on Twitter is not equal to your business demographic profile, can your efforts on the site really help you? Outreach should equate to sales and connections. On Twitter, as on any other platform mentioned, you have to figure out who these people are.

Currently, the best way to get this data is through a service from Schmap: Know Your Twitter Followers, a tool used by many Fortune 500 companies. You may know Schmap from their real-time city guides that cover more than 400 million locations worldwide. They have been producing these for the web since 2004.

In an interview with Mashable, Schmap CEO Paul Hallett said "Know Your Twitter Followers fills the void for audience measurement in social media and provides a breakdown of your followers so that you can understand how to target your audience."

By going to `http://knowyourfollowers.com`, anyone can get immediate access to a free summary demographic analysis of a portion of their Twitter followers. The price for a full, in-depth analysis is based on the number of your followers: $3.95 for accounts with up to 5,000 followers to $249.95 for accounts with more than 2 million followers. A portion of my Twitter account summary is shown in Figure 8-12.

| 📊 Age | | | 📊 Likes & Interests | | | 📊 Professions | | |
|---|---|---|---|---|---|---|---|---|
| 16 and under | 226 | 7.3% | Wining & dining | 9,443 | 19.7% | Sales/marketing | 7,507 | 18.8% |
| 17 to 19 | 181 | 5.9% | Music | 8,583 | 17.9% | Entrepreneurs | 4,042 | 10.1% |
| 20 to 24 | 264 | 8.6% | Technology | 8,289 | 17.3% | Senior managers | 3,868 | 9.7% |
| 25 to 29 | 475 | 15.4% | Travel | 8,168 | 17.1% | Authors/writers | 3,491 | 8.8% |
| 30 to 34 | 388 | 12.6% | Health issues | 7,444 | 15.6% | Consultants | 3,198 | 8.0% |
| 35 to 39 | 431 | 14.0% | Books/reading | 7,300 | 15.3% | Journalists | 2,976 | 7.5% |
| 40 to 49 | 668 | 21.7% | Art/culture | 6,792 | 14.2% | Web developers | 1,667 | 4.2% |
| 50 to 59 | 279 | 9.0% | News | 6,682 | 14.0% | Musicians | 1,339 | 3.4% |
| Other *expand* | | | Other *expand* | | | Other *expand* | | |
| Total analyzed: | 3,085 | 100% | Total analyzed: | 47,820 | 100% | Total analyzed: | 39,896 | 100% |

| 📊 Eat/drink at... | | | 📊 Shop at... | | | 📊 Dressed by... | | |
|---|---|---|---|---|---|---|---|---|
| Starbucks | 7,860 | 35.0% | Walmart | 5,793 | 22.3% | Macy's | 1,601 | 16.4% |
| McDonald's | 5,587 | 24.9% | Best Buy | 3,210 | 12.4% | Nordstrom | 1,229 | 12.6% |
| Hard Rock Cafe | 2,036 | 9.1% | Apple Store | 3,038 | 11.7% | Old Navy | 989 | 10.1% |
| Burger King | 1,743 | 7.8% | Target | 3,007 | 11.6% | Victoria's Secret | 768 | 7.9% |
| Taco Bell | 1,717 | 7.6% | Whole Foods | 2,592 | 10.0% | Burberry | 725 | 7.4% |
| Dominos | 1,395 | 6.2% | Ikea | 2,562 | 9.9% | Urban Outfitters | 549 | 5.6% |
| Chipotle | 1,341 | 6.0% | Barnes & Noble | 2,147 | 8.3% | Forever 21 | 520 | 5.3% |
| Dunkin Donuts | 1,298 | 5.8% | Costco | 1,901 | 7.3% | Patagonia | 492 | 5.0% |
| Other *expand* | | | Other *expand* | | | Other *expand* | | |
| Total analyzed: | 22,466 | 100% | Total analyzed: | 25,990 | 100% | Total analyzed: | 9,758 | 100% |

| 📊 They also use... | | | 📊 First languages | | | 📊 Twitter settings | | |
|---|---|---|---|---|---|---|---|---|
| Hootsuite | 14,273 | 29.8% | English | 44,482 | 93.0% | Profile image | 46,710 | 97.7% |
| Tweetdeck | 9,613 | 20.1% | Spanish | 1,230 | 2.6% | Website set | 36,892 | 77.1% |
| Youtube | 6,398 | 13.4% | Japanese | 843 | 1.8% | Geo-enabled | 12,053 | 25.2% |
| Twitpic | 6,133 | 12.8% | Portuguese | 326 | 0.7% | Verified | 264 | 0.6% |
| Facebook | 6,130 | 12.8% | German | 292 | 0.6% | Protected | 944 | 2.0% |

**Figure 8-12:**
Summary
of a full
analysis of
my Twitter
account.

After you buy a report, you can compare your demographics to Twitter averages, graph and map these comparisons, and then print or download the statistics to a PDF file or a CSV file (for use in Microsoft Excel, Microsoft Access, and most other spreadsheet or database software) so you can seriously dive in.

Data is available for many data points aside from demographics, including where your followers shop, buy clothing, and eat as well as their hobbies, professions, likes, and interests. This information could be invaluable if you are trying to see whether you have built the right audience for your brand or business.

Schmap makes no bones about where the data comes from — they use the data we make public from posts and social media reference. The magic lies in their use of a series of fuzzy logic algorithms developed by their own team.

Fuzzy logic, first theorized in 1965, is based on probabilities and reasoning (and is also applied to artificial intelligence systems).

From their website:

> *Put simply, we make statistically sensible deductions based on multiple bits of data. The multi-signal statistical approach is necessary, because computers, by and large, still suck at interpreting natural language, particularly the kind of culturally diverse and informal language your followers use on Twitter.*
>
> *In terms of accuracy, we strive to make sure that any given conclusion (regarding marital status, profession, location etc.) for any given follower has at least a 95% chance of being correct. As a result, an aggregate analysis for an account with even just a few hundred followers stands up very well indeed.*

Although the information isn't as accurate as the data you would get if every follower filled out a form, it's as accurate as any system mentioned here — and perhaps even more accurate.

## Unfollowing the excess

To boost your influence, remove dead accounts from your Twitter stream. After all, following a bunch of people who aren't Tweeting or, worse, are spammers is just a waste of time. When it comes to Internet metrics, following these types of accounts can lower your numbers.

### Losing dead accounts

When you've researched the people you follow on Twitter and feel it's time to unfollow some of them, check out Untweeps (www.untweeps.com). The program uses the Twitter API (application programming interface) to unfollow those you select from a list of people who haven't updated their account in a set number of days.

The site requests that you to sign in to your Twitter account. Do so, and the site whirs and grinds for a while and then presents a list of dead accounts, like the one shown in Figure 8-13, along with the last date the accounts updated on the site. You may be shocked at the number of results.

The only fly in the ointment is that you have to click to add a check mark next to each account you want to unfollow. After you've completed all the clicks, click the Unfollow Selected Tweeps button. While writing this, I unfollowed 493 dead Twitter accounts!

A superior free platform for finding spam-ridden and dead accounts is TwitCleaner, at `http://thetwitcleaner.com/`. Their approach — "Twitter is about quality not quantity" — mirrors my own and their reports are very detailed. After you sign in with your Twitter account on the site, they build a current report and direct-message you on Twitter when it is done.

They examine your account deeply and find not only dead accounts but also those who are using Twitter as a place to promote their own agendas. TwitCleaner finds the accounts who don't listen. Highly recommended.

### Disengaging from those who don't connect with you

Part of the fun and engagement on Twitter is following back those who choose to follow you. By using Twitter private lists, you can watch a group of select friends, be they customers or family (more on this feature in Chapter 9).

However, chances are that some people have followed you but you haven't followed back because you've been too busy with other things. Go to www. justunfollow.com and sign in with your Twitter account. You'll see lists of those who don't follow you back and those who are fans but you aren't following back, as shown in Figure 8-14.

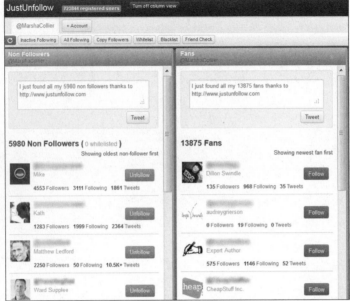

**Figure 8-14:**
Oops.
Seems I'm
not follow-
ing back
13,875
people.
My bad.

Below their IDs and avatars are the number of people they follow, the number that follow them, and their total number of Tweets. You'll find some who spew pointless Tweets or Tweet little in proportion to the number of people they follow; this info can be a tipping point as to whether you choose to follow them. One account I viewed had over 19,000 followers, followed more than 20,000, and has Tweeted just 643 times. Smells fishy to me. (I'm not following them back.) Generally, I check out accounts that bring up these flags for spammers.

You can unfollow or follow 25 people per visit to the site at no charge. For $9.99 a year, you can unfollow or follow an unlimited number of people per visit.

# Chapter 9

# Seizing the Social Media Conversation

*T*oday's social media interactions are not only where friends and family connect, but also where you meet new people. Today's conversations are seeds for future commerce harvests.

Social media networking conversations occur on many sites around the web. (See Chapter 2 for a figure showing them all.) In this chapter, you find out about the places where easy engagement can lead to customer enticement.

In this conversational atmosphere, you can expect to

- ✔ **Sell:** Promote online and offline sales by posting promotions, discounts, and offers

- ✔ **Find new customers:** Find people who are interested in a new vendor. Unhappy customers tend to be vocal on social media.

- ✔ **Build community:** Join with others in your industry to share information. Connect with prospective and current customers to ultimately help drive new business.

- ✔ **Observe the competition:** Follow friendly (or unfriendly) competition to see how they handle social media outreach.

- ✔ **Engage in customer service:** Through connecting online, you can successfully engage with customers who are in need of help.

This chapter talks about the sites where manners and creative thinking count. (After all, it takes a while to figure out how to get a point across in 140 characters on Twitter.) This overview should help you direct your outreach. Your social investment may take a bit of time to pay off, but pay off it will, if you just stick with it.

# Building a Community on Twitter

Twitter is a convenient format for building an online community. If the thought of short messages appeals to you, Twitter may be the place for your online customer connections.

Some quick Twitter stats:

- ✔ Twitter has an estimated 500 million registered users and 200 million active users.
- ✔ Estimated total Tweets average 400 million Tweets a day, 750 Tweets per second.
- ✔ 30 percent of Twitter users have an income of more than $100,000.
- ✔ Twitter handles more search queries than Microsoft's Bing and Yahoo! combined.

For Twitter to work for your social commerce, you have to follow people, listen, and take action by engaging in the conversation. Take the time to interact and foster relationships within the Twitter community. Later in the chapter, I show you how to find people to follow who will complement your brand.

Participating is not terribly hard because Tweets are limited to 140 characters. If you send text messages on your phone, you're given room for 160 characters, so moving from text messages to Tweeting isn't a big jump. After you get the hang of short messaging, Tweeting can become second nature.

Your plan for Twitter should be to engage a good number of followers, drawing them to your business and brand. Become their virtual friend and turn them into evangelists for you businesses. Twitter is not a numbers game unless you're a multinational company (and have the staff to run the account).

# Tweeting, top-ten style

On the bottom of your TV screen, you can often see the Twitter account of the show or the stars so that viewers can engage with the show online. The show wants to build buzz in this fast-moving and insanely viral medium.

The following top ten Twitter celebrities rarely reciprocate and follow back; I explain the follow-back issue later in this chapter. Note that although these users scream pop culture, 55 percent of Twitter users are 35 or older.

The list of top Twitter users (based on number of followers) reads like a who's who of pop culture:

- Lady Gaga (@ladygaga): 28,817,091 followers and 137,855 following

- Justin Bieber (@justinbieber): 27,155,092 followers and 123,056 following

- Katy Perry (@katyperry): 25,653,806 followers and 109 following

- Rihanna (@Rihanna): 24,845,744 followers and 867 following

- Britney Spears (@britneyspears): 19,814,113 followers and 413,537 following

- Barack Obama (@BarackObama): 18,946,850 followers and 673,721 following

- Shakira (@shakira): 18,004,546 followers and 67 following

- Taylor Swift (@taylorswift13): 17,894,054 followers and 81 following

- Kim Kardashian (@KimKardashian): 15,989,674 followers and 173 following

- YouTube (@YouTube): 15,677,621 followers and 425 following

The good news is you don't have to follow any of them. The bad news is that mimicking their Twitter habits probably won't help you at all.

Many celebrities and politicians have staff that manage the account and do their Tweeting for them. When the stars do interject Tweets of their own, they are usually carefully crafted to maintain the image of a brand.

Other celebrities take their Tweets into their own hands; often to the pleasure of the pop-culture media that enjoy nothing more than watching someone crash and burn. Alec Baldwin (@AB), Charlie Sheen (@charliesheen), and Gilbert Gottfried (see Chapter 2 to see why he's no longer on the site) build their brands through sensationalism. Luckily, you haven't any of their worries.

## Tweeting for business

You can have separate business and personal accounts on Twitter, but handling two accounts can be a challenge. I've found that I can consistently handle only one Twitter account at a time. (In Chapter 16, I describe some tools for handling multiple accounts.)

All the major brands are on Twitter. Big companies such as FedEx have a staff of people to handle Twitter and anther to handle Facebook. Use Twitter search to find your favorite brand, or go directly to http://twitter.com/MarshaCollier/brands-on-twitter for my public Twitter List of Brands. Follow that list to observe big business at work online.

Your presence on Twitter can personalize your business outreach — Tweets should sound like they're from a real, live person. Tweet about the ideas behind and value of your business to the community by sharing content. Share links to stories and pictures with your customers. Make your business transparent; make it real. (Chapter 18 gives you some more ideas for Tweets.) Here are some of the things you can do with a Twitter account:

- Organize *Tweetups*, which are live events that you sponsor for your Twitter followers and local community.
- Monitor your account through searches and see what people are saying about you.
- Respond publicly to customer queries and questions.
- Show that your business is not a cold, hard enterprise but is run by people.
- Spread the word easily if you're supporting a charity or cause.
- Learn from others in your line of work (find them through searches and hash tags as described shortly), and interact within that community.
- See who's doing innovative work in your field; you might get some good ideas to apply to your business.
- Build customers by friending like-minded people online.
- Handle customer service issues in a fresh and friendly way.

If the idea of typing words and phrases to people you don't know gives you the willies, check out Twitter's many examples of small businesses who reach their customers online.

In 2009, Co Co. Sala, a popular Washington, DC chocolate lounge and boutique — yes, you read right — joined Twitter (@cocosala). They've been using Twitter to build a customer base and connect with existing customers, as shown in Figure 9-1.

I asked Monica Sethi, head of social media outreach, about how they are using social media. She replied

> *Our passion lies in providing our customers with an experience which far surpasses their expectations. With the help of social media, we are able to deliver this exceptional customer experience not only at our venue but online, as well.*

> *With the emergence of social media, there has been a paradigm shift in communication. It is no longer about one-way communication. Social media allows us to engage with our customers in conversation. This provides us with the ability to understand our customers and connect with them on a deeper level.*

Another interesting example is @ChicagoCabbie, shown in Figure 9-2. This cab driver Tweets between calls and has built quite a following of Chicagoans. He also uses Twitter to set up appointments for rides. Smart!

**Figure 9-1:** Co Co. Sala's Twitter page shows warm content with followers and customers.

**Figure 9-2:** @Chicago Cabbie finds fares by making friends in his city.

The businesses (and people) who do the best on Twitter stay away from constant self-referential posts. Marketing and promotion must be couched between Tweets of interest to your followers.

## Choosing who to follow

Twitter can work only when you follow other people and they follow you back. How do you get people to follow you? By commenting on another Tweet, reTweeting, Tweeting content, or just jumping into a conversation that interests you.

Your first step is to go to the Twitter home page, at www.twitter.com, type your full name, your e-mail address, and a password. Then click Sign Up for Twitter, as shown in Figure 9-3.

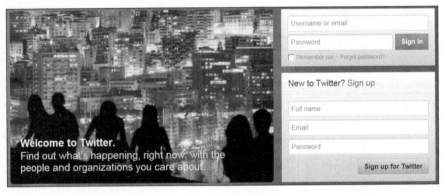

**Figure 9-3:** Enter a bit of data and you're in! Fill out your bio on the following page.

After you register on Twitter, things may seem a little lonely at first. I signed up in early 2008 and was befuddled by the blank page that stared back at me. Twitter posts suggestions for people you might want to follow. You can also try the following:

✔ **Followerwonk.com:** Use Followerwonk to search keywords in user bios as they have been input on Twitter. You can also search job titles, topics, or any specific keywords that may help you find someone you might be interested in following. Followerwonk presents search results in order of relevance to your keywords, so more valid results appear at the beginning. Most importantly? Note the Influence score next to each result, as shown in Figure 9-4. This proprietary rating metric, which ranges from 0 to 100 (higher scores indicate a person with greater influential activity), is based on a user's influence and engagement on Twitter.

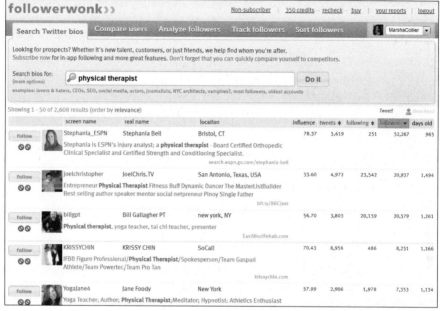

**Figure 9-4:**
Searching
for physical
therapists
on Twitter
through
Follower-
wonk.

✔ **Twellow.com:** Billing itself as the "Twitter Yellow Pages," this site has been indexing and categorizing Twitter since 2007. Twellow makes following new people a breeze. On the home page, select a category or subcategory from a drop-down menu to see a list of Twitter users whose bios (or personally selected categories on Twellow) match your search. You can also type in the search box the keyword of a topic you want to follow.

If you read the user's details and decide that you want to follow the person, click the Follow button below the user's profile picture, as shown in Figure 9-5.

**Figure 9-5:**
Click the
Follow but-
ton below
the profile
picture to
follow the
person.

You can narrow your keyword or topic searches to your immediate geographic area, which is particularly valuable if your business does not currently do online sales. On the search results page, click the city at the top right of the list and Twellow narrows the search to a reasonable distance. Note that the displayed city is generated from your Internet service provider and may not exactly match your location.

After you set up your Twitter account, select your topics and register them on Twellow so that they become indexed and available for others who search the site.

## Answering the "who should I follow back" question

When someone follows your account on Twitter, you receive an e-mail notification from the site. Take a minute to click through and view the user's bio and Tweets. If you see no bio or no real name, there is a chance that the account was set up with no intent of real engagement.

When you look at the user's Tweets, see if what the person says (and how it is phrased) is aligned with your personal and business culture. Are they your customer? Reading what someone writes gives you insight into the person and their background. But because Tweets are limited in length, you need to look at someone's Tweet stream to understand who they are.

People tell me that my writing style makes them feel as though I am sitting next to them chatting — not talking at them. If you look at my Tweets, you'll see that I Tweet news stories regularly. I get into conversations at least once a day, and I often share quotes. There. You know me. It's that easy.

Because social media is about inclusion, following back will help you build your audience. As a business or small brand, building an audience is the first step to building a community.

The decision to follow back is often different for major brands and celebrities than for small business owners. The legal department of some major brands prohibits following back. But reciprocation with the prospective customer is critical for a small business. As to celebrities, perhaps people are thrilled just to get a word from their heroes? I certainly was when Piers Morgan reTweeted me, but he never followed me (insert sad face here). But Kathy Ireland does!

Having tens of thousands (perhaps hundreds of thousands) of followers seems impossible to manage — and it would be for the average Twitter user. But in Chapter 16, I expose a trick of the pros and show you how to view a private Twitter list of just your close friends. You will still see anytime someone on Twitter addresses you personally.

# Making Friends and Fans on Facebook

Making friends with strangers can feel creepy, especially on a personal Facebook page. But your prospective customers are all strangers until you interact with them.

I hope you have a personal Facebook page where you connect with friends and family. I do, and since I had a personal page long before Facebook allowed business pages, I have many business contacts there as well. This is the perfect way to get a feel for how Facebook works. When you post personal items, however, be sure to post them to appear only on the news feeds of close friends and family.

But to build your brand on Facebook, you have to start a business page. The hard part is moving business friends away from your personal page to your fan page.

As I've said before, in today's social media, business has become personal. So unless you're new to Facebook, you will have some overlap between your personal and business pages.

## Why Facebook counts

If you're not yet convinced of the power of Facebook, check these statistics:

- Facebook has 900 million registered users worldwide and about 160 million in the United States.

- 50 percent of active users log in on any given day.

- The average Facebook user has more than 130 friends and spends 700 minutes per month on the site.

- Every 60 seconds, more than 500,000 comments are posted on an estimated 293,000 status updates and 136,000 photos.

- More than 30 billion pieces of content are shared each month.

- More than 55 million status updates are posted daily.

# Facebook business page benefits

A personal page is fun for connecting and sharing. Your business page takes a bit more finesse because it blends personal contact and marketing.

- ✔ You can have more than 5,000 friends (fans or likes on your business page). Do you want that many? The answer is yes if you plan on selling anything online.

- ✔ You can use your business name as the page title, making it easier for the page to be indexed by Google. This helps your business's SEO (search engine optimization) and may add strength to the listing position of your business website.

- ✔ Those who like the page are opting in for your updates. Treat this valuable resource with respect and don't barrage them with promotions.

- ✔ You can customize the page into a mini-site that includes contact forms, sales pages, blog feeds, contests, and even a store. In Chapter 10, I describe some tools that make setup quick and easy.

- ✔ Statistics are available on each individual post on your page, as shown in Figure 9-6.

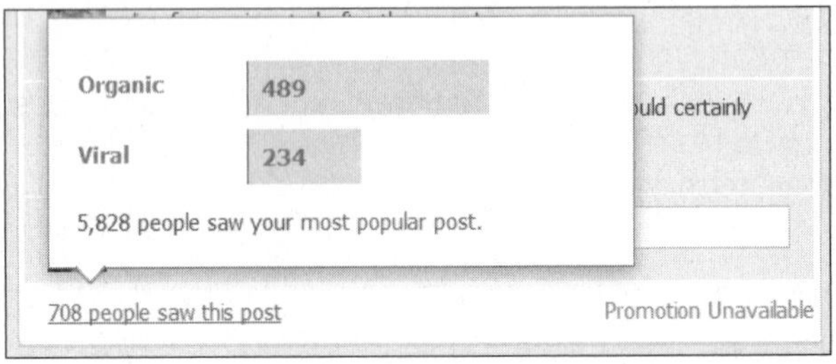

**Figure 9-6:**
See how far a post on your business page has spread.

Organic 489

Viral 234

5,828 people saw your most popular post.

708 people saw this post

Promotion Unavailable

- ✔ Status updates are filtered by Facebook's EdgeRank algorithm, which places what it deems to be the most relevant content in news feeds. Business pages can use a paid ad tool to enhance the views of a single post. (I have seen success with a budget as small as $5 a day.) Figure 9-7 shows how easy it is to start a three-day campaign.

- ✔ You can purchase ads that point to your business page or your website. These ads, which appear in Facebook's right-side border, can be targeted using 15 criteria and even more subcriteria, as shown in Figure 9-8. You can narrow the audience to city and even ZIP code. (Chapter 15 goes into buying and targeting your Facebook ads in depth.)

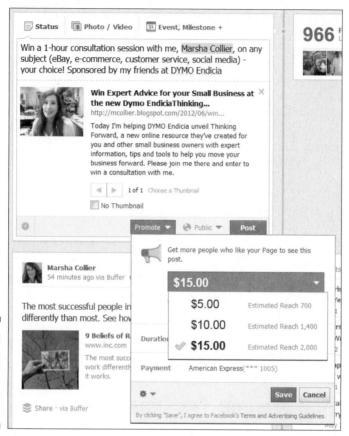

**Figure 9-7:**
Setting up a sponsored post on a business page.

✔ Gating is often used by brands running special promotions and is a function of apps (described in Chapter 10). The gate becomes the landing page for the page or promotion. To participate in a sweepstakes, giveaway, or special promotion, visitors must like your page before the information is revealed behind the gate page.

You always want the customer to visit your website. Link status updates to blog posts or to information that appears on your website. You want the customer to be engaged and understand your commitment to an online presence.

✔ Business pages are searchable in a Facebook search. When someone comes to your business location and sees a sign to join you on Facebook, they can type your business name and find the page without using a URL.

✔ Pages with more than 25 or more likes get valuable data, called Insights. Growth, demographics, engagement information, and activity can be tracked. Chapters 8 and 15 give you more insight on Insights.

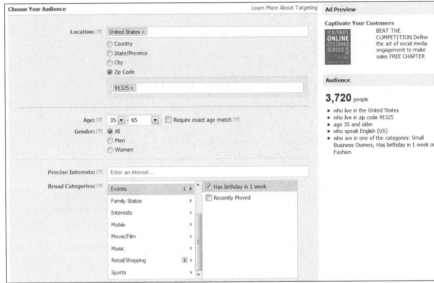

**Figure 9-8:** You can reach those with upcoming birthdays within your business ZIP code!

# Finding friends (or fans) for your business page

Facebook users are pretty loose with their friending habits, but liking a page is another story. This is the hard part.

I suggest that you first get your page together. Decide on a cover photo that best portrays your business. (You might want to use a picture of your staff or location.) Fill in all the blanks. After you launch the page, use the following methods to send out the word:

✔ Post an announcement of your new page on your personal Facebook page, inviting your online friends to join in on the fun!

✔ If you have an e-mail list, send out messages. If not, you can use a tool in the page's admin panel to import your contacts from most popular e-mail portals, such as Gmail, Yahoo!, and Hotmail.

✔ Tweet about your new page on Twitter, asking people, without pestering, to join you there. Perhaps say "come write on our Facebook wall."

✔ Leverage other social media sites where you already have an audience and mention that you have a new page. I've discovered a lot of new businesses this way.

✔ Put up a sign in your business asking your customers to join in the fun on Facebook. (Asking people to like your page is old-school marketing.) See Figure 9-9 for a good example from a local bakery.

**Figure 9-9:** Creative ways to get people to engage with your business.

✔ In your e-mail signature, add a link to your Facebook business page.

✔ Place a widget on your company website to let your customers know that you're on Facebook.

✔ From the Facebook admin page, invite friends from your personal page.

✔ Use Facebook search to find Facebook Groups that might be aligned to your type of business and then join them. From there, you can invite people to join you on your page.

✔ Buy a Facebook ad and regionalize it for your primary market area to promote your page. You can also target your ads to the fans of your competitors' page using Precise Interests (see Chapter 15 for details).

Building your base will take a while, so be patient. Continue to regularly post to the page. If you post good content, your fan count will grow.

## Engaging and building your audience

It's time to be your charming self. As the head of your business, your business page should reflect you. In the beginning, you may feel as though you're talking to yourself and a dozen or so family and friends. But don't give up. Slow and steady wins the race.

Social media scientist and data cruncher Dan Zarrella studies social media posts to find out which get the greatest attention. In contrast to Twitter, where information is exchanged among personal Tweets, Facebook posts with a higher number of self-referential words (such as *I* and *me*) tend to get more likes. Note that these posts aren't marketing ones; they're posts that involve you and your involvement with your business and customers.

Find other businesses, perhaps in your field or neighborhood, with which you are friendly and like their page from your business page, Here's how you do it:

1. **Click the down-facing arrow at the top-right of your Facebook page.**

2. **Select Use Facebook as *your page name,* as shown in Figure 9-10.**

   You are now using Facebook as your business page.

**Figure 9-10:** Your business page and personal profile.

3. **Now that you are using Facebook as your business page, visit a like-minded page and click its Like button.**

4. **Click Home in the top bar.**

   You see a news feed from the Fan page of the other business.

5. **If you see a post you like, click it and like it or add a comment.**

   Your participation in the social business community lets other business page owners know that you're interested in them; they may reciprocate.

Only one in five posts on your Facebook page should be promotional. The other four posts should be about something your audience will appreciate but not directly about your business.

You can post four basic items: photos, text, videos, and links. After you post, you can only hope that your fans will like, comment on, or share your post on another Facebook page. Dan Zarrella (aforementioned social media scientist) recently studied the types of Facebook post interactions that received the most traction. In Figure 9-11, you can clearly see that photos perform best. Second best is text (comments, notes, and ideas), with videos third and links fourth.

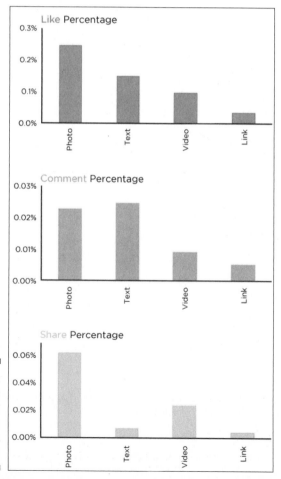

**Figure 9-11:** The results of Dan Zarella's Facebook study.

Facebook's EdgeRank weighs text-only posts lower by default. People like photos, so give them photos that will resonate with them or relate to your business. Also share photos from around the web on your page and see if including photos brings in new fans and stimulates engagement.

Post things on your page that will engage those who may become future customers. Here are some ideas:

✔ Offer special promotions or other perks only for participants on your Facebook page. (Only one in five updates should be promotions.)

✔ Ask questions by using the Facebook polling tool. Grab your audience's attention by asking questions about topics to which your audience can relate. Perhaps develop a conversation by asking questions about products, services, or items people would like you to add.

In the status update box, click the + to the right of Event, Milestone to display the three options shown in Figure 9-12. Then select Question, craft your question and some suggested answers, and launch the poll.

**Figure 9-12:**
The
Facebook
Question
tool on your
business
page.

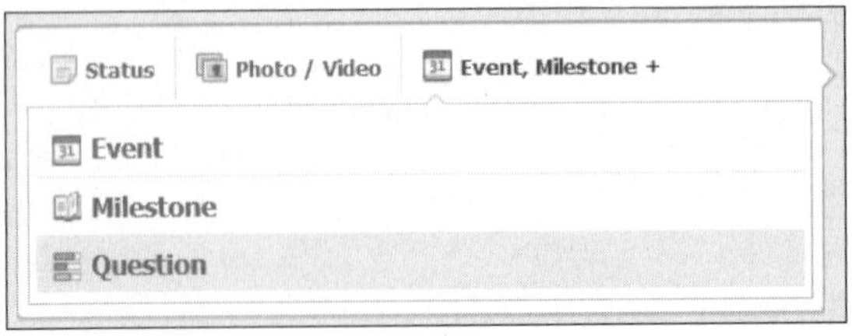

Status | Photo / Video | Event, Milestone +

Event

Milestone

Question

✔ Post information about progress in your business or industry or new information that relates to your work.

✔ Check your competition's page and see what they use to generate buzz and gain followers. Don't reinvent the wheel. Imitation is the sincerest form of flattery.

✔ Subscribe personally to a few blogs or news sites and post links to articles and pictures that your audience might enjoy. In Chapter 16, I show you tools to help you connect the posts.

✔ Pepper your posts with some personal updates. Tell your fans what you plan for the weekend and invite engagement by asking what they will be doing. (Personal updates do not count for your one in five promotions.)

✔ Respond, respond, respond. When someone comments on your page, be sure to respond. Customer service is pivotal in the twenty-first century; use Facebook as a platform for your company's transparency.

The key to growing a Facebook page is being there. If you don't have the time to commit to Facebook, I suggest that you wait and start with Twitter, which may fit in better with your schedule.

# Finding Other Social Media Sites

As much as I enjoy other social media sites, such as Google+ and LinkedIn, I have to weigh what works best for my business. For me, it's all about return on investment (ROI). I have a business to run and only so much time in the day. If I can't make a sale or build my customer base on one social media site, it's time to move on to another.

General Motors did exactly that. The company was rumored to have spent about $10 million for advertising on Facebook in 2010. This amount is a fraction of GM's total ad budget, which runs around $1.8 billion. However, GM was spending an additional $30 million on developing content and maintaining their "free" Facebook pages. In a budget cut, GM stopped advertising because they decided that paid ads on the site had little effect on consumers' buying decisions.

Facebook did not perform or bring in enough revenue for GM to justify the time and money they spent. This return on investment is something you must consider when entering social media sites. Granted, a small business does not have to carry the weight of General Motors, but your business will expend time and possibly money.

Think twice before entering other venues online. You don't want to be a jack-of-all-trades but master-of-none. Choose your target, and work it. If you find no payoff, it might be time to move on.

Google+ and LinkedIn are specialized sites. Google+ has had massive growth in the tech-savvy community but has yet to be a proven revenue builder for business. LinkedIn is the perfect place for professionals and business people to make connections. Neither is a site where you would sell directly. Think of them more as important listings in a business directory.

## Google+: The online networking directory

Major big brands and celebrities have pages on Google+ mainly because of its large user base. Estimates show that by the end of 2012, Google+ will have 400 million users. Almost everyone on the web has a Google account and we, as businesses, rely on Google page rank to list our sites in search.

Circles are the Google+ way for you to segment your community. Fans on Google+ are those people who put you in their circles on their pages.

If you have a local trade, you should know that Google+ Local (see Chapter 6) is a tab within Google+ and weaves your business into results when searching for venues on Google Maps and Places. Google+ Local has replaced Google Places altogether. Google+ also features Zagat scores and recommendations on the pages.

You might want to think of Google+ as a Yellow Pages of people and businesses. That reason alone might be enough for you to stake your claim and put up a page on the site. Go to `www.google.com/+/business` for more information and to start your page.

Here are some more stats:

- ✔ Student is the number-one occupation of Google+ users, with software engineer a far second and consultant third.
- ✔ Of Google+ users, 32 percent are from the United States.
- ✔ Globally, two-thirds of its users are male, and more than 42 percent are single.
- ✔ Google+ has 170 million reported users and is adding an estimated 625,000 users every day.
- ✔ Social reports on your +1 (Google's form of like) activity are available in your Google Analytics account.
- ✔ The Google +1 button is used more than 5 billion times per day.
- ✔ Websites using the +1 button generate three and a half times the Google+ visits than sites without the button.

## Building a professional profile on LinkedIn

If you're a speaker, consultant, or professional in your industry, I highly recommend that you (at the very least) post your profile on the LinkedIn site and join some industry groups. LinkedIn offers business connections and employment opportunities like no other site.

As of March 2012, LinkedIn counts executives from all 2011 Fortune 500 companies as members; its corporate hiring solutions are used by 82 of the Fortune 100 companies.

Some stats to know about LinkedIn:

- ✔ More than 2 million companies have LinkedIn pages.
- ✔ Every second, 2 new members sign up to LinkedIn.
- ✔ LinkedIn has 161 million members in more than 200 countries.
- ✔ Members are on track to make more than 5.3 billion searches on the platform in 2012.
- ✔ LinkedIn's revenue has doubled every quarter for the last two years.
- ✔ LinkedIn has more than 1 million groups.

# Chapter 10

# Cashing In: Doing Real Business Online

*In This Chapter*

▶ Making your site business-ready

▶ Using cloud services to enhance your existing business

▶ Adding stores to your presence

*W*hether or not a portion of or all your business depends on retail sales, the Internet offers many options for cashing in. In addition to selling your products and services, monetization can be in the form of facilitating your customers to find you and making appointments (handle pre-appointment paperwork).

In this chapter, I show you some web apps that can you save time, so you can attend to your other real-world business tasks.

## Making It Easy for Your Customer to Do Business Online

Today's web-enabled customers aren't going to search too hard to find your business. If your listing doesn't show up on the first or perhaps the second page of search results, they'll click elsewhere. If your web pages don't load fast enough — bam! — they're off to the next guy. If your online customer service ratings aren't sterling or you charge shipping but your competition doesn't, guess where customers will go?

If you're so busy managing your customers and studying statistics and reports, you won't realize where your potential customers are hanging out. I recommend personalizing your web offerings based on stats, but don't get buried in the science of numbers. Fulfill your customers' needs on your website, your Facebook page, and any other place where the social media customer will find you.

Time is of the essence when it comes to capturing the attention of today's consumer. Let your landing pages do some of the work for you by adding some of these features:

✔ **Forms:** If you need paperwork filled out before an appointment, why not replicate the form as a clickable link from a New Clients information page on your website? You can make an editable PDF form for your customers to fill out.

Let your clients fill out the forms at their leisure online before they come in. Then let them upload the forms directly to your office or print the forms and bring them to the appointment.

✔ **Wish lists:** Depending on your business, a wish list can be as simple as customers clicking items or services to add to an online list. You can use the list to learn more about your customers, or offer them the option to receive more information by e-mail.

✔ **Gift certificates:** If your business sells gift certificates, why not let your website visitor click to buy one as a gift? Embeddable widgets can help you enable this, as shown in Figure 10-1.

**Figure 10-1:**
Make appointments and buy gift certificates online from Carabella Cosmetics.

✔ **Location and mapping:** Want to make it easier for your customers to find you? Are you a real estate agent with several homes for sale? Embed a map with optional driving directions on your pages. Doing so is easy.

1. **Locate your business on Google Maps, and then click the link icon in the top-left panel.**

2. **Select Customize and Preview Embedded Map, and then find the best size map for your web page.**

**3. Copy the HTML that appears in the bottom of the window and paste it into your web page.**

For more detailed information, go to `http://maps.google.com/help/maps/getmaps/`.

Allen's Retail Liquor's site (based on the Blogger platform) has the location map shown in Figure 10-2. If you don't want to mess with code to embed a widget, at the very least add a link to a Google map and driving directions page.

**Figure 10-2:** Clicking this map takes you to a Google map page with driving directions.

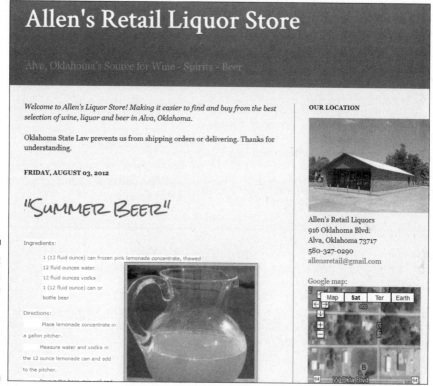

**Transportation:** A customer may need transportation to your place of business. A restaurant may want to offer a car service as a sideline to a dinner reservation. A doctor's office may want to give patients the option to get transportation by taxi or another service before or after a procedure. Make an arrangement with a local company and put their widget on your website.

## Car-in-the-driveway pricing

As long as I have been doing business on the web, I have seen companies that do not post prices on their site for their products and services. You can't find out the cost until you contact them (commonly under the guise that they want to "customize" a plan for you).

*Car-in-the-driveway pricing* refers to those who decide on the price based on the type of car in your driveway. Websites that practice this form of pricing need to know a lot of information about your business before they quote you a price.

Granted, enterprise-level business may have more complex needs and may be able to get a discount based on high usage. But as a small business, you should have a right to know the minimum it would cost you to get involved at the outset. Do you really have the time for e-mail exchanges or listening to a sales pitch on the phone?

Jamie Crager, CEO of Crowdshifter Media, had an opinion on this topic as well:

*When dealing with web platforms or SaaS [software as a service] providers, though they may state that they offer complete solutions and services online, those that don't include pricing information not only waste the prospect's time but most likely cause that person or business to move on to another site that does include pricing.*

*Businesses do not have the time to spend their day calling SaaS providers to see if their solutions are a good fit. The potential customer needs to be able to view many choices and make the best decision quickly. Having all the information up front shows that the SaaS provider values the time of those who might choose to use their products and services.*

Steer to the companies that respect your time and let you know up front the costs of using their services.

Extending access to your products and services in a self-serve fashion gives your consumers a sense of exclusivity with your brand. Adding these features to your website also shows your clients that you respect their time and pocketbook. Your website hosting provider may have widgets for your site, or a web search may bring up premade widgets. Adding web-enabled niceties increases your bottom line.

# *Using Cost-Effective SaaS Cloud Services*

Everything seems to be *in the cloud*. What does that really mean to you? Now you, too, have the opportunity to manage tasks on web servers, such as those from Microsoft, Amazon, or Google.

You're probably using the cloud if you use Gmail, Hotmail, or another web-based e-mail service. Also, if you've downloaded music from Amazon, your music can be accessed by their cloud player via Wi-Fi, versus downloading all your music to every device you own.

Let me throw another possibly new phrase your way: SaaS, or *software as a service*. When a company has software or a platform that you want to use but have no need to buy, you can pay a monthly fee for using it from the vendor's site. When they upgrade their offering, you benefit from updates without changing a thing on your computer.

The application is hosted by the service provider and made available to you through a special login or an installable widget on your site. You don't install the app on your site.

Now, spending big money on expensive custom software applications for your business may no longer be needed. A SaaS platform that can perform the tasks you want may already be available. The barriers to entry have fallen and an entrepreneur (like you, only techier) can develop a solid product, thereby reducing the expenditure for small business.

Consider the following before using a SaaS application:

✔ Does the service have an introductory level? Can you dip your toe in the water with a starter account? Can you do business with them on a month-to-month basis?

✔ Can you track success from an online dashboard? You want to know when and how people are accessing your application.

✔ Check the provider's online references. Don't just rely on a sales pitch.

✔ Be aware of your costs from the start. Factor in any ups and extras.

✔ Know where your data will be stored and the reliability of the servers.

✔ Be sure that you own all data generated from your site. Have all your questions regarding their privacy policies been answered? Are you okay with disclosure of your data to third parties?

✔ Ask about downtimes. Run your own web search regarding previous security breaches.

Cloud software is a boon to small businesses. Next up, a few examples. Perhaps others apps are available on the web that are better suited to your business? Think about it.

## Implementing real-time restaurant reservations

From what I've heard, any automation in the hospitality industry that can help meet a challenge is welcome. Whether a restaurant is a startup or an established eatery, innovations are hard to find. When it comes to reservation management, OpenTable was established as a leader early on. Taking web reservations for restaurants since 1999, they've had a stronghold on the market.

Their Electronic Reservation Book (ERB) essentially replaced the traditional paper reservation system for many restaurants. OpenTable provides ERB as an integrated software and hardware solution that computerizes restaurant host-stand operations. The restaurant pays for the hardware and an initial installation, as well as a monthly subscription fee and a per-guest reservation fee.

What about the little guy, or those who may be a bit more tech savvy? Enter Urbanspoon, developers of the insanely popular iPhone and Android apps, shown in Figure 10-3. The unique Shake Your Phone to decide where to eat has been gaining fans online since its inception in 2008. The app has been shaken over a billion times.

**Figure 10-3:** The iPhone version of the Urbanspoon app has been downloaded more than 20 million times.

In 2011, web traffic for Urbanspoon was up 80 percent, the mobile side of Urbanspoon saw 112 percent year-over-year growth, and the company had 255 million visits (up from 141 million in 2010).

If your restaurant has an iPad (needed for the restaurant's working view), you can avail yourself of Urbanspoon's iPad app, RezBook, which enables online reservations. RezBook, similar to the OpenTable software, is also capable of storing customer information, seating requests, and more. Currently available in many cities (and launching in more), the service lets customers book tables at restaurants online by using the Urbanspoon mobile app or a widget placed on a restaurant's home page (see Figure 10-4).

**Figure 10-4:** Reservation management on your iPad from Urbanspoon.

Right Now, a newly launched feature, enables prospective diners to view immediate table availability at a restaurant. The feature supports real-time availability for both reservations and walk-ins.

There's no big software to buy and your business can get up and running in 15 minutes. A customizable widget can also take reservations from your website. Currently, Urbanspoon charges a reasonable per-user subscription fee. Want to just give it a try? You can use it based on performance only at $2 a seat. For more information, go to http://rez.urbanspoon.com/ or e-mail them at rezbook@urbanspoon.com.

## Booking personal services with a click

Beauty and wellness professionals such as trainers, stylists, massage therapists, and estheticians rarely sit around a desk waiting for the phone to ring. Time is money and, if they are lucky, their time is booked with customers.

These types of professionals may lease space in a salon, spa, or gym or run their business as an independent. An SaaS platform such as StyleSeat is perfect for the mobile professional.

StyleSeat provides a fully customizable online platform. Not only do they provide a back end for professionals, the website (shown in Figure 10-5) is a directory-style portal that prospective clients can use to discover new options and to book appointments online. Site visitors can search available professionals and sort by price, availability, offers, location, and capability to book online.

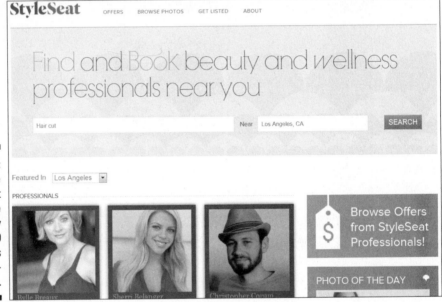

**Figure 10-5:**
The StyleSeat website currently lists 55,000 wellness professionals.

As of this writing, StyleSeat represents 55,000 salons, spas, and professionals. Their 2 million page views have generated $45 million in bookings for those on the site.

On the website, a registered professional can

- ✔ Use the online booking feature, which includes automatic e-mail and text message reminders plus follow-up e-mails
- ✔ Use the Facebook and Twitter share features
- ✔ Create custom online deals and seasonal specials
- ✔ Design a web page

✔ Upload photos to a gallery

✔ Turn on automatic client confirmations, reminders, and thank-you notes set up through the customizable dashboard shown in Figure 10-6

✔ Access industry articles and tips designed to boost business

✔ Download a StyleSeat app that enables a business to manage appointments and day-to-day activities as well as track schedules, ongoing business statistics, and daily data on iPhone, iPad, or Android devices

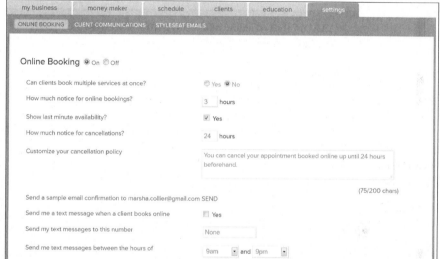

**Figure 10-6:**
Customizable
booking
settings on
StyleSeat.

Many of the tools are free for a small business. Premium subscriptions with more features are available for a reasonable monthly fee, starting at $25. Check their website at www.styleseat.com for more details and current pricing.

# *Boosting Your Web Presence with Apps and the Facebook Store*

Whether you actively sell items through e-commerce or are a service business that sells just a few items, including a shopping cart opens up new opportunities. Are you a dentist who sells a fancy electric toothbrush to your patients? A doctor with a favorite homeopathic remedy that you recommend? A travel agent who loves a particular line of travel accessories and can buy them wholesale to resell? If you have even a few products to sell, putting together a one-time small store can be worthwhile.

Selling items related to your service business can bring in unexpected revenue.

The more places your items for sale appear, the more chance you have of selling them and making additional profits — as long as you aren't paying for an expensive shopping cart system. Unless you're an online retailer with a large store, you don't need to spend a monthly fee for even a basic shopping cart.

## Website store integration without the cost or hassle

Two things irk me: paying for something that doesn't give me a return on investment and turning a simple task into a big deal. Both issues are prevalent when it comes to expensive software and putting together a small online store. In this section, I describe a way to include a small web store on your site, without recurring fees. You integrate your store once and don't have to touch it again, unless you want to change your prices.

In one of my websites, I sell a few inexpensive versions of professional products that help online sellers take better pictures. I don't push sales; the products simply accompany the content on the site. A separate store page lists the items, along with PayPal Buy Now buttons. Checkout is simple, as in shown in Figure 10-7.

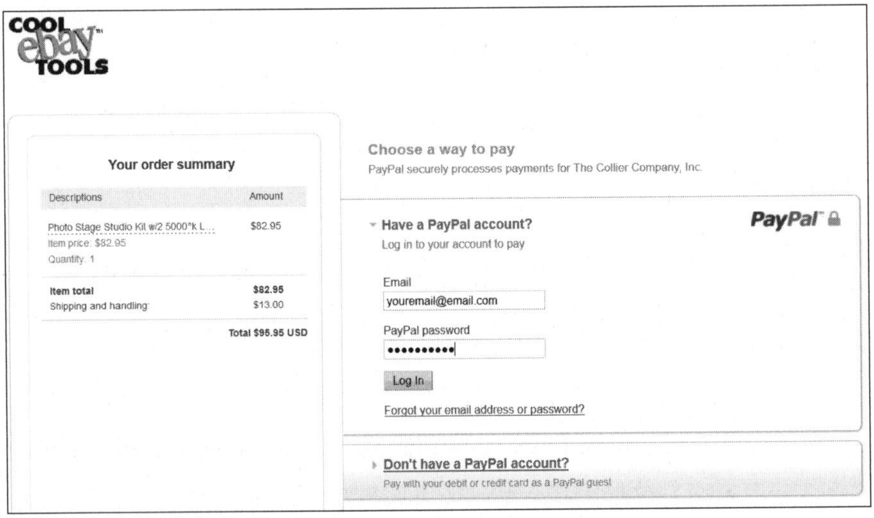

**Figure 10-7:** My single-page checkout enables a customer to pay using PayPal.

COOL ebay TOOLS

**Your order summary**

| Descriptions | Amount |
| --- | --- |
| Photo Stage Studio Kit w/2 5000°k L... Item price: $82.95 Quantity: 1 | $82.95 |
| **Item total** | **$82.95** |
| Shipping and handling | $13.00 |
| | Total $95.95 USD |

**Choose a way to pay**
PayPal securely processes payments for The Collier Company, Inc.

PayPal ▾ **Have a PayPal account?**
Log in to your account to pay

Email
youremail@email.com

PayPal password
••••••••••

Log In

Forgot your email address or password?

▸ **Don't have a PayPal account?**
Pay with your debit or credit card as a PayPal guest

You need to be a merchant member of PayPal to use these buttons, but PayPal enables a simple credit or debit card checkout for your customers. The system is well worth the few minutes it takes to sign up. The most it costs you to process your PayPal orders is 2.9 percent of the total plus $0.30 per transaction.

You can install Buy Now, Add to Cart, or Subscription buttons, as shown in Figure 10-8:

✔ **Buy Now:** For use with a single item, this button directs the buyer to immediately pay with PayPal.

✔ **Add to Cart:** This button enables your customers to buy several items. When they finish selecting items to purchase, they go to your PayPal payment page and pay.

✔ **Subscription:** Use this button for recurring payments.

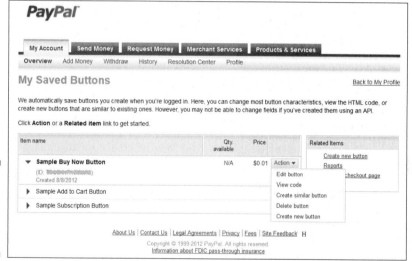

**Figure 10-8:**
Setting up
PayPal
buttons
is easy.

To install these buttons on your website, you don't need to have a computer science degree but you do need a rudimentary knowledge of web page HTML. This task is not for advanced users — you *can* do this.

To install a PayPal buttons on your website, follow these steps:

1. **Log in to your PayPal Premier or Business account at** `https://www.paypal.com.`

    The My Account Overview page appears.

2. **Click the My Business Setup link.**

3. **On the resulting page, under the Set Up my payment solution, select PayPal Payments Standard.**

4. **Click the Merchant Services tab.**

   The Merchant Services page appears.

5. **Under the Tools and Settings heading, click the My Saved Buttons link.**

   The My Saved Buttons page appears with the three sample PayPal buttons: Buy Now, Add to Cart, and Subscription.

6. **Select the button you'd like to use and edit appropriately.**

   Enter the payment details of your item, the price, and more.

7. **Click Create Button.**

   Your button code is displayed.

8. **On the Websites tab, click the Select Code button to select the generated HTML code.**

9. **Copy the selected text to the clipboard.**

   To copy, press Ctrl+C or right-click and select Copy.

10. **Position your cursor on your web page (in HTML edit mode) where you want the button to appear and paste the selected text.**

    To paste, press Ctrl+V or right-click and select Paste.

11. **Save the web page with your new payment button installed!**

After you have payment buttons set up on your site, you'll be able to sell. For detailed instructions and more information, go to www.paypal.com and click the Business tab at the top of the page.

## Building a store and adding apps on Facebook

You've created a business Facebook page and have worked it to build followers. I hope you are engaging them regularly and they are eager to visit your page. It's not a bad idea at this point to add an F-commerce (Facebook-commerce) store or other apps to your Facebook page. If you're a professional, it might be good for visitors to be able to see your resume on an additional page.

Many apps are available to help you promote your business on Facebook. Fanpage Toolkit, for example, is an all-in-one suite of applications that is reasonably priced (the basic version is free) and offers many options to enhance your Facebook engagement with your fans. Visit their website at http://fanpagetoolkit.com/.

The wizard-driven Fanpage Toolkit enables you to create a media-rich promotional Facebook landing page step by step, with no coding knowledge. All pages are designed through templates and an onscreen editor.

Some of the features of this application suite follow:

- ✔ **Resume page:** Use a prebuilt set of templates for resumes or bios. If you already have your resume on LinkedIn, use the app's one-click sync function and synchronize your entire LinkedIn profile.

- ✔ **F-commerce store:** Start a store from scratch or import an existing eBay or Magento store catalog through Toolkit's one-click sync. Other online stores can be imported through the import/export tool. The free version of this platform allows for up to 10 items for sale. All transactions are completed in Facebook and payments are enabled by PayPal. Figure 10-9 shows my basic level F-commerce store on my business page.

**Figure 10-9:** Go from my Facebook business page to my F-commerce store with one click.

✔ **Promotions:** Use predesigned templates to create customized coupons, with start and end dates. These coupons can be redeemed in person at your place of business or through your Facebook F-commerce store.

✔ **Sweepstakes app:** Enable your fans to enter a custom sweepstakes in which you plan a promotional giveaway. You can choose from a variety of different sweepstake formats that abide by Facebook's rules. The app selects a winner at random at the end of the promotion. Running a sweepstakes gives you an opportunity to capture lead data while increasing likes.

✔ **Digital downloads:** Give away freebies in the form of digital good, such as an e-book, a song track, or a white paper.

✔ **Analytics:** Get a powerful analytics system over and above Facebook's Insights. The app builds graphs, tables, maps, tag clouds, and much more.

Adding these platforms to your online outreach can only increase your opportunities to cash in on your web presence.

# Chapter 11

# Building Revenue through Links and Deals

......................................................

......................................................

*T*his chapter is going to take you into a new direction: selling through images and content you share on popular sites. I'm not suggesting that you merely link products. Instead, you discover how to monetize your original content. You'll generate revenue on your website and social media through ads and links. If you produce valuable, read-worthy content, your audience grows by following your social media account and then visiting your website.

Consider the definition of social commerce from Wikipedia:

> *Social commerce is a subset of electronic commerce that involves using social media and online media to support social interaction and user contributions, to assist in the online buying and selling of products and services.*

This is what you can accomplish through your social media outreach and from your website. In this chapter, I give you the basics; it's up to you to apply this advice. I show you several ways to sell products through social media outreach. If your stockroom has no products, read on to find out how to profit from affiliate links.

## Helping Amazon Help You

If you don't have a product to sell, you can find items related to your service or profession on Amazon, link to them (through Amazon Associates) on your website or blog, and make a commission when the product is sold (more on that in the section that follows). Amazon's prices are often the lowest on the web, and when your visitors see an Amazon ad for a related product on your site, they may click and buy.

If you *do* have a singular or unique product (perhaps you're a dentist with a special formula to whiten teeth or a personal trainer with a gizmo to protect hands while doing presses), you can sell that individual product on Amazon as well as on your website. You also might have the opportunity to buy product from one of your suppliers and resell it online. Know that with Amazon (or eBay for that matter), you don't have to pay for a store or pay monthly fees; you can just sell an item and pay the site a small percentage of the sale.

Amazon doesn't want to share inside numbers on how many people shop at their website, but comScore recently released results from a study. "One in five Internet users worldwide visited an Amazon site in the month of June, making Amazon the most visited retail property on the Web with 282 million visitors." Mobile customers are also taking online shopping seriously. According to comScore, 44 million unique visitors accessed Amazon from a mobile device in March 2002. People love and trust Amazon, so partnering with them should be a good complement to your brand.

You don't have to be a big brand or an online retailer to list an item for sale on Amazon. Anyone can do so.

## *Linking products from Amazon*

I know a lawyer who gives new clients a copy of a specific book to help them understand the legal process. Obstetricians also offer recommendations for books to read during pregnancy. A tailor I go to recommended a book on fabrics when I asked a question. A friend's physical therapist recommends a specific exercise device. My dentist recommends a special electric toothbrush.

Are you starting to formulate ideas about business-related items to sell through your business? Thinking about merchandise should also help you think about business-related content for your website and social media outreach. When someone becomes your client or customer, you can give them a product if you want. But those who visit your website are there to consume content — content that they consider valuable. Why not offer them something to buy? You don't have to do a thing but put the Amazon-supplied code on your site.

If your customers purchase anything else when they visit Amazon to buy your featured item, you'll get a percentage of those items. For example, someone who purchased one of my books from a link also bought an iPad from a third party on Amazon. I got $24.34, or 6 percent of the purchase price.

Follow these steps to find merchandise on Amazon that may pertain to your business or give you an idea of the type of merchandise to procure from suppliers:

1. **List the keywords or items you think would complement your business and be relevant to your social media followers and website visitors.**

2. **Go to Amazon and search for the keywords and items in your list.**

   In Figure 11-1, I searched for *clean teeth* and netted more than 8,600 results spread over 30 categories. (I'm not sure what a white iPod touch has to do with clean teeth, but just go with me on this.) On the left side of the screen, Amazon has products related to my search in distinct categories.

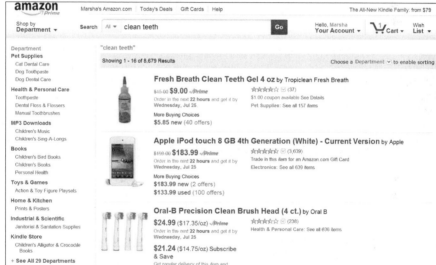

**Figure 11-1:** Amazon has more than 30 categories that stock items related to clean teeth.

3. **If you want to narrow your search to a category, click the category name.**

4. **When you see a product that appeals to you (and your brand) and that might interest your website visitors, click the title to read the details.**

   Take note of the sales rank as you review an item. If you have a choice between two similar products, why not select the one that is the most popular?

**5. If the product meets your requirements, copy and paste the item name to a list in another window.**

Alternatively, copy and paste the UPC or ASIN, which is usually in the product details section at the bottom of the item's page, as shown in Figure 11-2.

**Figure 11-2:**
Product
Details
contain SKU
(stock-keep-
ing unit)
numbers.

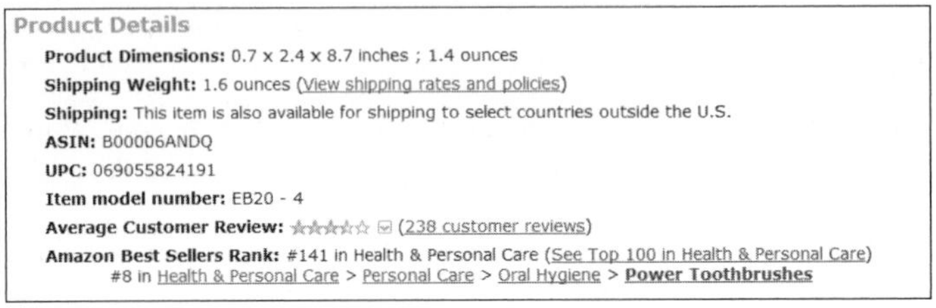

> **Product Details**
> **Product Dimensions:** 0.7 x 2.4 x 8.7 inches ; 1.4 ounces
> **Shipping Weight:** 1.6 ounces (View shipping rates and policies)
> **Shipping:** This item is also available for shipping to select countries outside the U.S.
> **ASIN:** B00006ANDQ
> **UPC:** 069055824191
> **Item model number:** EB20 - 4
> **Average Customer Review:** ★★★☆☆ ☑ (238 customer reviews)
> **Amazon Best Sellers Rank:** #141 in Health & Personal Care (See Top 100 in Health & Personal Care)
> #8 in Health & Personal Care > Personal Care > Oral Hygiene > **Power Toothbrushes**

Now that you have an idea of the types of items you want to feature on your website, it's time to join Amazon Associates.

## *Joining Amazon Associates*

I'm taking a leap here and assuming that you already shop at Amazon. As you can see by the Associates hub page in Figure 11-3, Amazon sells almost any conceivable item of merchandise. If you don't shop at Amazon, you'll have to open an account.

To become an Amazon associate, do the following:

**1. Go to Amazon's home page (**www.amazon.com**) and click the Become an Affiliate link at the bottom of the page.**

Alternatively, you can go directly to http://affiliate-program.amazon.com/. The Amazon Associates hub screen appears.

As of this writing, if you're a resident of Arkansas, Colorado, Illinois, North Carolina, Rhode Island, or Connecticut, you are ineligible to join the Associates Program due to current state sales tax laws. This may change, but for now you are out of luck as far as an affiliate account.

**2. Click the Join Now for Free button.**

**3. Fill in the required forms.**

Be sure to read the Terms of Service. Payments are made by direct deposit to your bank, or you can opt to receive payment by Amazon gift cards (which can be convenient if you're a regular Amazon shopper).

While filling out the forms, you are required to give Amazon a link to your website. Upon examining your application, Amazon visits your website to approve your content before they permit you to become an associate. Amazon's site requirements are in the Program Operating Agreement at `https://affiliate-program.amazon.com/gp/associates/agreement/`. Their rules are pretty fair, so you should have no problem being approved.

Assuming your site passes muster, you'll get an e-mail confirmation from Amazon.

Now that you're an associate, you are eligible to make varying percentages (advertising fees) on sales. Figuring out your percentage is a bit challenging, because Amazon rates (just like your mileage) will vary. The payout is based on the number and category of products that are shipped, streamed, or downloaded in a month.

As a member, you have access to the Associates hub page, at `https://affiliate-program.amazon.com/`, from where you can manage your account.

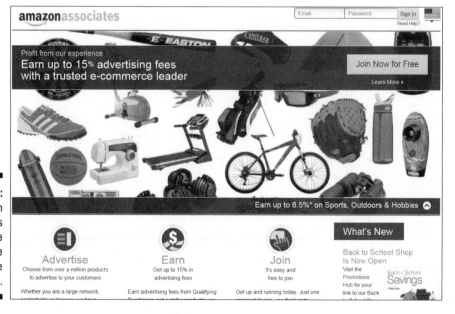

**Figure 11-3:**
Amazon
Associates
home page
for the
affiliate
program.

## Touring the Associates site stripe

When you become an associate and sign into your Amazon account to browse, your pages have an Associates stripe at the top. You can turn off the bar, but I find it handy because it allows me to make affiliate links on-the-fly.

The Associates bar is broken up into nine parts. The portions of the bar most relevant to social media commerce are shown in Figure 11-4 and described in the following:

- ✔ **Link to This Page:** Opens a window where you can create put a product link on your website.

- ✔ **Add to Widget:** Adds an additional item to a widget you've already created for an item.

- ✔ **Share:** Provides a long link to share on Twitter. I use this option when I'm in a conversation with someone and recommend a book or product. I copy and paste the supplied link (which includes code to identify your Associate account) into a URL shortener such as bitly or Tweetdeck (to automatically shorten the link), and craft a conversational Tweet.

- ✔ **Your Earnings Summary:** Shows whether anyone is clicking your links and how much you've earned on sold items. Use this button to see how your links are performing.

**Figure 11-4:**
Click the bar to monetize.

You can accomplish these tasks when you sign in on the main Associates page at `https://affiliate-program.amazon.com/`, but using the bar is usually faster.

## Making links and widgets

After you've passed inspection and been approved for the Associates program, it's time to add links or widgets on your site. *Links* are text-based hyperlinks that are part of your content. *Widgets* are rectangular and show an image of the item (or more than one item) for sale. In Figure 11-5, I've inserted a widget at the bottom of a blog post in case someone wants to buy one of my books after they've finished reading.

**Figure 11-5:**
I've inserted links to related products for sale on my blog post.

After you are a member of Amazon, your browser (via cookies) automatically recognizes your Amazon sign-in and the Associates stripe appears automatically when you browse the site.

To get a link or widget for your website or blog, do the following:

1. **Browse to the product page of the item you want to link.**

2. **Click the Link to This Page button on the Associate's bar.**

    The screen shown in Figure 11-6 appears.

3. **Click one of the tabs at the top of the screen — Text and Image, Text Only, or Image Only — depending on what you want to link.**

4. **Make any color adjustments and select other options as desired.**

    Your affiliate information is embedded in the code, and the link widget or text link is ready to paste in your blog or website.

5. **Click Highlight Link.**

6. **Press Ctrl +C (⌘+C) to put the link on your clipboard.**

7. **In your blog or website, position your cursor where you want the widget or link to appear and press Ctrl+V (⌘+V).**

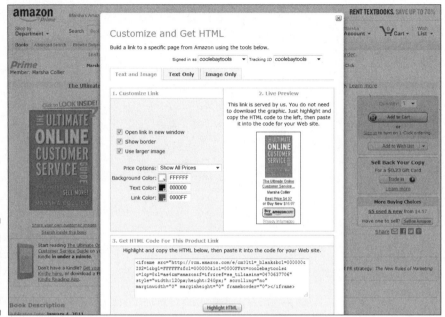

**Figure 11-6:** A widget is generated automatically.

If you already have a widget on a page and want to add another item, click Add to Widget and your new item appears. Widgets update dynamically from the Amazon website.

To share on Facebook or Twitter, follow these steps:

1. **Browse to the product page of the item you want to share.**

2. **Click the Share button on the Associate's bar.**

3. **Make a selection from the drop-down menu:**

   • **Facebook:** If you choose Facebook, you see the standard Share This Link window, as shown in Figure 11-7. Add your comment and then click Share Link.

   • **Twitter:** If you choose Twitter, a Tweet window opens containing your associate's code and a promotional Tweet. Because Tweets are short and must be concise, I recommend that you write the Tweet in a more social manner than Amazon's proposed Tweet and use a URL shortener. (Nothing looks less social than Tweeting a referral link.) Copy and paste this link and Tweet from another site so you have control over shortening the URL.

**Figure 11-7:**
Share on
Facebook.

# Pinning on Pinterest

The best way to describe Pinterest is as a cross between an overpopulated refrigerator door and a scrapbook. As of this writing, it is the newest, hottest social network. Members "pin" images and other media content (graphics or videos) from their computers or shared from the web.

A picture is worth a thousand words, right? That could be why Pinterest had 90 million unique (180 million total) visits in July 2012. Pinterest is currently the third most popular social media network, behind Twitter and Facebook.

The site is incredibly successful for brands such as Whole Foods, Women's Health, Better Homes and Gardens, Southwest Airlines, and Martha Stewart. For example, Pinterest is the top social media referrer for MarthaStewart.com and MarthaStewartWedding.com. For those brands, Pinterest is sending more referrals than Facebook and Twitter combined.

Pinterest is best for businesses that lend themselves to a visual format, such as those in the following areas:

- ✔ Interior design
- ✔ Fashion stylists
- ✔ Photographers
- ✔ Travel agents
- ✔ Restaurants
- ✔ Veterinarians and animal lovers

✔ Event planners

✔ Real estate agents

As an example, the AARP Pinterest page, shown in Figure 11-8, follows most of the accepted best practices for Pinterest. It is a visually appealing page. Currently, their board has only about 1,600 followers. For a small business, consider the percentage of members who are liking your page to measure the page's worth in time investment.

For the most engagement and sharing on Pinterest, follow someone back when they follow. Repin items from other users to gain follows. Social networking is all about interaction.

If you have the impression that more women than men are using Pinterest, you're correct. Their user base is 80 percent women. But a survey from Compete.com exposes that more men (37 percent) than women (17 percent) make purchases as a consequence of seeing something they like on Pinterest. However, a total of only 25 percent of survey respondents said they had actually made a purchase due to viewing a product on Pinterest.

Pinterest is not ideal for every business. If you enjoy using it, that's great. But adding one more network to your social arsenal may be too time-consuming.

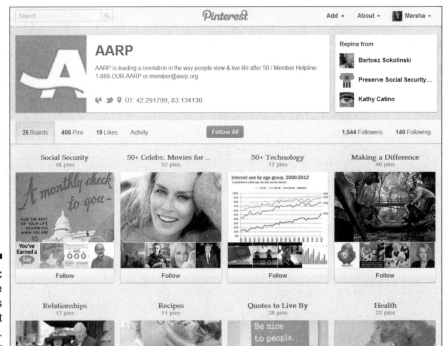

**Figure 11-8:**
Even the AARP has a Pinterest page.

## Making it personal

Pinterest is a very personal platform. Photos touch people visually, and when pictures of products are interlaced with consumable ideas, the subtlety pays off. When you follow people (and they follow you back, because they connect emotionally to your pins), they share by repinning your pins on their pages. This repinning increases the viral nature of your posts.

The images that are most shared, liked, and commented on are those that relate to the audience. Post images that resonate with you and your business. Take a look at my page, which is shown in Figure 11-9. I try to share only images that relate to my readers' lifestyle, while interspersing my business products (and Amazon items) for sale with links.

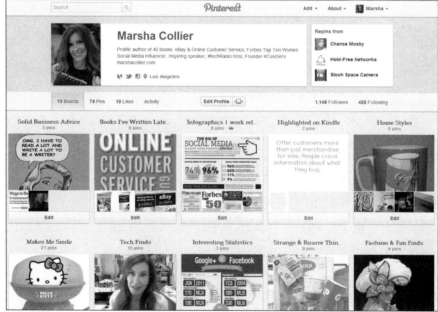

**Figure 11-9:** My Pinterest page has boards that should engage my readers.

## Linking back to content

There's money to be made in this form of social media sharing because products you sell (and pin) can be linked back to your own website. If you don't sell specific products, you can use Pinterest to increase your fan base by posting intriguing, relevant content. If your content is good, you increase the chance that consumers will click through your pins.

After uploading an image of an item I have for sale to Pinterest, I edit the pin, and edit the link back to point to my site. In Figure 11-10, for example, I am linking the image back to my Facebook store. If viewers like the posted item, they can click it to see it on the selling page. That's where the commerce part kicks in.

| | |
|---|---|
| Search | **Pinterest**  Add +  About +  Marsha + |

**Edit Pin**  Delete Pin

Description

Love! VINTAGE Block Signed Andy Warhol Campbell's Soup POP Art Mug selling it in my Facebook store under

Link  https://www.facebook.com/MarshaCollierFa

Board  Home Styles

**Save Pin**

Love! VINTAGE Block Signed Andy Warhol Campbell's Soup POP Art Mug selling it in my Facebook store under daily Deals

**Figure 11-10:** Inserting a link to my store, where someone might buy this item.

If you have the time, Pinterest may be a profitable social media platform to try out — after you've conquered at least one of the others.

# Joining a Local Social Platform: MerchantCircle

I ran a small advertising and marketing agency for many years, and from that experience, I can tell you that being a member of your local chamber of commerce is the first step you should take when promoting your business locally. Nothing is more social that person-to-person contact. When people know you, recommending you becomes that much easier.

Places on the Internet can work just like your local chamber. They may not be as social as being face-to-face, but you can make some solid business contacts and perhaps promote sales.

MerchantCircle (www.merchantcircle.com) is a small business social network that hones in on local. They are an online business directory, social business network, and marketing platform. The site was founded in 2005 as a business-to-business site (B2B), not unlike a chamber of commerce. They built their brand mostly in small towns where larger sites don't cover the locale. For example, in 2010, 50 percent of local businesses in Wasilla, Alaska were actively engaging on the site.

Their website states that "MerchantCircle is the largest online network of local business owners in the nation" and they probably are. Your company is probably listed because they originally gleaned business listings from the Yellow Pages and other sources. Businesses that "claim" their page on the site get a web page listing, a blogging platform, and an e-mail newsletter application — all under the MerchantCircle brand.

This year, MerchantCircle relaunched the site to be more consumer-focused, like Yelp. Now potential customers can search for and find providers across all business categories, including home repair and improvement; health and beauty; financial and professional services; construction and real estate services; and restaurants. Customer can also request quotes, access ratings, and provide reviews.

The site is growing quickly, so you should really take a moment to claim your company page. The process takes about five minutes. Follow these steps for the most efficient path to joining:

1. **Go to** `www.merchantcircle.com` **(as I did in Figure 11-11) and type your business name and city in the search box.**

   You could also click Join Now in the upper-right corner.

**Figure 11-11:** The Merchant Circle home page.

2. **When your business appears, click the red Claim Your Business banner.**

3. **On the next page, create a MerchantCircle login by typing your e-mail address and a password. Then click Submit.**

   The resulting page displays three pricing plans cost.

4. **Scroll down the page to the tiny letters at the bottom that read No, Thanks and click there.**

   (If you want a paid plan, you can always sign up for it later.) Annoyingly, the next page populates with even more offers for you to purchase. (Trust me, they will always be available.)

5. **Just say no: Scroll again to the tiny letters at the bottom of the page and click No, Thanks.**

   At this point, MerchantCircle sends you an e-mail to confirm your e-mail address. The dashboard shown in Figure 11-12 appears.

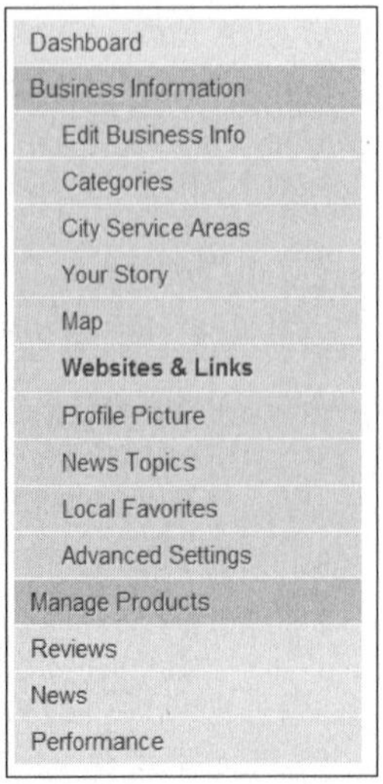

**Figure 11-12:**
Your
Merchant
Circle
Dashboard
options.

Dashboard

Business Information

   Edit Business Info

   Categories

   City Service Areas

   Your Story

   Map

   **Websites & Links**

   Profile Picture

   News Topics

   Local Favorites

   Advanced Settings

Manage Products

Reviews

News

Performance

6. **Edit your listing and your dashboard and add bells and whistles to your page.**

7. **When you receive the MerchantCircle e-mail, confirm your e-mail address by following the instructions in the message.**

When you confirm your address, you can add more of the aforementioned bells and whistles and save your work.

Your business now has a page on MerchantCircle. After you've claimed your page, you should do the following immediately:

- ✔ **Make sure your business name is correct.** Your business name may have been drawn from an abbreviated version in the Yellow Pages.

- ✔ **Check your address listing.** If you have a home-based business and you don't want your address shown in the listing, remove it using the Edit Business tab.

- ✔ **Upload a few photos.** Upload a photo as your profile picture as well as three others to populate the gray boxes on the side of your listing. These photos might show your place of business, sample projects, or food items if you own a restaurant.

- ✔ **Check to see that you were categorized properly.** Go to the Categories tab to select additional categories that best describe your services.

- ✔ **Connect your Twitter and Facebook Business pages.** If you don't want MerchantCircle to be posting to these accounts, you can choose not to export posts from MerchantCircle to these pages.

- ✔ **Create your custom MerchantCircle web address and add a link to your website**. On the Websites and Link page, type your company name to make a more personalized URL address.

None of these tasks take long. After I completed them, my company's page looked like Figure 11-13.

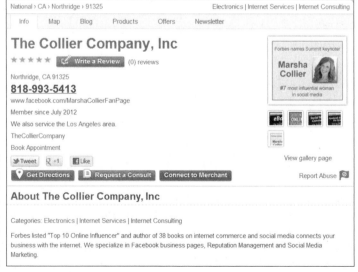

**Figure 11-13:**
The Collier Company page, all set and ready to go.

If you have time, you can search for businesses within your community where you have friends. If they've claimed their business page, you see a color picture or logo in their listing. I looked up my business friends, along with my dentist, doctor, insurance guy, mechanic, and beauty salon. No one had claimed their page. It's kind of cool to be the first of your friends (and also gives you an advantage).

# Chapter 12

# Making a Direct Hit with Mobile

As of June 2012, 55 percent of mobile subscribers owned a smartphone and two out of three Americans who acquired a new mobile phone in the last three months chose a smartphone. Feature phones still sell but will certainly be going the way of the cassette player in a few years.

Did you know that 80 percent of those who own a smartphone won't leave the house without it? They realize that they can save time and accomplish tasks on the run. Maybe they're researching restaurants and making reservations for dinner tomorrow. Or perhaps they're checking e-mail while picking up a pizza.

Tablets are flying off the shelves too, with nearly 100 million devices sold worldwide in 2011. This market is estimated to top $20 billion in 2012. Although tablets and smartphones will not replace PCs, they have basic computing power, a cheaper price point, and are uncomplicated to use. Best of all? They're portable.

eBay Inc. President and CEO John Donahoe has said that

> We now expect eBay and PayPal mobile to each transact $10 billion in volume in 2012 — that's more than double 2011, a staggering surge in mobile shopping and payments on devices that did not exist just a few years ago. Retail is at an inflection point, and we are helping to reshape how people around the world shop and pay.

From these stats, it's clear that folks are shopping with mobile devices. But what about advertising reach? Interactive Advertising Bureau (IAB) and its Mobile Marketing Center of Excellence recently released "Mobile's Role in the Consumer's Media Day," an in-depth research report that reveals how receptiveness to advertising and media consumption varies by device, time of day, and location. According to the report,

- A strong degree of ad interaction exists among tablet users, with nearly half (47 percent) saying that they engage with ads on that device more than once a week.

- One in four (25 percent) smartphone users also said that they interact with ads at that same frequency.

- When mobile device users engage with an ad, they are extremely likely to take action (80 percent of smartphone users and 89 percent of tablet users).

These numbers should help convince you that you need not only social media for commerce but also a plan for mobile users as well. It's time to adapt, adopt, and enhance your mobile connections to your customer. In this chapter, I give you a few ideas of where to start.

# Making Your Site Mobile-Friendly

If you've used a smartphone to visit a website, you'll understand the importance of a mobile-friendly site. Complex, content-heavy web pages with many photographs, elements, or videos present challenges to mobile viewing.

You may think that you could simply add an app for your business instead of creating a mobile version of your website, but apps are not as functional as a website. Apps are fun and useful for a single purpose, but 81 percent of mobile users prefer mobile sites to apps when researching purchases. And more than 40 percent of users turn to a competitor's website after a bad mobile experience.

A Compuware study found that on mobile devices

- 71 percent of users expect a mobile site to load as fast as a desktop site

- 60 percent of users expect a mobile site to load in three seconds or less

- 78 percent retry a site two times or less if it does not load initially

In our want-it-now world, people expect those with a presence on the web to keep up with technology. I must confess that not every website I am involved with is up to snuff when it comes to mobile. Like many of you, I don't have the time or resources to stay on top of every technological trend. But as the number of smartphone users continues to grow, my lackadaisical attitude will change and I will make it happen!

Luckily, my sites work great on tablets, and I believe the trend will be toward larger screens for active web browsing. Those who try tablets want the full web experience.

The goal when making an alternate mobile commerce site is to eliminate extraneous features and words, without limiting your selection of products. A mobile site should have less information about each product and fewer things users can do with the products, but the range of items should remain the same as on the full site. If users can't find a product on a mobile site, they assume the company doesn't sell it and go elsewhere.

Don't make a push for mobile a priority over the other strategies described in this book. Keep things simple and remember that people visit your website or blog for the value of your content.

The main reasons that your full website does not translate automatically to mobile are as follows:

- ✔ The screen on a phone (or small-format tablet) is considerably smaller than most computer displays.

- ✔ Small screens generally equal lower resolutions, so unless you have a mobile design, items may look distorted or have missing elements when viewed in a mobile browser.

- ✔ Cellular data networks process data more slowly than your computer, which can result in interminably long page load times. Your customers will not wait around; they'll just exit.

- ✔ Mobile subscribers who aren't connected to Wi-Fi accrue higher data usage when they come to a data-heavy page. The moment they notice the slow page load, they leave.

- ✔ Flash, a common browser add-on for viewing videos on website sites, is not compatible with Apple's iOS (iPhone and iPad devices). In addition, Flash is not always included as part of a mobile browser.

- ✔ HTML5, the latest version of HyperText Markup Language (the code used to build web pages), translates web pages for most operating systems. This new version is still in its infancy but looks promising in allowing far more flexibility and putting far less strain on mobile processors.

Most blogging platforms automatically format your pages for mobile viewing. Figure 12-1 shows you how my Marsha Collier's Musings blog (a Blogger site) looks on a computer monitor. In Figure 12-2, you see the same blog on a phone. The figure on the left is the mobile version of my Blogger site. The one on the right shows my blog on Posterous; that site isn't quite as enticing, but it is clear and loads quickly.

# Marsha Collier's Musings

I'm the author of the "For Dummies" series of books about eBay and **Customer Service**, Host of **Computer and Technology Radio.** I blog on eBay, useful products and anything fun. Also please visit my eBay book website **Cool eBay Tools**

Tuesday, July 24, 2012

## Six Things You Can Do to Better Manage Your Time

Time management is a recurring issue around here. It comes up constantly as one of the great struggles. We've got lots to do and insufficient time to do it.

Here are my best time management tips (they work for me).

1. *Keep a list*. You've got to have a comprehensive list of your outstanding obligations. It can be on paper or contained in a fancy task management system. Personally, I use Wunderlist: it falls somewhere between paper and fancy. You'll find all kinds of systems for organizing the list. It's essential that you get the list out of your head and into your system. Until you get it all down somewhere, you'll spend tremendous energy worrying about what you're forgetting

2. *Delegate*. Go through your list weekly and decide what you can give away. Don't wait until you're on overload to delegate: do it now. The more time you give your team to do the work, the more likely it is to get done right. The more time you allow, the more likely you are to hand it off since you'll hesitate to let it go

### Pages

Marsha Collier's Books

Connect with Your Customers To Sell More!

Twittamentary the Movie

Join me Saturdays on Computer and Technology Radio

Home

### Search This Blog

[ ] Search

**Figure 12-1:** My blog as viewed on a computer monitor.

To see how your site looks on a smartphone, go to www.howtogomo.com/en/d/test-your-site/. Just type your website URL in the Test Your Website text box, and you are presented with the smartphone version (as I did for Figure 12-2).

When viewing websites on tablets, you serve the simplified version of the website that better applies to mobile devices. But performing this task gets complicated. Many tablet users are looking for a rich user experience. To stay clear of disgruntled web visitors, offer a clear link from your mobile site to your full site for those who prefer the features found only on the full site.

**Figure 12-2:**
My mobile-
optimized
blogs.

# Developing Your Own App

Many businesses use apps for promotions or as ways to funnel business to their websites. If you think an app is something only the big guys have, you'll be surprised at the reasonable the price for developing one.

Finding an experienced freelancer to develop an app isn't too difficult these days. Several popular sites serve as directories for self-employed tech types. I visited two of my favorites to check things out. A search for *app developer* on www.elance.com netted almost 1,500 app pros. A visit to www.odesk.com came up with 2,950 app contractors from all parts of the world.

You may wonder how an app can fit into your business profile. Here are a few examples to get your creative juices flowing.

The publisher of the *For Dummies* series found a creative way to give people a taste of my book, *eBay For Dummies,* in an iOS device app available in the iTunes store (`http://itunes.apple.com/us/book/ebay-for-dummies/id488574053`). Figure 12-3 shows the opening layout. Each tile links to a summary of a section from the book, to entice people to discover more — and buy the book.

**Figure 12-3:**
My *eBay For Dummies* book app.

Rosen Law Firm (described in Chapter 4) produced the app shown in Figure 12-4 to calculate child support for the state in which they practice, North Carolina. "Our goal has always been to make the divorce process less of a mystery. Divorce is never easy and we hope that by making the tools more accessible, you can take control and get on with your life sooner," says Lee Rosen. The app is available for Android and iPhone, free of charge, and available for immediate download by visiting app stores or Rosen's North Carolina Child Support page (`www.rosen.com/childsupport/`).

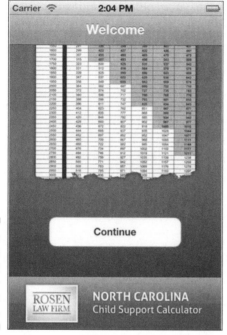

**Figure 12-4:**
Calculate
how much
child sup-
port you
have to pay.

I have several other business apps on my phone:

- ✔ **GroundLink:** A handy app from a car service that works in every city I've ever visited. If I need a car, I can use this app to book my ride to or from the airport.

- ✔ **Uber:** For a car-on-demand when I travel, I open Uber (when I am in a supported city) and can get a car easier than a taxi.

- ✔ **Dominos Pizza:** Want pizza in a hurry? Log in to the app, order your pizza, and even watch as it's being made.

# Checking In by Mobile

Some social apps reward their users for checking in from smartphones as they go from place to place in the bricks-and-mortar world. This mobile check-in activity is popular with those who connect online.

The current leader in the market is Foursquare, a social geolocation-based application that allows users to check in when they arrive at almost any location. Currently, more than 20 million people use Foursquare, so if you have a retail location, odds are some of your customers are checking in. I've checked in to Foursquare on a plane (with a flight number), at a restaurant, at a bank, in the doctor's office . . . pretty much from everywhere.

When users arrive at a location and check in, their friends may be notified of their location (based on the individual user's privacy settings). Repeat visits earn users badges of honor (in Figure 12-5, see my badge for visiting three bakeries) and place them higher in an internal ranking system.

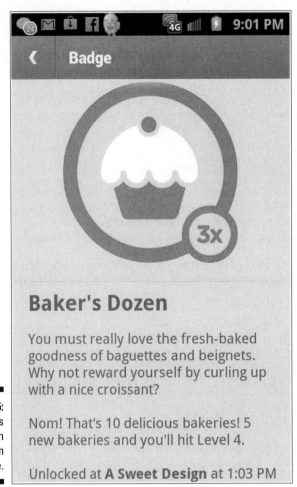

**Figure 12-5:** My Baker's Dozen badge from Foursquare.

Foursquare allows the user to become the Mayor of a business or spot she frequents by being the person who checks in at a single location most often. This high status is coveted by participants. When someone gets ousted, a scramble sometimes ensues to be reinstated by making another visit.

All this activity occurs using a game mechanism: Users earn points, get discounts, win Mayorships, and unlock badges for trying new places and revisiting old favorites.

In June 2010, the *Wall Street Journal's* website became the first to experiment with an Add to Foursquare button. If you're reading a restaurant review or other cultural coverage on WSJ.com, you can click a button to add the venue mentioned in the article to your Foursquare to-do list, along with a tip written by a WSJ editor that links to the original article.

How does this feature translate into developing customers? Smart businesses take advantage of the titular Mayoral status by offering discounts and bonuses to Mayors and repeat visitors, such as free dessert with a meal. A clever idea might be to speed up some of your slower business hours with a special, such as "Check in between 4:00 and 6:00 PM for a free draft beer." You can promote the bonus easily on Facebook, Twitter, or your website — and you can have Foursquare do it as well.

If you register your business to be eligible to bestow Foursquare's Mayoral discount, the smartphone mobile application notifies the Mayor of the discount whenever he checks in from your location. To claim your venue on Foursquare and offer mobile specials, go to `https://foursquare.com/business/merchants`.

After you register your business, you gain access to the following (be on the lookout for more):

- ✔ **Dashboard:** You get full access to real-time data about your customers, including

  Total daily check-ins over time

  Your most recent visitors

  Your most frequent visitors

  Customer breakdown by gender

  The time of day people check in

  The portion of your venue's Foursquare check-ins that are broadcast to Twitter and Facebook

- ✔ **Updates:** You can share text, photos, or promotions with customers who are physically close to your location as well as on Facebook and Twitter.

- ✔ **Specials:** You can run specials (and target different groups) for those who check in at your place of business. For example, Mayor specials can be unlocked only by the current Mayor, and check-in specials are awarded when a customer checks in a prescribed number of times.

  Not only does your special appear on Foursquare at no charge to you, but you are free to advertise your specials on the web using download-able Foursquare graphics available on the site. Also, with a few clicks, you can promote the special on your Facebook page or Tweet it to your followers.

If people check in at a location near your business, they may receive a notification that a Mayor or check-in discount awaits nearby if they stop by your location.

Big business has also been parlaying the service and marketing slant of these games. Starbucks, for example, offers a Barista badge to customers who attain a prescribed number of check-ins at a Starbucks location. Currently, the company is even toying with the idea of tying the badge and the number of check-ins to an in-store rewards program. Not a bad idea to emulate!

Although gamification may seem like fun and games, it can have a serious influence on how often game players frequent your business.

# Part IV
# Supporting Your Social Media Commerce Efforts

The 5th Wave                    By Rich Tennant

"Just how accurately should my website reflect my place of business?"

# In this part . . .

Customers are now demanding online customer service. In Part IV I show you how to make them happy. You also discover how to measure your online sentiment and build your following and online reputation. Remember that your character and perceived trust level sell your products in social media. I address how to advertise and promote, social media style. You also find out about platform clients and apps that will save you time when it comes to your social media execution.

# Chapter 13

# Handling Customer Service without Picking Up the Phone (Well, Almost)

*1* wrote a book on online customer service more than a year ago, when big business was just beginning to reach out to their customers through social media. Big brands have big budgets to spend trying out new ways of reaching their customers. Social media customer service doesn't require a huge budget. In this way, it is a level playing field where small business can successfully compete head-to-head with brands.

One of the ways small businesses can improve their customer service and overall bottom line is to study the new media trends and see what is working. You can conduct community outreach on a far smaller scale without having to staff a department.

This chapter introduces you to new ways to handle your customer service issues efficiently and transparently online.

## Handling Customer Service Issues Online

When customers know that they can communicate directly with a business on social media, they may connect with them for any number of reasons. But as soon as they realize that a customer service issue or product question can be addressed via a single Tweet or post, they're more likely to do business with the businesses that respond online.

A recent infographic from Zendesk, shown in Figure 13-1, shows some remarkable numbers.

**Figure 13-1:**
A surprising
62 percent
of consum-
ers have
used social
media for
support.

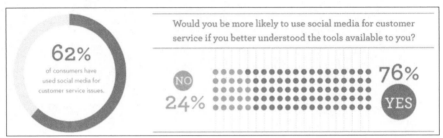

As more people discover and participate in social media, they realize how easy it is to use this new medium for customer service. Savvy business owners who monitor Twitter or Facebook can have texts sent to their smartphone when a customer mentions their business — and can respond immediately on the spot.

Social media is no longer an option when dealing with today's tech-savvy customer. When renowned financial adviser (and respected blogger) Josh Brown was interviewed for *Investment News*, he had an interesting slant on why we, as businesses, need to connect on social media:

> *We're all talking about this like it's optional. It's not. If you're a financial adviser and you meet a Gen Y guy at a party, a 30-year-old who's making some real money, and he goes to look you up on Google and doesn't find you, to him you don't exist. This is not optional.*
>
> *It doesn't mean you have to be Tweeting all day and spending all your time on Facebook. That's not necessary. But you should have a beachhead somewhere, and you should have some social clout. You should have people following you and conversing with you. You should have some stuff out there that seems like you're engaged, because otherwise you'll come off like you're asleep.*

In April 2012, Maritz Research asked questions of an online panel of U.S. Internet users about their awareness and use of several consumer feedback mechanisms. Table 13-1 shows some interesting data from the 1,400 respondents.

From the numbers in Table 13-1, you might think that social media was a lagging technology in business communication. But consider that e-mail first gained popularity through CompuServe in 1992. Social media has been recognized only since MySpace transitioned from a file storage service to a social networking site in 2004. Facebook opened its doors to the public in late 2006, and Twitter became its own company in 2007.

| Table 13-1 | Channels for Contacting or Providing Feedback to Business | | |
|---|---|---|---|
| **Channel** | **Aware Of** | **Have Used** | **Prefer** |
| Facebook | 91% | 29% | 8% |
| E-mail company | 83% | 75% | 52% |
| Twitter | 79% | 8% | 1% |
| Phone call | 76% | 66% | 31% |
| Write letter | 69% | 38% | 3% |
| Google+ | 60% | 8% | 1% |
| LinkedIn | 52% | 6% | 0% |

The 2012 American Express Global Customer Service Barometer found that consumers who have used social media for service wield the greatest amount of influence. They tell significantly more people about their service experiences, and say they'd spend 21 percent more with companies who deliver great service — compared to 13 percent on average.

In an interview, Jim Bush, executive vice president of world service, American Express, remarked further about the data:

> Consumers who have used social media for service in the last year are willing to pay a 21% premium at companies that provide great service. They also tell three times as many people about positive service experiences compared to the general population. Ultimately, getting service right with these social media savvy consumers can help a business grow.

Figure 13-2 was designed by eMarketer.com based on the American Express data. It graphically demonstrates why Internet users are flocking to social media for customer service.

A telling piece of information has been repeated twice. If those who use social media for customer service are willing to pay more for your product or service, you ought to get something going online in a hurry.

Use your online posts as a way to inform a large group of people at once. Your transparency in public is respected. When you admit to a mistake in front of an online community, making it right on the public network reflects well on you and your business.

Table 13-2 provides some additional information from the study about the power of social media customer service that is worth considering.

| Table 13-2 | Impact of Social Media on Customer Service | | |
|---|---|---|---|
| **Service Topic** | **Consumers Who Have Used Social Media for Customer Service** | **Consumers Who Haven't Used Social Media for Customer Service** | **General Population** |
| Additional amount consumers are willing to spend for excellent service | 21% more | 11% more | 13% more |
| Have not completed an intended purchase because of a poor customer service experience in the past year | 83% | 49% | 55% |
| Number of people consumers tell about good customer service experiences | 42 people | 9 people | 15 people |
| Number of people consumers tell about bad customer service experiences | 53 people | 17 people | 24 people |

*From the 2012 American Express Global Customer Service Barometer

# *Participating in Customer Service, Social Media-Style*

Social media is a community activity. When one member has a problem, others join in to help, often commenting to a business until it responds.

When companies step forward during a public relations crisis, they score in public perception. A company that responds promptly and effectively to customer issues prevents the online buzz that otherwise might escalate into large-scale customer concerns.

Recently, Southwest Airlines reached 3 million Facebook fans. As a thank-you, they ran a highly discounted sale on fares. But when customers booked their flights, their bookings were overcharged. To add insult to injury, many had their credit and debit cards charged multiple times.

Although Southwest worked diligently to correct the charges, the social media networks were on fire with customer complaints. I watched the @SouthwestAir Twitter team valiantly and humbly respond to what seemed to be unending complaints, long into the night and throughout the next day. Efforts like that do not go unnoticed in the social media community.

Many big companies such as Southwest have a team of people whose sole responsibility is to respond to comments on social media. In many cases, each team member signs her Tweets with initials to personalize the outreach. Note that many just respond and don't invoke conversation.

As a small business, your customer service outreach needs to be integrated into a regular stream of content (see Chapter 9 for subject matter suggestions). It's not enough for you to respond or react. You need to give consumers a reason to stick with you in social media.

A recent blog post from my friend Michael Pace, a customer service executive, discussed the importance of blending customer service and participating in online conversations:

> *Conversations lead to Relationships, Relationships lead to Retention, and Retention is the main goal of every Customer Service organization. If you do it well, that Retention becomes Word of Mouth, Word of Mouth refills your funnel at a phenomenal conversion rate with near nominal costs. All this becomes a virtuous cycle: more followers, more transparent conversations, more viral spread of your brand, more activity of products, services and communities, more reputational value...*

Customers expect good service and prompt resolution to problems. Companies that dedicate themselves to monitoring mentions and intervening with customer issues online practice a winning customer service formula. Responding appropriately and swiftly develops trust.

## Defusing issues before they escalate

Social media comments go by quickly on Twitter. Some major brands and businesses do not monitor their mentions and comments from unhappy customers go unanswered. Not every call for help ends up in a public relations fiasco because people new to social media don't always have the skill it takes to get a brand's attention. A customer who doesn't hear back feels ignored and disrespected, and no doubt spreads the word to people they know in the offline world.

Most companies who take social media seriously respond quickly on Twitter (more so than on Facebook), perhaps because reactions are observed by many on such a public forum. Twitter's stream also is tracked by Google, and much of what is Tweeted appears as part of Google searches. The speed at which social media comments spread (through Tweets, reTweets, and Google) should signify that if you don't show that you care about a customer's concern as fast as humanly possible, you might end up in viral hell.

The other day, I had an issue with FedEx. I Tweeted one of the FedEx Twitter representatives: "@fedexrobin Help! I have a fedex problem!" As shown in Figure 13-3, she had the problem worked out before I could make the phone call!

**Figure 13-3:**
Twitter
responses
from
@FedExRobin.

Had I not Tweeted to Robin directly and just mentioned FedEx, my Tweet would have been answered with equal speed because FedEx monitors social media streams constantly. For example, without having to look very hard, I found @FedExRobin hard at work (see Figure 13-4). A young woman was bemoaning in a Tweet that her FedEx delivery hadn't arrived. FedEx monitoring paid off: Within a few moments, she got a response from FedEx and Robin was able to track the package and appease the customer.

**Figure 13-4:**
An unhappy
customer
who payed
(sic) extra.

FedEx's social media monitoring allows them to find customers who make an off-hand comment about the brand. The company has a team on Twitter and another on Facebook, ready to help with delivery or pickup issues. They try to fully embrace the FedEx employee Purple Promise, which is: "I will make every FedEx experience outstanding."

Impressed with FedEx's social media outreach, I spoke with Sheila T. Harrell, vice president of customer service operations for FedEx. Social media is clearly important to the company. Sheila told me that "every call, chat, Tweet, and interaction is an opportunity to make a difference."

Many consumers aren't comfortable when they are asked to follow or friend a business online. But when a business reaches out to help with an issue, they subconsciously bond with the brand.

The other side of the coin is the exchange in Figure 13-5, in which a disgruntled Twitter user comments about dissatisfaction with a company's customer service response. The reply from the brand made me gasp. It caused others to gasp as well; this screen shot has been around the Internet for quite a while (without the names obscured). That exposure can't be helping the business's reputation.

When engaging with your customers through social media, be transparent and be authentic. By doing so, your customers come to trust you and you build loyalty.

# Unhappy consumers target social media in record numbers

In 2011, 49 days after the HP TouchPad was launched in the United States, Hewlett Packard decided to liquidate stock of their state-of-the-art Touchpad tablet in a historic fire sale set to begin on August 20. Prices were unprecedented: $149.00 for the 32GB tablet and $99.00 for the 16GB version (introductory prices were $599.99 and $499.99, respectively). Interest in the sale immediately reached a fever pitch. For example, in less than 24 hours, SlickDeals had over three million views and nine thousand posts from people wanting to get their hands on the tablet. I was one of those people.

I stayed on the computer trying to purchase nonstop for hours. I watched HP's Small Business site crash continually during my order process. I finally got my order to stick on August 21, but got no confirmation of the order. On August 23 I was able to find my order on the site, with *Shipping soon* in the detail. While I was waiting to find out if my order had registered, I looked for other places to order. OnSale was selling their stock on Amazon as well as on their own site. Their Amazon offer on August 21 sold out in 20 minutes. I was able to purchase on the site at 2:19pm, only to have my order cancelled on August 24. Another company, Datavis, sold units on eBay on August 20; within 10 minutes they crashed the site. On August 22, PayPal was

refunding payments. Barnes & Noble sold out; on August 22 they started cancelling orders and posted to Twitter.

It was reported that HP incorrectly sent extended allocation amounts to some of its retailers. The retailers who sold allocated amounts realized that they would be unable to fulfill thousands of orders. Those who thought they had secure orders passed up opportunities to purchase from other sources. Other websites and retailers got into the fray; one received 4,500 orders for the 1,000 units they had in stock. *Sold out* and *Out of stock* messages were a common sight across e-retailers.

According to Mashable, on August 22, Twitter mentions on the issue were running at 50,000 Tweets a day. It is rumored that more than 200,000 units were sold within a week, but orders far exceeded the actual stock. On the same day, Groubal, the consumer complaint website, started an online petition entitled "Barnes & Noble Screwed Me Out of My TouchPad." The petition filled up with 1,727 signatures. Hundreds (perhaps thousands) of unhappy buyers lit up Twitter and Facebook.

HP was heroic enough to step forward. On August 20, Bryna Corcoran (@BrynaAtHP), of HP's social media team, bravely sent the

Tweet pictured. For months, she Tweeted facts and tried to help whenever she could. I spoke to Bryna, and here is her advice for the small business owner:

> "The biggest challenge for any business owner jumping into social media is balancing the needs/wants of the community with the interest of your company. You'll have to build up a thick skin as it can be an internal struggle with yourself, especially if you are someone who easily sympathizes with the frustrations or plight of others. You will want to give everyone the answers and resolutions they need but there are going to be times when you simply cannot comment or share information that could put your company at risk.
>
> I think most people with whom you deal are kind and understand that it's not the fault of the person they are speaking with on social media that they are having a poor experience with a company or product. When you are authentic, sincere, and genuine with what you can share with a customer, you may find they simply appreciate being heard and acknowledged by a company spokesperson. In my experience, this approach has turned a very frustrated customer into one who is endeared to you because you are treating them as you would want to be treated if the shoe was on the other foot."

My personal update: I finally got an e-mail from HP saying that all orders would be shipped by October 31. My order was shipped to me, two months after ordering, on October 24. Yes, I was one of the voices graciously handled in public by Bryna.

# Posting publicly in social media

Your initial contact with a customer through social media is public and open for anyone to see who is connected to you or the consumer. Your reputation is fair game to the residents of the web. Monitoring your social media accounts and responding quickly and publicly to online mentions should be your first line of defense against customer dissatisfaction.

Those who are part of online media wield power when sharing feedback or complaints. Customer can band together in solidarity. Whether your company responds publicly or not, online comments have staying power.

After you've engaged a customer, the only currently acceptable reason for making the discussion secret is confidentiality. When the information necessary to solve an issue requires personal or private information, making the chat private or continuing by e-mail is satisfactory.

In 2010, David Armano (@armano), executive vice president of Edelman Digital, came up with an interesting flowchart that maps out the engagement process. This simple decision tree, shown in Figure 13-6, can help you understand the best-practices flow of social engagement.

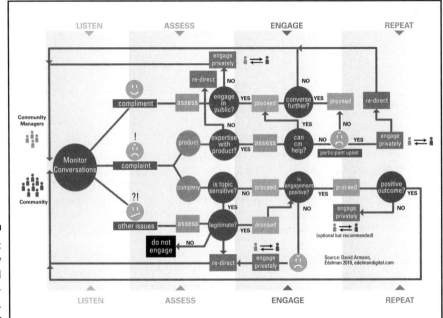

**Figure 13-6:** The flow of social engagement.

Note, though, that taking the conversation into a phone call may not be what the customer wants. Voice calls have been losing favor with those under 30. They are embedded in the newest technologies and are loathe to connect on the telephone. Today's tech-savvy customers want to conduct their business on the web.

In the aforementioned Maritz study, 27 percent of customers whose issues were addressed on a public forum said they were delighted to get a public response from a company. The "delight" factor dwindled to 6 percent when issues were solved through traditional direct methods (phone call or e-mail).

# Building Your Own Community

When you arrive at a well-produced website, you often see a link to a community area. This area is where the customer service and FAQs pages live. You might also find a customer-to-customer community that encourages participation from those who visit the business site.

Whether you choose to have a customer community attached to your site is up to you. In a self-service community, customers come and go and make comments. In a managed community, you or one of your employees acts as a moderator, guiding the conversation. Your presence signifies to visitors that you want to connect.

When deciding how to design a community — or whether to even have one — base your choice on your available time and resources. If you are short on time, you might be able to manage a Facebook page, Twitter, or a blog and accomplish the same goals.

You can build a small-business customer community quickly with tools from Get Satisfaction, at www.getsatisfaction.com. The company was launched to solve a problem that the founders had with their original website. They knew the pain of delivering customer service by e-mail and, in contrast, had amazing experiences answering questions in public and through their blog. The outcome was the platform they now offer. Think of your community as an online support or feedback forum that becomes part of your site.

Community powered support can be more results-oriented and perceived to be more social than the alternate (traditional) ways of dealing with customer issues. Figure 13-7 shows Get Satisfaction's own community-powered support page.

Their easy-to-manage option for building customer interaction is based on organically driven customer-to-customer support. It affords you the benefit of publicly displaying issues that you are currently addressing and have already solved.

Get Satisfaction offers a $19 per month small-business solution to help you get started. The platform is a great way to start a community. It enhances your customer service by allowing open comments and by engaging your customers through simple FAQs. As you grow, the site offers graduated steps, so you can upgrade to a more robust platform as needed.

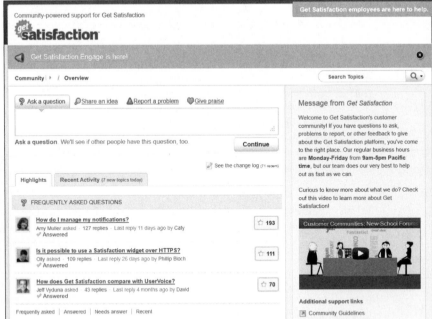

**Figure 13-7:**
Visitors
can ask a
question or
see previ-
ously asked
questions
and the
answers.

## Handling support issues with help desk tools

After you're aware of your company's issues, an online service desk can be a real boon to efficiency. Having a platform to handle customer queries from a browser window or mobile device is a great idea. For businesses that handle many requests, help desk software can be the answer. In this way, you can respond promptly to customer inquiries, complaints, and service queries.

A few web-based help desk options are available, including the popular Zendesk. Their software suite enables those who provide customer service to receive, process, and respond to service requests in one centralized area. The platform is currently used by more than 20,000 organizations worldwide. Zendesk facilitates conversations via web, e-mail, phone, Twitter, Facebook, mobile devices, online chat, community forums, knowledge bases, and more.

Zendesk integrates with more than 90 solutions. For example, many grow-ing businesses integrate Zendesk support with Salesforce or Get Satisfaction community platforms.

Another popular solution comes from UserVoice. As an alternate to FAQ pages, your customers can get answers from the UserVoice widget, which is shown in Figure 13-8. A customer types a question, and UserVoice Instant

Answers pulls the answer from an online knowledge base that you've set up. Your business dashboard shows you which answers in your knowledge base are the best-performing, so you can edit information as needed.

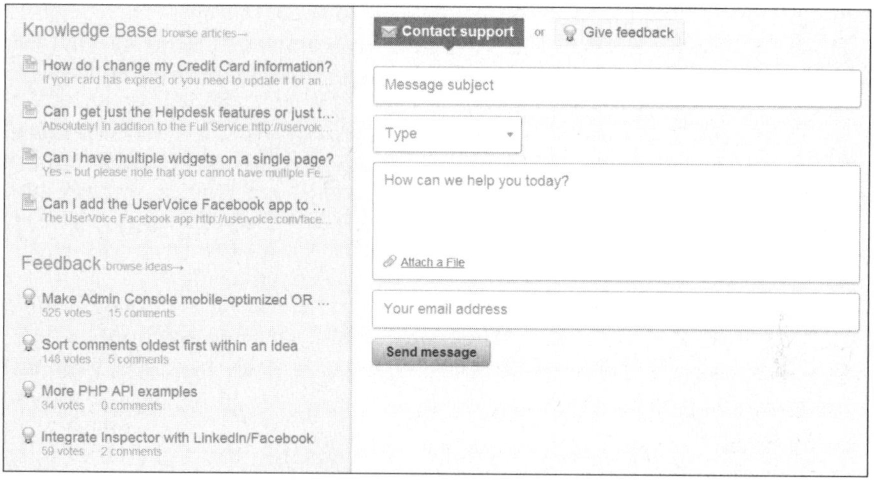

**Figure 13-8:**
The UserVoice web widget can help your customers help themselves.

Both platforms provide an integrated help desk and customer support portal. Help desk software is web-based (also available on mobile devices) and covers customer support, trouble tickets, and a knowledge base.

UserVoice offers a free basic plan that includes their feedback and help desk modules for one agent as well as the Inspector, a tool that aggregates information about your customer from your own systems as well as publicly available data from social networks on the fly. This data is helpful when you have no information at hand about the person making the request. To find out more, go to www.uservoice.com.

The Zendesk starter package costs $20 per year for three agents and includes native mobile apps, such as iPad, iPhone, Android, BlackBerry, and Windows Phone. For more information, visit www.zendesk.com.

## Helping customers is everyone's job

For your customers, the most important aspect in a transaction is the experience they have, not the attributes of your product or service. Online or in person, your employees are your first-level, frontline customer service representatives.

When employees discuss your business with a friend, post to a blog, or Tweet on Twitter, they can — in mere seconds — make your company shine or seriously damage your business's reputation.

Each staff member who helps your business run on a daily basis should have a hand in your customer service. How your employees feel about you, as their leader, and the culture in which they work has a lot to do with whether they take pride in their work. If they have a positive attitude when speaking to or connecting online with customers, they put their best foot forward.

Hiring employees who care — who are as emotionally invested in your dream as you are — can make all the difference in your customer service success.

As a small-business person, you are your own human resources department. You have to hire and fire based on your instincts — and the task is never easy. In my business, I am an employee to my clients, and my employees are there to help me make the magic happen. Customer magic goes on 24/7; a "wow" lasts only a moment or two.

To make the magic happen for your customers, you need loyal employees who support you. And although finding employees who think like you and have the same level of commitment to customer service is tough, keeping them happy is even tougher.

By using the ideas and tools in this chapter, you and your employees can reach out to many more customers!

# Chapter 14

# Monitoring Your Online Reputation

*W*hether or not you've taken the plunge into social media, your business is likely being mentioned online. One source of customer comments are review sites (which I describe in Chapter 6), but those evaluations are just the tip of the iceberg (as they saw on the *Titanic*).

Millions of blogs, helps desks, user groups, and retail sites have comment areas. Wherever your customers go, they may mention your business in a positive or negative vein. Nothing disappears from the Internet, so it certainly behooves you to know when and where you and your business are mentioned.

In this chapter, I recommend some top-notch free tools for monitoring social media. You'll find that they'll save you time and money.

## Free Speech and the Law

You might think that negative comments can be erased. Alas, not in the world of new media. Everyone has an opinion, and the law says they have a right to voice their thoughts. You might think that sites that host comments would have some accountability, but they cannot be held responsible for comments posted by users. Section 230 of the 1996 Communication Decency Act protects providers of "interactive computer services" (who publish information provided by others) from suits seeking to make them responsible for the speech of their users.

Groups such as the Electronic Frontier Foundation actively support litigation to preserve First Amendment rights in computing and telecommunications technology.

As far as people posting comments, they are covered too. SLAPP (short for Strategic Lawsuit Against Public Participation) lawsuits can be filed as retaliation for criticizing a person or business in a public forum. Rarely do SLAPP lawsuits end up in court or win if prosecuted. The purpose of this legal action is to intimidate the critic with the fear of litigation and the cost of defending such an action. However, if you lose a SLAPP lawsuit, it may cost you a bundle and you may be responsible for the opposition's legal costs as well as your own.

To defend First Amendment rights, 28 states have enacted anti-SLAPP legislation. For example, in California, you have the right to file a motion to strike a complaint filed against you based on an "act in furtherance of [your] right of petition or free speech under the United States or California Constitution in connection with a public issue." If you win your motion against a SLAPP and believe that you can show that the plaintiff filed the lawsuit to harass or silence you, rather than to resolve a legitimate legal claim, you might consider filing an anti-SLAPP suit against your opponent. Keep in mind that anti-SLAPP laws do not cover harassing, defamation, or threatening statements.

The best defense against damage to your business reputation is to find online comments as soon as they are posted. A negative comment can't be erased, but you do have the opportunity to reach out to the customer and make things right before the comments spiral out of control.

A negative comment will not disappear from the web, but it can be outweighed by many more positive comments. Here's where the value of a social media community comes in. After you have a relationship with your online community, happy customers and those who believe in you and your business can be encouraged to help out and post positive missives.

Don't get bogged down in the negatives. When customers say good things about you, their comments are worthy of praise. Smart businesses actively seek out positive commenters as well and thank them, privately and publically if is appropriate.

Learning about your customers (commenters) can be as simple as a Google search. Finding them on social media and giving them a public "thank you" on Twitter or Facebook is perceived as a pleasant surprise.

Fish where the fish are — find your customers where they spend time on the web and interact with them. By doing so, you've positioned your business to build a loyal community.

# Monitoring Comments with Google

If you listen to many so-called experts online, you might be assured that a surefire way exists to catch any web mention of your company. That assertion is simply *not* true. Some monitoring services find a few instances, others find more, and yet another may find something different. But in the ten years in which I've been looking to monitor my own brand, I have found complete results to be fairly elusive.

The good side of all this is that after you register for monitoring on more than one service or RSS feed (more on RSS further on), most e-mail you the results and the costs are nil or minimal. You get notifications daily or as they occur (I recommend once a day).

Sometimes the most obvious answers slip our minds. Doing a web search on Google or Bing can help you find up-to-the moment as well as archived postings on the web. (I've found posts as far back as the early 90s.)

The problem is, performing a simple and accurate search on the web isn't quite so easy. Think about this: Of the 7 billion people in the world, 315 million live in the United States. A projected 80 percent of the U.S. population is online (an estimated 175 million on Facebook alone). Imagine the number of online entries if each person posts one sentence a week. Studies show that an average visit to a web page triggers 56 instances of data collection — that's a lot of files.

It's difficult to fathom how much information is out there, but a huge portion is at your fingertips if you know a few search tricks to streamline your results. In this section, you discover how to fine-tune your online searches.

When performing web searches, capital letters are not read by the query engine, so capitalization is not required. The only place capitalization does count is in the few search operands mentioned in this section.

## Improving search results

My first website (shown in Figure 14-1) went online in 1996. I learned early about the wealth of knowledge that can be found by performing in-depth searches. Finding esoteric information online became a passion. I use the information in my business and when researching for the books I write. In this section, I provide some inside tricks of the search gurus.

The Collier Company served the retail marketing community from 1984 to 2002. The president, Marsha Collier - has gone full time into writing and eBay. Now the Collier Company's child-web, coolebaytools.com, is the main site. Please click on the banner below to get there. Thank you for visiting.

**Figure 14-1:** My first business website, circa 1996.

*What Did We Do?*

We produced printed materials; such as ads, catalogs, posters, buttons, tabloids, magazines, and more for over eighteen years. We also planned and executed some very successful and exciting ad campaigns.

**We've been online since 1984,** when we had an old Kaypro computer, changing floppies *(there was NO hard drive)* and were working with CPM *(pre MS DOS)*. We heard about something called CompuServe, and how you could talk to people from all over the world with the computer and a modem *(300 bps.. whew)*. That's how our online experience began, we're hooked on the Internet, it is *THE* way to promote your business. We design custom graphics and your WWW site, as well as offering state of the art, high-speed Web Hosting packages!

**Marsha Collier**, president, has over twenty five years experience in advertising and marketing, previously working for *The Miami Herald*, Miami, Florida; *The Daily News*, Los Angeles; (also general manager of *Dodger Blue*, the official newspaper of the Los Angeles Dodgers from 1982 to 1983) and finally founding the Collier Company in 1984. Marsha also acted as publisher of "*Southern California Auto Racing*", from 1985 through 1987. The Collier Company won the "Small Business of the Year" award from California State Assemblyman Richard Katz in 1990, and Marsha was named "Citizen of the Year" in 1992 by the Northridge Chamber of Commerce, the California State Assembly and it was resolved in the US Senate by Ed Davis, Senator from the State of California. She is also the author

If you are in a pinch and don't remember the search operators described in this section, go to Google's Advanced Search page at `www.google.com/ advanced_search`. From that page, you can include and exclude words and phrases and even find free images to use.

### Explicit phrases

You want to search for a phrase, not the single words. but Google wants to give you every result of each word in the same web page, You can imagine a search like that could possibly come up with millions of results. When searching the web for a name or phrase that has more than one word, be explicit, try the following tricks to refine your search:

✔ **Use AND or +.** When combining words, use AND (all uppercase) or the + character. Do not include a space after the + character. For example,

```
marsha AND collier
marsha +collier
```

✔ **Enclose the phrase in quotation marks.** When you place your search terms within quotes, the search engine retrieves results with those words, exactly in the order you wrote them. For example,

```
"marsha collier"
```

## Excluding words

To exclude a word in a search phrase, use – (the minus sign). Suppose you and several other people or businesses have the same or a similar name, such as Brownes Coffee Shop and Brownes Coffee & Tea Shop. If you use the minus sign before the word you want to exclude from the results, you optimize your results; note, however, that you do not add a space after the minus sign. For example:

```
brownes coffee shop -tea
"brownes coffee" -tea
```

## Unique spelling

If you want to search for a word or name with a unique spelling, like *Stanly's Restaurant,* Google changes your search to the more common spelling, *Stanley's Restaurant.* Google attempts to read your mind and guess your intent by correcting your spelling. Use Google's verbatim tool to get the results want. Should your search be for a name or word with a unique spelling, do the following:

1. **On the left side of a Google search results page, click Show Search Tools.**

2. **In the resulting list, click Verbatim.**

3. **In the search box, type your search terms, and then click the magnifying glass icon.**

## Site search

If you'd like to find results in a certain website, you use the word *site,* a colon (:), and the search word or phrase. Note that there is no space before or after the colon. For example, if I wanted to search for my name on the Yelp review site, I would type

```
site:yelp.com "marsha collier"
```

## Show search tools

On the left side of a Google search page, you see a category list: Web, Images, Maps, Videos, News, Shopping, Books, and More (clicking More displays more categories). Below that list you might see name of the city you are in, and an option to change the location (in the case of a location search). At the very bottom of these links is a Show Search Tools link. Clicking this link displays the menu shown in Figure 14-2 so you can select the timeframe in which you'd like to search.

| | |
|---|---|
| Any time | **Twitter / jmspool: She has realized that European ...** |
| Past hour | twitter.com/jmspool/statuses/2433859822699927424 |
| Past 24 hours | 6 hours ago - @jmspool that's bad, considering hair dryers should blow. Details Expand |
| Past week | Collapse. Reply; RetweetedRetweet; Delete; FavoritedFavorite. 4m · **Marsha Collier** ... |
| Past month | Jared Spool shared this |
| Past year | |
| Custom range... | **Linked Income , Archive » To Klout or not to Klout, that is the question** |
| | www.linked-income.com/.../to-klout-or-not-to-klout-that-is-th ... |
| Sorted by | 16 hours ago - Neal Schaffer of Windmill Networking (Number 28 on the Forbes Top 50 |
| relevance | list) and**Marsha Collier** (Number 31 on the Forbes Top 50 list) both have high Klout ... |
| Sorted by date | |
| | **Q3: If you have a customer service staff at your biz, how much - inagist** |
| All results | inagist.com/all/2431559437460520096/ |
| Sites with images | 21 hours ago - inagist · **Marsha Collier** as @MarshaCollier. Q3: If you have a customer |
| Related searches | service staff at your biz, how much training do they receive during their SECOND YEAR |
| Visited pages | ... |
| Not yet visited | |
| Dictionary | **How does lack of employee training contribute to poor customer ...** |
| Reading level | www.scribd.com › Business/Law › Marketing |
| Personal | 20 hours ago - Readcasts. 0. Embed Views. This is a private document. Published by. |
| Nearby | **Marsha Collier**. Follow. Search. TIP Press Ctrl-F⌘F to search anywhere in the |
| Translated foreign | document. |
| pages | |
| Verbatim | **Margie's Moments of Tiyoweh** |
| | www.margieclayman.com/ |
| Reset tools | 14 hours ago - **Marsha Collier** (@marshacollier) – supportive beyond measure, |
| | co-founder of #custserv, prolific author. 86. Jeffrey J. Kingman (@jeffreyjkingman) – |
| | co-founder ... |
| | From your Google Reader subscriptions. |

**Figure 14-2:** The Show Search Tools link displays many handy variables for this 24-hour search.

# *Setting up Google Alerts*

The kind folks at Google have a service that notifies you when Google finds new results, web pages, newspaper articles, or blogs that match your selected search term or phrase. Google e-mails you results or sends them as they happen to Google Reader via an RSS feed.

Here are my recommendations and how to set up a Google alert. Follow these steps:

1. **Type** www.google.com/alerts **in your web browser.**

   The Google Alerts page is displayed.

   You might also want to set up alerts for your competition or for news stories that relate to your business.

2. **In the Search Query box, type your keyword query (search word or phrase) using the operands mentioned in the preceding section.**

   For example, in Figure 14-3, I searched for one of my book titles.

3. **In the Result Type drop-down menu, select Everything.**

   The Everything choice includes results from anything and everything on the web that Google finds matching your query. Or you can select a single category: Blogs, News, Video, Discussions, or Books.

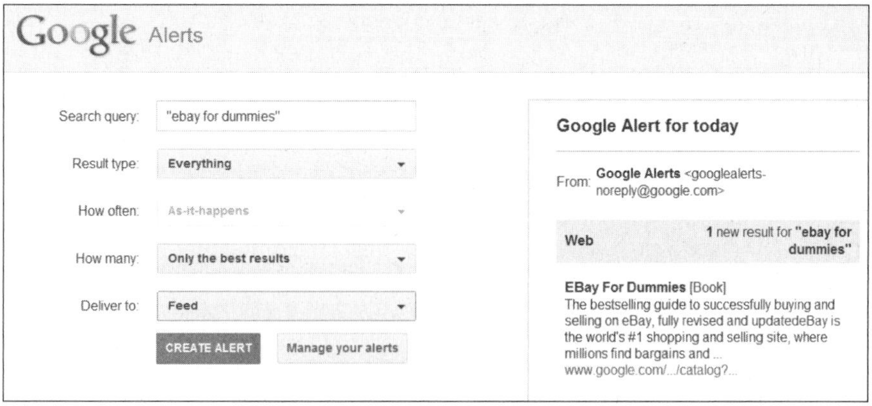

Google Alerts

Search query: "ebay for dummies"

Result type: Everything

How often: As-it-happens

How many: Only the best results

Deliver to: Feed

CREATE ALERT    Manage your alerts

**Google Alert for today**

From: **Google Alerts** <googlealerts-noreply@google.com>

**Web**                    1 new result for **"ebay for dummies"**

**EBay For Dummies** [Book]
The bestselling guide to successfully buying and selling on eBay, fully revised and updatedeBay is the world's #1 shopping and selling site, where millions find bargains and ...
www.google.com/.../catalog?...

**Figure 14-3:**
Setting up
a Google
alert.

4. **In the How Often drop-down menu, select the frequency of the notifications.**

   If you want the alert as soon as Google finds something, select As-It-Happens. Realize that you may get interruptions at odd hours. If you'd prefer more of a digest, select Once a Day or Once a Week. I recommend Once a Day because the point of doing this is to stay on top of sentiment.

5. **In the How Many drop-down menu, determine whether you want Google to decide which results are important.**

   Only the Best Results is the first option, but I recommend choosing the alternate, All Results. You don't want to miss a thing.

6. **In the Deliver To drop-down menu, select your e-mail address from the e-mail addresses that Google has on record for you or indicate that you would like to have a feed sent to Google Reader.**

   In Figure 14-3, all result notifications go to my Google Reader.

7. **Click Create Alert.**

8. **Repeat this process for as many alerts as you want to generate.**

After you've created an alert, you can click the Manage Your Alerts button (or go to www.google.com/alerts/manage) to make changes, additions, or deletions.

Google alerts find quite a bit if helpful information on the web. In addition to Google alerts, however, I like the more in-depth results I get by adding the services described next.

# Listening in on Blogs and Twitter

So much information is moving around the Internet that it often takes more than one product to get the most accurate read of your brand (or your name) on the web.

Knowing where your customers hang out on the web gives you a leg up on figuring out where you want to search. For example, if your customers are on Twitter, using its built-in site search is not the most accurate. Twitter updates the search database daily, but searches only go back a few days, and you may not see all the information you want. Every day, close to 350 million Tweets are posted on Twitter and many regularly refer to businesses and brands.

You can set your Twitter account to alert you via text messaging on your mobile device or by e-mail anytime someone mentions or @ replies to you. This feature is great for day-to-day conversations, but someone may mention you or your business (or a competitor) in a Tweet and refer to you by name, not by your Twitter account.

Also, Facebook is a pretty closed platform, so not a lot that is posted on Facebook appears on the web. You're going to need an app for that. In this section, I provide a few recommendations for platforms to enhance your searches. Using one, two or even all these platforms helps you — at little or no cost — keep an eye on any web comments made about your company (or you).

## TweetReports

TweetReports, at `http://tweetreports.com`, is an effective search and monitoring tool for Twitter. Just type your business name in the text box in the center of the page, as shown in Figure 14-4, and press Return to search. You are presented with the most accurate and thorough data of mentions on Twitter that I have seen. You are free to browse through all the results of your search and click through to follow or view the person making the comments on Twitter.

You can go back to the home page and perform as many searches as you want. For $5, you can purchase a copy of a report you've run (based on the last seven days of activity or 25,000 Tweets). Simply click Buy Report, in the upper-right corner of your search results.

Figure 14-5 shows the results of my search. On the right side of the screen, note the Related Conversations section, which contains the terms that appear most often accompanying my search keywords.

**Figure 14-4:**
The Tweet
Reports
home
page with
a search
typed and
ready to go.

**Figure 14-5:**
Results of
my Tweet
Reports
search.

TweetReports has many other features besides the basic search, such as keyword monitoring, brand monitoring, sentiment analysis, and search filtering. The company offers a seven-day free trial, and an individual account costs $9 a month. You can cancel at any time. No contracts.

## Twilert

Twilert is a free web app that e-mails you results at a prescribed time whenever mentions appear on Twitter (see Figure 14-6). They monitor for keywords, Twitter accounts or Twitter hash tags. When you set up a twilert, you can also limit your search to Tweets that are sent from a specific city (within a certain number of miles) from where the Tweets were sent.

The e-mail includes links and can also let you know whether the Tweet was asking a question and whether the sentiment of the Tweet was positive or negative. Just go to www.twilert.com and sign in with your Twitter ID.

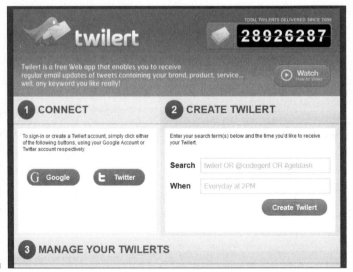

**Figure 14-6:**
Type your search words and let Twilert know what time you'd like the report.

## Social Mention

The Social Mention site has a wide reach and produces broad results, with as many as 81 platforms included in the search, as shown in Figure 14-7. To search them all, select All at the top-right of the screen. To limit your search to specific sources, select them by adding a add check mark in the box before their name.

Your search results are accompanied by sentiment graphs and the top keywords associated with your search, as shown on the left in Figure 14-8.

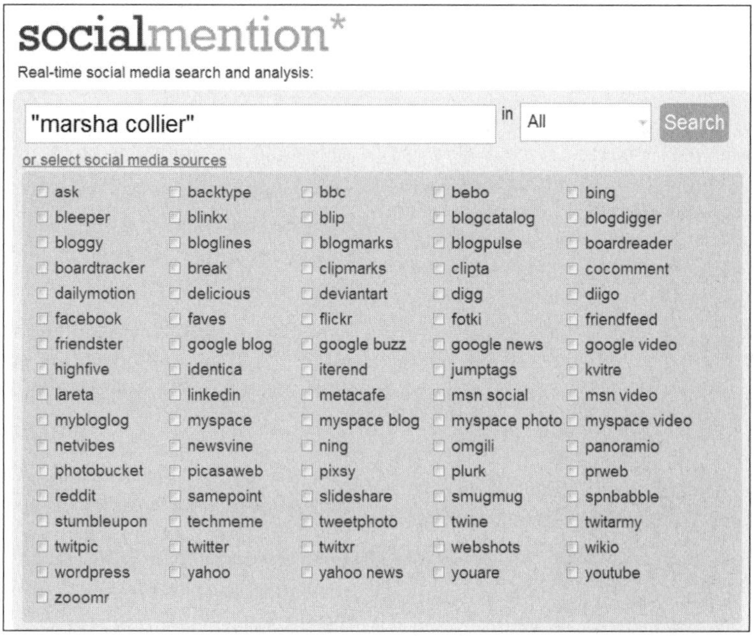

**Figure 14-7:**
Social
Mention
searches a
large num-
ber of sites.

**Figure 14-8:**
The results
of my
search,
along with
sentiment
information.

If you hone in on your search operands and are happy with the results, save the search to an RSS feed.

# Adding an RSS feed to Google Reader

After you sign up with Google, you have access to many Google applications and services, including Google Reader, an excellent RSS reader. RSS (Really Simple Syndication) is a no-fuss way to get updates from a page or blog that support RSS feeds. An RSS reader is a platform that constantly checks the feeds to which you subscribe for updates and posts them in a read-able format. By using Reader, you can access your feeds wherever you are, not just at your home computer.

When you're on a site that displays an RSS link, you can subscribe to new updates. (An example RSS link is shown in the upper-right corner of Figure 14-8.) When you click the RSS link or symbol, the site whirs and grinds for a few sec-onds and you see either a page full of code (see

the first figure) or a page asking what reader you would like the feed to go to.

If the resulting page asks where you'd like to view the feed, select the Google logo for Google Reader, and the Reader automatically installs the feed on your page.

If you see a page of code, don't panic. At the top of the page, in the web URL space, high-light and copy the address for the feed (it begins with *http*). Next, go to Google Reader at www.google.com/reader, and mouse over your Subscriptions column. When a down arrow appears on the right, click and select Add a Subscription (see the second figure). In the small text box that appears, paste the address you copied and press Return. The feed is added to your feedlist.

```
← → C  ⓘ www.icerocket.com/search?tab=blog&q=marsha+collier&rss=1                    ☆ ♡ ⬚ 🖪 🖪 🔊 ⬚ 🔔 📇 ♻ ⬚ ⬚ ⬚
ⓢ Sony Support  📰 eBay  📄 Personalize w/...  ⓒ Pin It  📄 TwitterKeys  📄 The Economics ...  ⓒ Share on Poster...  ⓒ Google Bookm...   »  ☐ Other bookmar

This XML file does not appear to have any style information associated with it. The document tree is shown below.

▼<rss xmlns:dc="http://purl.org/dc/elements/1.1/" version="2.0">
  ▼<channel>
    <title>Icerocket blog search: marsha collier</title>
    <link>http://www.icerocket.com/search?q=marsha+collier</link>
    <description>Blogs Search from IceRocket.com</description>
    <language>en-us</language>
    <copyright>Copyright 2012, IceRocket.com</copyright>
    ▼<item>
      ▼<title>
        <![CDATA[ 9 More Social Media Customer Service Tips ]]>
      </title>
      ▼<description>
        ▼<![CDATA[
          I have had many conversations lately with friends, brands, and fellow community managers/engagers about
          customer service and social media. Perhaps my recent recap of 9 customer service tips from an awesome
          webinar with Frank Eliason also has me thinking about the topic. And so, I'm dedicating more o <b>...</b>
        ]]>
      </description>
      ▼<link>
        ▼<![CDATA[
          http://www.radian6.com/blog/2012/07/9-more-social-media-customer-service-tips/
```

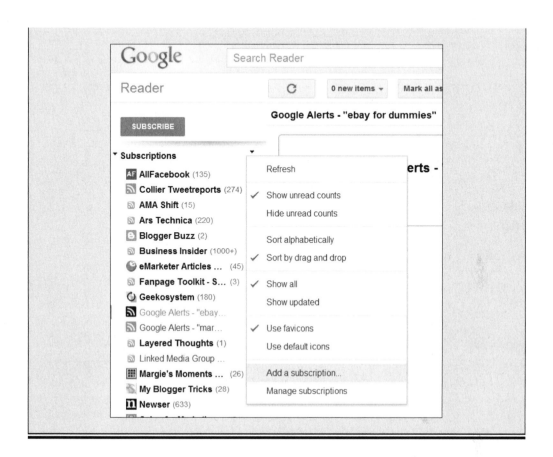

# Samepoint

Samepoint has been tracking the web since 2008. To create an account, go to www.samepoint.com. Alternatively, you can sign in with your Google, Twitter, Facebook, Yahoo!, AOL, or Open ID credentials. Signing in with a universal login is safe and becoming more the norm on the Internet.

Samepoint provides three types of searches:

✔ **Social Mentions (on Web):** This type of search provides results like the ones shown in Figure 14-9. Each post is measured for sentiment and has a color-coded bar indicating social tone, with red for negative and green for positive; you also see a list of any negative or positive words found in the post. (Good data!)

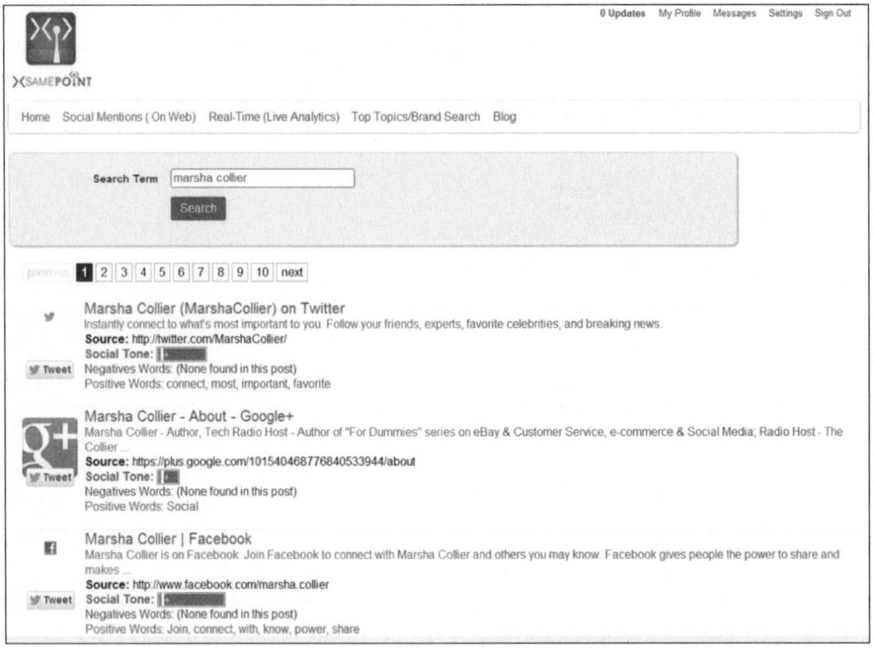

**Figure 14-9:**
Search results from the web indicating positive and negative tone.

✔ **Real-Time (Live Analytics):** This search returns an executive-style summary based on your keywords. You see graphs that show top conversation points, top influencers to engage, your social media ecosystem, and more.

✔ **Top Topics/Brand Search:** Input your search keywords and perform the search. Your results look like those in Figure 14-10 and are from all sources. Note that you can rerun your search selecting one of the sites listed in the drop-down menu.

All this information is available at no charge.

## IceRocket

IceRocket, at www.icerocket.com, is a nifty free resource for monitoring your brand that crawls more than 200 million blogs, news stories, videos, and more.

IceRocket has been around since 2004 and was originally backed by Mark Cuban. Recently, it was acquired by Meltwater Group, a purveyor of enterprise-level social media and news monitoring applications, and they integrated portions of their subscriber technology into the platform. They plan to let the funky little IceRocket site continue to operate.

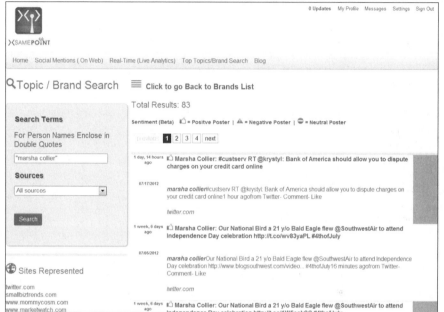

**Figure 14-10:** Samepoint brand search.

On the home page, you have your choice of searching blogs, Twitter, Facebook, Images, and the Big Buzz (a compendium of all the searches). I performed a search of blogs; Figure 14-11 shows the results.

From the results page, you can narrow your results by date and also subscribe to receive an RSS feed of ongoing results.

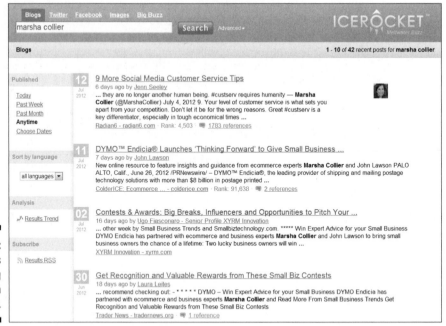

**Figure 14-11:**
Results
of a blog
search on
IceRocket.

# Chapter 15

# Marketing in a Social Way: New Media Advertising

*In This Chapter*

▶ Using e-mail to build sales

▶ Promoting on Facebook

*T*his book's title doesn't include the word *marketing,* which is traditionally the act of promoting your business and selling your products or services. Instead, this book is more about the new media style of marketing via the social web. Conceptually, this is a 180-degree turnaround from customary practices of hitting the customer and hitting them hard. Now our goal is to develop a community with our customers.

Developing a community enhances your relationships with your local customers and also expedites your outreach to extend your customer base across the Internet. Broadening your customer base in this fashion is not only desirable but profitable.

Many time-tested marketing conventions, including e-mail, have taken a new twist. This chapter should help you wrap your mind around some fresh new ways of accomplishing some important marketing goals.

## Building Sales through E-Mail

Have you heard about the death of e-mail? I've been seeing many scholarly articles on the web and in blogs with catchy headlines like "How does the death of e-mail disrupt the status quo?"

True, new channels of communicating are far more efficient than e-mail. A post on Facebook or Twitter can deliver a powerful message to an audience you've already worked hard to cultivate. As much as the social media proponents would like you to believe, however, e-mail is not dead — we just have more ways to connect with our customers. Although not a real-time social tool, e-mail can facilitate these new modes of real-time communication.

Since the first e-mail was sent in 1971 by Ray Tomlinson, a lot has changed. Here are a few fast facts on the state of e-mail today:

- ✔ A 2010 study by the Radicati Group showed that there were approximately 1.9 billion e-mail users worldwide. In a 2012 IBM-sponsored white paper, IDC reported that by 2014, the estimated number of worldwide e-mail accounts would be 2.4 billion.

- ✔ 92 percent of Internet users send or read e-mail.

- ✔ 89.6 million Americans use their mobile device to access e-mail, 64 percent do so every day.

- ✔ According to Forrester Research, U.S. marketers will spend almost $2.5 billion on e-mail marketing alone by 2016.

- ✔ The estimated average return on $1 invested in e-mail marketing in 2011 was $44.25.

As a one-to-one communication tool, e-mail remains one of the most effective ways to drive online and offline sales. Studies show e-mail is also the preferred method by which consumers want to be notified of offers. The key here is to apply the social rules of new media to an established mode of communication.

## Commercial e-mail and the law

Many laws regulate the sending of e-mail, both within the United States and internationally. As you can imagine, each law is subject to individual interpretation. If it weren't for all the legalese and courtroom wrangling, we most likely would have no spam e-mail at all. But we do.

The safest policy that a small-business owner can adhere to is to not send out unsolicited or unwanted e-mails, period. If someone subscribes to your newsletter, why not use a two-step e-mail confirmation, as shown in Figure 15-1?

If you'd prefer not to offer a double opt-in, have an auto-responder send out a quick e-mail to remind your customers that they signed up for your e-mail list. Send one the same day someone signs up, and follow up once a week for two weeks after the person signs up. Each e-mail should include some content plus bonus material or a special offer to reward the customer for signing up.

**Figure 15-1:**
Clear
confirmation
that I have
subscribed.

To stay within the law before you send commercial e-mails, visit the Federal Trade Commission's Bureau of Consumer Protection Business Center and download their compliance guide at `http://business.ftc.gov/documents/bus61-can-spam-act-compliance-guide-business/`.

The Federal Communications Commission also has a few words to say about e-mail. Under the FCC's rules, commercial e-mail messages may be sent via the Internet only if the recipients have provided their "express prior authorization." Each separate e-mail in violation of the CAN-SPAM Act is subject to penalties of up to $16,000, so noncompliance can be costly. But following the law isn't complicated. Here's a rundown of CAN-SPAM's main requirements from the FTC:

- **Don't use false or misleading header information.** Your "From," "To," "Reply-To," and routing information — including the originating domain name and e-mail address — must be accurate and identify the person or business who initiated the message.

- **Don't use deceptive subject lines.** The subject line must accurately reflect the content of the message.

- **Identify the message as an ad.** The law gives you a lot of leeway in how to do this, but you must disclose clearly and conspicuously that your message is an advertisement.

- **Tell recipients where you're located.** Your message must include your valid physical postal address, which can be your current street address, a post office box you've registered with the U.S. Postal Service, or a private mailbox you've registered with a commercial mail-receiving agency established under Postal Service regulations.

✔ **Tell recipients how to opt out of receiving future e-mail from you.**
Your message must include a clear and conspicuous explanation of how
the recipient can opt out of getting e-mail from you in the future. Craft
the notice in a way that's easy for an ordinary person to recognize, read,
and understand. Give a return e-mail address or another easy Internet-
based way to allow people to communicate their choice to you. You
may create a menu to allow a recipient to opt out of certain types of
messages, but you must include the option to stop all commercial messages from you. Make sure your spam filter doesn't block these opt-out
requests.

✔ **Honor opt-out requests promptly.** Any opt-out mechanism you offer
must be able to process opt-out requests for at least 30 days after you
send your message. You must honor a recipient's opt-out request within
10 business days. You can't charge a fee, require the recipient to give
you any personally identifying information beyond an e-mail address,
or make the recipient take any step other than sending a reply e-mail or
visiting a single page on an Internet website as a condition for honoring
an opt-out request. After people tell you they don't want to receive more
messages from you, you can't sell or transfer their e-mail addresses,
even in the form of a mailing list. The only exception is that you may
transfer the addresses to a company you've hired to help you comply
with the CAN-SPAM Act.

✔ **Monitor what others are doing on your behalf.** The law makes clear that
even if you hire another company to handle your e-mail marketing, you
can't contract away your legal responsibility to comply with the law. Both
the company whose product is promoted in the message and the company that actually sends the message may be held legally responsible.

## Less marketing and more connecting

Just the thought of opening my e-mail inbox every morning gives me the
chills. I admit to being one of the millions who first access e-mail on my
tablet with my morning coffee. I go through the list and delete commercial
e-mails that I have no time to read, and then I look at the ones I can handle
via mobile, and finally I leave the last few to answer from my desk. Deleting
e-mails to save time is the modus operandi for web-connected folks in business these days.

When I purchase from companies, some of them feel it gives them a right to
send daily deals and brass-band-accompanied promotions. Is it even possible
for a business to have that many sales that they need to contact me daily?
Like my Mom used to tell me, "Don't cry wolf."

# Compiling your e-mail list

Building a solid e-mail list takes time, but your efforts pay off. E-mail lists purchased or rented from brokers may not be reliable, even when they claim the list is targeted and that all the addresses are opt-in. Do you really think that if someone had a highly performing e-mail list they would be selling or renting it? Would you share addresses of your customers who had opted-in to your e-mails in good faith? I think not.

You also have no idea of how many times e-mail list addresses have been e-mailed or how many recipients have reported previous e-mails as spam. Spam traps are commonly set up to recognize e-mails sent to an address that is no longer valid but still receives consistent e-mail traffic. When you send e-mails to dead addresses on a list, your company's reputation is at risk. ISPs summarily block e-mail accounts that are identified as spamming; can you afford to risk nondeliverability of your company e-mails?

Combine your offline marketing skills with these new media ideas:

- Start a loyalty program and offer discounts to repeat customers.

- Print a QR code on your receipts that leads to a sign-up discounts page.

- At a physical business location, have an old-fashioned sign-up list or request sign ups from customers as they check out.

- Run a sweepstakes on your website to gain Facebook likes as well as e-mail addresses.

- Promote an irresistible offer in social media and place it front and center on your website – just for e-mail subscribers.

- Sponsor a Facebook post and combine helpful content with a valuable offer that requires a clickthrough to your website and an e-mail correspondence.

- Piggyback by advertising a special in an e-mail from a related noncompetitor; have a call to action on the offer's landing page on your site.

- Attend a local chamber of commerce meeting, exchange cards, and ask permission to make contact via e-mail.

Admittedly, the blame for the bulk mail in my inbox falls on me. When I'm ordering online, often a bit of tiny text next to a prechecked box says something like "Keep me posted on new products and sales," and I forget to deselect it. Mea culpa.

How important can your message be to your customer that you have to e-mail them every day? Deleting e-mails can become rote. Until I can get around to opting-out of an e-mail list, I tend to blindly delete, especially if I'm in a hurry. Instead of e-mailing your customers daily, why not reach out to them when you have an offer that stands out from the crowd? A weekly deal on a specific product or service would be appreciated by regular and new customers. Vary your messages and layout; send readable content as well. Give your customers a reason to want to open your e-mails.

There are experts who claim the more e-mail the better — that is, sending frequency doesn't affect the unsubscribe rate. The data on both sides of the argument is conflicting. What isn't taken into consideration is that many people use filters to get rid of commercial e-mails or just delete without unsubscribing.

The chart in Figure 15-2 from eMarketer.com shows some important statistics derived from a March 2012 study. Note that the number-one reason why people subscribe is to receive discounts, followed by taking part in a specific promotion. Discounts are a known draw, but creative promotions on a Facebook page or a social media network are where your newest customers find you.

**Figure 15-2:** Reasons for subscribing to e-mails from a business or nonprofit.

Reasons US Email Users Subscribe to Emails from a Business or Nonprofit, Q4 2011
% of respondents

| | |
|---|---|
| To receive discounts and special offers | 58% |
| To take part in a specific promotion | 39% |
| I am a customer/supporter of the business/nonprofit | 37% |
| To gain access to exclusive content | 26% |
| The desire to stay informed on an ongoing basis | 26% |
| Want to support a business/nonprofit I like | 25% |

Source: Chadwick Martin Bailey and Constant Contact, "10 Facts About Why and How Consumers 'Like' and Subscribe," March 27, 2012
138432
www.eMarketer.com

Source: Chadwick Martin Bailey and Constant Contact's "10 Facts about Why and How Consumers Like' and 'Subscribe'"

From the same study comes this telling statistic: 69 percent of U.S. e-mail users unsubscribe from a business or nonprofit e-mail because the organization sends too many e-mails.

In my opinion, the amount of monitored "opens" tells the story of whether your message is getting through to your audience. Be sure your e-mail opens can be tracked. This also lets you know which e-mails are resonating with your customers.

Give your customers some credit. If they were kind enough to give you permission to connect with them through e-mail, why would you abuse the privilege? Your e-mails need to carry meaning and value.

## Best practices for e-mail marketing

The subject matter of your e-mails should be about fulfilling the interests of your customers. You know your customers better than anyone. If they want recipes, for example, include a recipe in your e-mail. Have content that relates to your business and the customer's needs. Build on the loyalty proposition and make your customer feel like part of an exclusive club.

Define your objectives before you compose your e-mail. Wanting to build customer loyalty or generating sales isn't enough. Follow the tips below for a more cohesive, successful campaign:

- ✔ **Keep your layout clean.** Professional looking, easy-to-read pages have no more than three typefaces. Refrain from overdoing text effects.

- ✔ **Use an appropriate size font.** Use a font that is large enough to read while sitting back in your seat and looking at the monitor. Most folks don't have great vision and causing them to squint won't make them want to read anything you include in your e-mail (or post on your website).

- ✔ **Emphasize your call to action.** Define your key message and stick to it. Don't bury your call to action; put it in the top third of your e-mail. Repeat it twice more in the body of the e-mail.

- ✔ **Keep the look and feel consistent.** The landing page should carry forward the look and feel of your e-mail. Don't make customers think they've landed on a different planet when they click your links.

- ✔ **Include teasers.** Rather than running entire stories in your e-mails, consider putting teasers for interesting stories that cause the reader to click to finish the story. The action of clicking the link brings them to the landing page on your website.

✔ **Test your list.** Split your mailing list and test two different e-mails to find out which message resonates best with your readers.

✔ **Study Tweets of major brands.** See how the big boys squeeze a sales message into a Tweet of fewer than 140 characters. Visit the site `www.retailtweets.com` to view the current aggregation of Tweets from major e-commerce and bricks-and-mortar retailers.

✔ **Give customers a reason to read.** Increase your open rates by giving your reader a subject line with an incentive to open the e-mail. Create a sense of urgency.

✔ **Charm your customers.** This e-mail is from *you*, not from some faceless business. Stay away from jargon and don't try to sound too professional. Use the social media standard of just being real; your personality will come through in your e-mail.

✔ **Include your logo.** Place your logo in the top third of the e-mail, preferably to the left of your headline copy.

✔ **Conduct a blink test.** Before sending the e-mail, send it to a couple of trusted colleagues. Ask them if they can define your key message at first glance. (If they can't, go back to the drawing board.)

Always give your e-mails a five-point test. Does the subject line give the recipient a reason to want to open the e-mail? Is the e-mail itself visually appealing? Is there a call to action? Is the content worth reading? Last, would you like to receive this e-mail?

Whether you send your e-mails with e-mail software or use an online service, keep respect for the customer at the top of your mind. After a customer unsubscribes, you've lost e-mail as a contact point.

# Targeting Your Audience on Facebook

Facebook is an odd duck. No one blanket way exists to describe what will work for *your* fans. Posts that work on one Facebook page may be death on another. One thing is for sure, though: Posts with a personal slant get the most traction.

One person I always read for the latest data on social media is Dan Zarrella (@DanZarrella). This author and Hubspot's social media scientist loves to pore over data more than I do.

This past year, Dan collected a database of more than 1.3 million Facebook posts from the top 10,000 most-liked pages, and his analysis was staggering.

He identified the characteristics that correlated with the most likes, comments, and shares.

Following is a condensation of his findings:

- ✔ Photo posts garnered the highest amounts of likes and shares when compared to text, video, or link posts.
- ✔ Text posts edged out photo posts slightly when it came to receiving comments.
- ✔ Links, unfortunately, scored the lowest of the three.

Dan also found that Facebook posts with a high number of self-referential words (*I* or *me*), unlike posts on other social media platforms, get more likes, as shown in Figure 15-3, which is from his blog at www.danzarrella.com. Talking about yourself drives people away on other sites, but Facebook is that touchy-feely place where everybody knows your name.

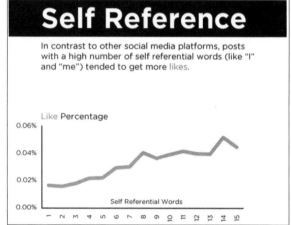

**Figure 15-3:** Self-reference and how it affects likes.

Also, people on Facebook love photos! If you're a veterinarian, you should post pictures of your patients along with an endearing story. Hair stylists, put up pictures of your best creations. Keep it visual and personal on Facebook.

I checked my Facebook Insights and, indeed, the photos I've posted on my Facebook fan page are the most viral of my posts.

## Sponsoring posts and stories

I think that sponsored posts are the best, no-brainer entry point into Facebook promotions. Status updates are filtered by Facebook's EdgeRank algorithm, which places in news feeds what it deems to be the most relevant content. Business pages pay a small amount to enhance the views of a single update. I can't imagine a better way to spend less than $10 when you can get the kind of results shown in Figure 15-4.

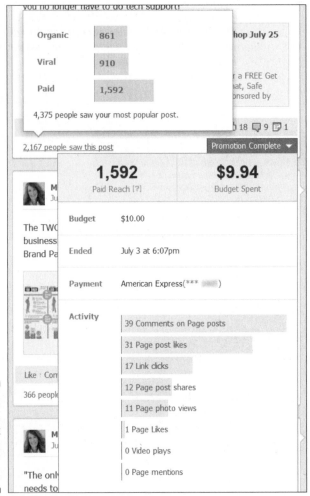

**Figure 15-4:**
For $9.94, this post received a total of 2,167 views.

The three types of post views shown in Figure 15-4 represent unique users:

- ✔ **Organic:** The number of people who visited your post or saw the post in their home page news feed.

- ✔ **Viral:** The people who saw your post when it was shared by a friend. Viral reach also counts the likes, comments, and further shares by others.

- ✔ **Paid:** The number of unique people who saw the post from a sponsored story position.

When you prepare your sponsored post, clicking Promote at the bottom of the text box displays a menu where you can decide on your budget (based on Facebook's reach estimates) and the duration (1 to 3 days) of the promotion, as shown in Figure 15-5.

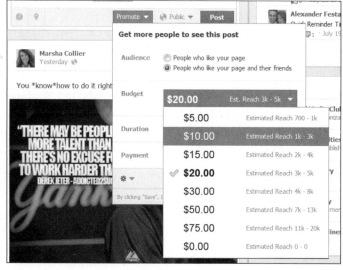

**Figure 15-5:**
Selecting
the budget
for your
sponsored
post.

You may schedule what time or date your post (promoted or not) launches on your business page. At the bottom of the text box in the left corner, click the small clock to display the year, month, date, and time. Make your selections, and then click the Schedule button, shown in Figure 15-6, to schedule the post.

Estimating the best time to post isn't easy. When you have engagement on your fan page, Facebook's Insights give you quite a bit of data on your posts. If you correspond individual posts with the data on visitor actions, you can analyze which content (and time of posting) performs best on your page. To dive in and get a clearer look, click your page's Insights link, which appears in your admin panel at the top of the page, and then export and download a CSV or Excel file of the last 28 days' worth of data (see Figure 15-7).

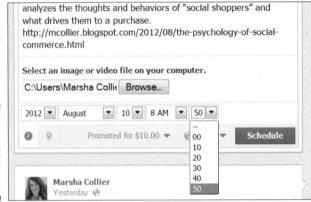

**Figure 15-6:**
Scheduling
your post
for a future
date.

## Sponsored stories

Facebook offers businesses the opportunity to sponsor their pages or individual posts through sponsored stories. These differ from the sponsored posts, which appear in the news feed. A sponsored story (linking to a page or a specific post) appears as an ad in the right column of the home news feed or in the right column next to your timeline.

Sponsored stories offer targeting options so that you can greatly narrow the audience for your ad. You can target the post to a multitude of parameters, such as age, gender, interests, relationship status, language, education level, and workplace or location (country, state, city). Many further targeting options are available, and the cost of your ad varies based on your selections.

People visit Facebook for social interaction and are less likely to click an ad unless the ad is for something that really interests them. Ads (and sponsored stories) consist of a picture and a line of text, making it difficult to select just the right words to attract clicks. Sponsored stories look like Facebook ads and do a better job of honing in on those who are not fans (or friends of fans) of your business page.

I tested a sponsored (promoted) post versus a sponsored story. The promoted post cost far less and garnered more results. For a small business, I recommend that you start small. Stick with quality content and occasional sponsored posts.

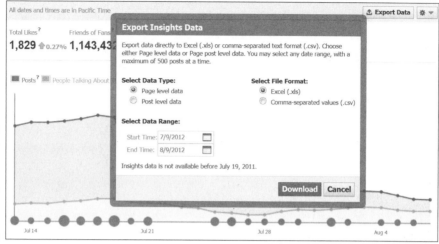

**Figure 15-7:**
Requesting
a download
of your
data from
Insights.

One caveat: I exported this data from my puny fan page and was overwhelmed with one of the largest Excel data packages I've ever seen, with at least 16 sheets and numerous columns of never-ending data points. Each data point is split into three sets: daily, weekly, and 28 days.

The tone and mood of Facebook users move too fast for long-term data examination. On Facebook, 28 days is a long time. I recommend deleting most of the long-term data. Keep the daily numbers and 7-day data points and you still have way too much data!

Luckily, I found out about a comprehensive online service that does the analysis for me. EdgeRank Checker, at www.edgerankchecker.com, can analyze your posts and translate their effectiveness into easy-to-understand, straightforward metrics, as shown in Figure 15-8.

The Facebook EdgeRank is explained on their site:

> *EdgeRank is an algorithm that ranks objects in the Facebook News Feed. Pages with high EdgeRank Scores will be more likely to show up in the news feed, than Pages with low EdgeRank Scores.*

> *EdgeRank is made up of 3 variables: Affinity, Weight, and Time Decay. Affinity is dependent on a user's relationship with an object in the news feed. Weight is determined by the type of object, such as a photo/video/link/etc. The last variable is Time Decay, as an object gets older, the lower the value.*

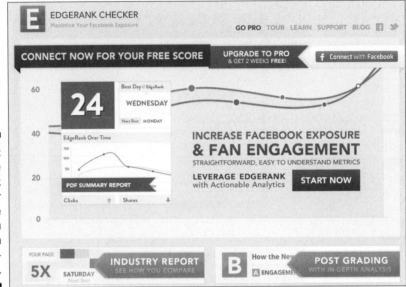

**Figure 15-8:**
The
EdgeRank
Checker
website
gives you
free data on
your busi-
ness page.

Each post is compared to others you have posted. By studying their analysis, you can figure out which type of post resonates most with your Facebook audience. I must admit that reading their examination of my posts was a big dose of tough love. If you subscribe to their Pro plan, you not only find out what you've done wrong or right in your engagement but are also given constructive criticism (through data analysis) along the way.

Log in to your Facebook page from their site and you can automatically avail yourself of their free plan. You immediately see these stats for your page:

- EdgeRank score
- Best average day of the week
- Worst average day of the week
- Average day of the week for most new fans
- Average day of the week for most fan loss

Should you choose to subscribe to the Pro plan, you get the following specific page data analysis:

- Real-time monitor
- Page-specific recommendations

✔ Industry report

✔ Post grading from A to F

✔ EdgeRank score over time

✔ Visual analysis of the engagement progress

✔ Best day plus best time plus best keyword

✔ Best post type: status, photo, link, video

As a small-business owner, you don't have hours to spend trying to analyze Facebook's reams of data. Use EdgeRank Checker instead. I highly recommend their site.

## Promoting through Facebook ads

Regarding Facebook ads, I have good news and bad news. The good news is that an advertiser can tightly target an ad's appearance. The bad news is that people on Facebook rarely click ads; they're on Facebook for social interaction.

Many major brands have pulled their paid advertising from Facebook (they still find value from their free fan pages for customer engagement) due to the lack of return. At this point, the best way for a small business to use Facebook ads is to target customers for items in your Facebook store (see Chapter 10). People are on Facebook to visit their friends' posts and don't want to leave the site for outside clicks. If your product is in a Facebook store, odds of getting some results from your ads may be pretty good.

Should you decide to run a Facebook ad, you can select your budget based on CPC (cost per click). Just be sure you don't set the cost per click too high. The web has been rampant with reports of bots clicking ads on Facebook. You don't need to be paying for worthless clicks.

If you want to give ads a try, try this approach: Open your ad at the Facebook suggested cost per click, and then lower what you will pay per click after a few clicks. Monitor whether you are continuing to get clicks and then adjust your pricing again.

Sponsored posts, as described earlier, give you more control of your ad dollar and better results.

# Chapter 16

# Improving Productivity with Apps and Widgets

*A* recurring message in every book I've written for small business is: save time, save money, and run lean. In the many years I've spent in my own business, I know that keeping a balance between time and money makes for success in the long run. Sometimes, purchasing software, apps, or tools is necessary. Your ROI (return on investment) in such tools is measured by your increased efficiency.

A new, shiny social media tool shows up every month or so. Young, snappy startups have great ideas and often develop tools on a shoestring. They get publicity from social media experts who promote these tools within their community; their job is to keep their finger on the pulse of what is new. Your job is to run your business efficiently. I recommend staying away from technology in its beta form. As with any new invention, the developer may not have the funding to continue developing the tool. If an application you use is abandoned, you may be stuck having to learn a new one.

Start small when you're beginning your efforts to institute your online outreach. Using a highly reputed, enterprise-level program can seem appealing, but you may find yourself caught in a learning curve that takes far more time than you care to invest. Most offer a tempting 30-day free trial. Vendors know that after you've devoted hours to setting up an application, you'll probably feel invested enough to carry on with their service. A better solution is a freemium model, in which the basics are free. If the product performs as you intended, you can upgrade to the paid version with more features.

Several applications are available for managing your Twitter feed and Facebook posts. In this chapter, I outline a few tried-and-true applications to shorten the time needed to capture an audience for social media commerce.

# Using Client Apps to Manage Twitter

After you are following and being followed by a few hundred people on Twitter and Facebook, you may wonder why you ever followed back so many people. Your personal Facebook page allows you to place your friends into groups, but for Twitter you need a tool that can help you segregate your customers from your closest friends, family, and online friends in separate feeds.

As of this writing, I have more than 55,000 followers on Twitter. (I follow back about 45,000.) This crowd can get unwieldy without a management tool. Many apps can help with your Twitter outreach. For mobile, many find that the basic Twitter app serves them well, but third-party clients are also popular.

Twitterrific (see Figure 16-1) was the first great Twitter client for the iPhone (now on iPad as well) and still remains a favorite with iOS users. For Android, I use Seesmic (shown in Figure 16-1) for its speed and many valuable features: sharing photos, videos, and the use of bitly-shortened links. Seesmic also takes advantage of Twitter web features such as lists, trending topics, and search.

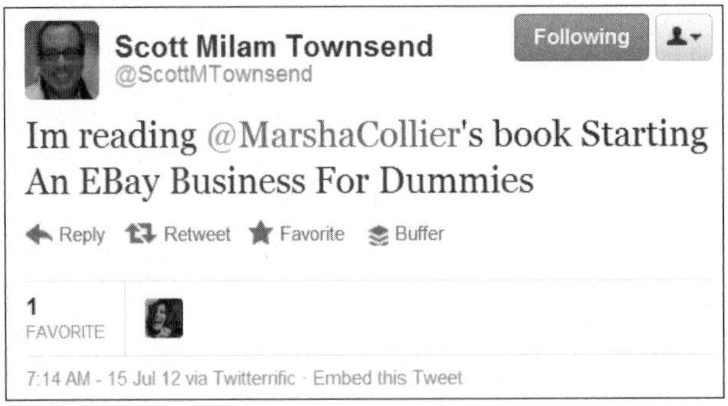

**Figure 16-1:** Twitterific is a favorite on the iPhone.

**Scott Milam Townsend**
@ScottMTownsend
Following

Im reading @MarshaCollier's book Starting An EBay Business For Dummies

Reply    Retweet    Favorite    Buffer

1
FAVORITE

7:14 AM - 15 Jul 12 via Twitterrific · Embed this Tweet

For my desktop, I am a loyal user of the no-cost TweetDeck. Recently acquired by Twitter, TweetDeck is available for Mac OSX and Windows at www.tweetdeck.com. The desktop client has added many valuable functions to its dashboard:

✔ **Customize stream columns:** You can choose to follow topics, hashtag subjects, lists that you have set up on Twitter, or even particular users, each within their own columns.

✔ **Schedule Tweets:** You can schedule a Tweet for a later day or time. Instead of clicking Send after you type your Tweet, click the small clock icon next to the Send button, and set the time and date for the post to appear. I use this function occasionally for reTweets, but have moved my Tweet scheduling to BufferApp, described later in this chapter.

✔ **Move columns:** Select the order in which you'd like to view your columns. Change their order by clicking the sideways arrows at the bottom of the column you want to move to the right or left.

✔ **Shorten URLs:** Links shared on Twitter.com are automatically shortened to a t.co link. If you want to have tracking capabilities for links you Tweet, use a bitly account. TweetDeck can be authorized to use your bitly credentials (found in your bitly account). More on using bitly in the next section.

✔ **Customize background colors and text size**. I'm not a fan of white text on a black background. With TweetDeck, I can have black text on a white background and change the text size.

✔ **Monitor and manage unlimited social media accounts:** In Figure 16-2, you can see how easy it is to add other social media networks to TweetDeck.

**Figure 16-2:** Adding a LinkedIn account to TweetDeck is a one-click proposition.

Set up Twitter searches for your products, your industry, and especially your competition so that they appear as columns in TweetDeck. Be proactive here; not every topic has its own hashtag or Twitter handle.

When following your competitor's Twitter streams, it's not a bad idea to jump into their Tweet stream and attract customers to you. Any time you see someone comment on a topic that interests you, click the user's avatar (in the upper-left corner) to reply. New points of view are what fuel conversations on Twitter. Folks enjoy shout-outs and appreciate that you took the time to connect.

By following your industry and figuring out what customers are looking for, you might get a leg up on the competition. For example, if you're a baker and you see comments about *pink velvet cupcakes,* you may find it worthwhile to find the recipe and jump on this trend before your competition.

# Tracking Your Links with bitly

If you, by choice or circumstance, end up using several platforms to send posts, receiving statistics on the success of your link can be problematic. Each platform may have its own built-in shortener, and unless you set the link to be abbreviated by a shortener that tracks the link's progress, you may never know which type of links resonate best on social networks.

I've used bitly on all platforms and have found the statistical information useful when tracking the popularity of links I've posted. When bitly is used for shortening, the bitly.com stats page of your account show an aggregate of clicks on your link over a period of time (hour, day, week, month). By clicking the link on the stats page, the stats of individual posts appear. Figure 16-3 shows a week's activity on one link that I sent out.

bitly also shows you from where people saw the link and from which platform they clicked, as shown in Figure 16-4. You can use this information to determine which types of links and information do best on the various networks.

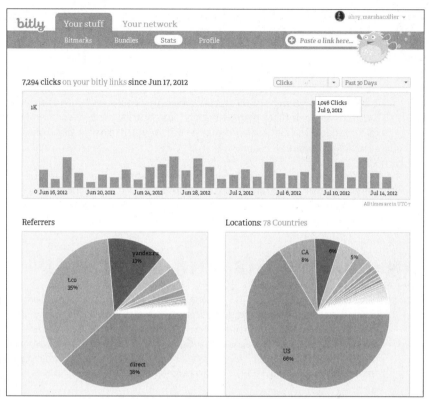

**Figure 16-3:**
One week's activity on a particularly popular link.

**Figure 16-4:**
You can get valuable information about which platforms clicked your link.

| Referrer | Click(s) | Country | Click(s) |
|---|---|---|---|
| Email Clients, IM, AIR Apps, and Direct | 709 | United States ( US ) | 666 |
| t.co | 483 | Canada ( CA ) | 108 |
| twitter.com | 35 | Australia ( AU ) | 28 |
| www.facebook.com | 12 | United Kingdom ( GB ) | 24 |
| m.facebook.com | 12 | France ( FR ) | 13 |
| iconfactory.com | 7 | Germany ( DE ) | 13 |
| hootsuite.com | 2 | Spain ( ES ) | 10 |
| tweetlist.com | 1 | Russian Federation ( RU ) | 9 |
| bit.ly | 1 | Netherlands ( NL ) | 9 |
| empireavenue.com | 1 | Mexico ( MX ) | 7 |
| my.yahoo.com | 1 | Belgium ( BE ) | 5 |
| www.twittergadget.com | 1 | Philippines ( PH ) | 4 |
| mobile.twitter.com | 1 | South Africa ( ZA ) | 4 |
| www.celebritytweet.com | 1 | Singapore ( SG ) | 4 |

To integrate bitly into any of your dashboards, you first need to sign up for a free account at www.bitly.com. During the setup process, you see instructions on how to connect your various social media accounts.

If you want to use bitly independently of any posting platforms, you can get a shortened link and post links to social networks from your web browser. They offer a handy tool (at www.bitly.com/a/tools) called a bitmarklet, which you can drag from the bitly page into your browser bookmark bar. (If you don't see your bookmarks bar in your browser, choose View⇨Show Bookmarks Bar.)

When you come across a web page that you want to share, just click the bitkmarklet and a sidebar appears showing you the preshortened (custom) code for your post. Your bitly account tracks this code whenever it's used on the web.

# Scheduling Posts with BufferApp

I'm a big fan of BufferApp, which enables you to queue up posts for Facebook (business or personal pages), multiple Twitter accounts, and LinkedIn (other social networks are in the works) and launch them at prescribed times. It optimizes your time because updates can be queued from any browser or mobile device. When I find a story to share, I post it to BufferApp via apps or extensions. I can also edit or change the order of the updates on any device.

BufferApp (also referred to as Buffer) does a fantastic job of managing the basics of sharing articles and quotes in my Twitter account. I also often use the program to buffer (schedule) reTweets and Facebook shares to Twitter. You set the post's timing patterns and frequency from your dashboard. BufferApp is free to try, and $10 a month to subscribe.

By viewing your Buffer account's analytics page, you can see how many folks clicked or reTweeted your post. You can also follow back such users, and comment (thank them) right from the analytics page.

After you have signed up for Buffer, download the extension for your browser. To get the mobile app (I use it on my tablet), visit your App store. Buffer buttons now appear in your browser wherever you need them, next to the Tweet and reTweet buttons on Twitter and the Facebook share and post buttons.

When you find a particularly interesting story or quote while browsing the web — or in a newsreader — you can buffer it from your browser (as in Figure 16-5) and set up a post. On your mobile device, Buffer appears as an option when you click to share.

**Figure 16-5:**
One click
adds this
story to your
scheduled
list.

When engaging in social media, you have to be there and participate in the conversation, so the idea of scheduling every post is soulless. Space out your Tweets with a reasonable amount of time to give your followers an opportunity to see your updates. If you barrage them with post after post, you will have more unfollows than follows.

A few rules for scheduled posts:

- ✔ Schedule interesting articles and quotes that your followers will find worthwhile.

- ✔ When it comes to self-promotion, don't send one post after another. Keep your audience engaged; don't broadcast to them.

- ✔ Balance your schedule. Don't use Buffer for every update. Post time-sensitive material as it happens from your mobile device or computer.

- ✔ Jump into the conversation and answer all @ replies manually.

- ✔ Thank your followers for any reTweets of your posts.

- ✔ Don't sacrifice your online interaction by scheduling. Real-time communication is your ultimate goal.

Remember to keep your posts social. Networking now is a world of social business and social interaction. Use BufferApp, as I do, to lighten the load. You'll be much happier in your online engagement if you do.

# Managing with HootSuite

HootSuite is a social media management system for executing outreach and monitoring across social networks from a single web-based dashboard. Although HootSuite is used by social media teams with multiple agents, many individual users like it as well.

When you're looking for a robust platform that keeps everything in one place, HootSuite is a perfect option. HootSuite offers a free basic plan for up to five social profiles. (Note that HootSuite has its own link shortener, so you will not be able to connect to bitly.)The basic account gives you access to data on your Twitter account, but you need to upgrade to the Pro plan for Facebook Insights and Google Analytics. I have a basic account with HootSuite (see Figure 16-6) and find it easy to use.

The Pro plan, at $9.99 a month, gives you a complete management platform. From a Pro (or Enterprise level) account, you can connect HootSuite to Instagram, YouTube, Tumblr, Flickr, Trendspottr, Digg, MailChimp, LinkedIn, Get Satisfaction, Constant Contact, and more.

When it comes to reaching your customers online, putting time-saving systems in place early on makes your move into social media easier. Small businesses can benefit from starter packages. The bigger your business gets, the more you'll need to use these online platforms to organize your outreach.

**Figure 16-6:**
Monitoring
my
Facebook
account on
HootSuite.

# Part V
# The Part of Tens

The 5th Wave     By Rich Tennant

"...and then one day it hit Tarzan,
Lord of Jungle – where future in that?"

# In this part . . .

You can't have a *For Dummies* book without a Part of Tens. Here, I give you ten steps to social media outreach. I also tip you off to the best ways to get feedback on products — and your business. In addition, a glossary clues you in on terms you may not know but will definitely hear as you make your rise to social media maven.

# Chapter 17

# Ten Ways to Build an Online Presence Now

· · · · · · · · · · · · · · · · · · · · · · · · · · · · · · · · · · · · · · · · · · · · · ·

*In This Chapter*

▶ Go to a search engine

▶ Find listings on review sites

▶ Get your website up to snuff

▶ Sign up for a Facebook business page

▶ Study your competition

▶ Identify your community through keyword searches

▶ Update your LinkedIn page

▶ Promote with friends and associates

▶ Schedule social media time

▶ Enjoy social media

· · · · · · · · · · · · · · · · · · · · · · · · · · · · · · · · · · · · · · · · · · · · · ·

*I* hope all the information in this book doesn't seem daunting. Just take a step-by-step approach to stake your claim on the web. Your web presence is what carries your business into the future: your marketing and income streams depend on it.

In this chapter, I provide a quick outline of the ten steps to take to secure your online position. The sooner you start, the sooner you will kick-off your climb to inevitable online domination in your field.

## Go to a Search Engine

If you haven't thought about how much you can find on the web, let me remind you. People go to the Internet to discover almost every kind of business. Whether they're looking for cupcakes or dentists, their first stop is a search engine. How many people go to these sites? The numbers are staggering.

The three most popular search engines — Google, Bing, and Yahoo! — have become the Yellow Pages of the Internet. These sites guard their own traffic data. The numbers that follow are estimates from third-party analytics sites. These numbers might help convince you as to why you need to beef up your online presence. The customer is looking for you on these sites, but do you show up?

- ✔ **Google** is the undisputed leader in swiftly retrieving large numbers of fast and relevant results.

  Alexa traffic rank: 1

  Compete rank: 1

  Quantcast rank: 1

  Alexa traffic rank in the United States: 1

  Alexa, number of sites linking in: 4,916,599

  Compete, estimated U.S. unique monthly visitors: 166,472,109

- ✔ **Bing** used to be called MSN Search, but Microsoft successfully rebranded the site in 2009.

  Alexa traffic rank: 25

  Compete rank: 5

  Quantcast rank: 13

  Alexa traffic rank in the United States: 13

  Alexa, number of sites linking in: 173,184

  Compete, estimated U.S. unique monthly visitors: 134,101,020

- ✔ **Yahoo!** began in 2002 and has since become a global favorite.

  Alexa traffic rank: 4

  Compete rank: 3

  Quantcast rank: 5

  Alexa traffic rank in the United States: 3

  Alexa, number of sites linking in: 1,961,427

  Compete, estimated U.S. unique monthly visitors: 157,558,013

Suppose folks in your community are looking for someone in your area of expertise. When they do a search, does your business name appear in the results?

In Figures 17-1, 17-2, and 17-3, I searched for a dentist in a suburb of Los Angeles. In each search, a different group of dentists show on the first page. Why? Some dentists have bought ads that appear on the page. At the very least, they businesses claimed their business listing on review sites (see Chapter 6). When you run your search on the big three, see where your business name is listed. The first page of results is clearly the most desirable.

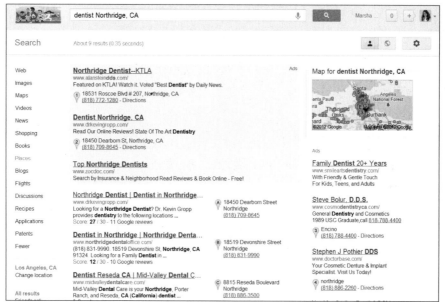

**Figure 17-1:** A Google search for a dentist in Northridge, CA.

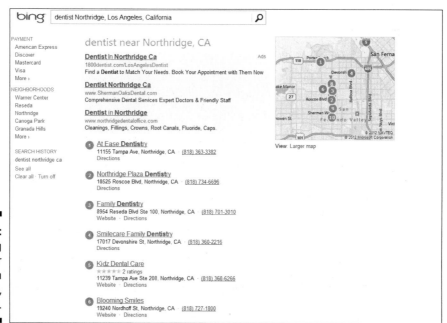

**Figure 17-2:** A Bing search for a dentist in Northridge, CA.

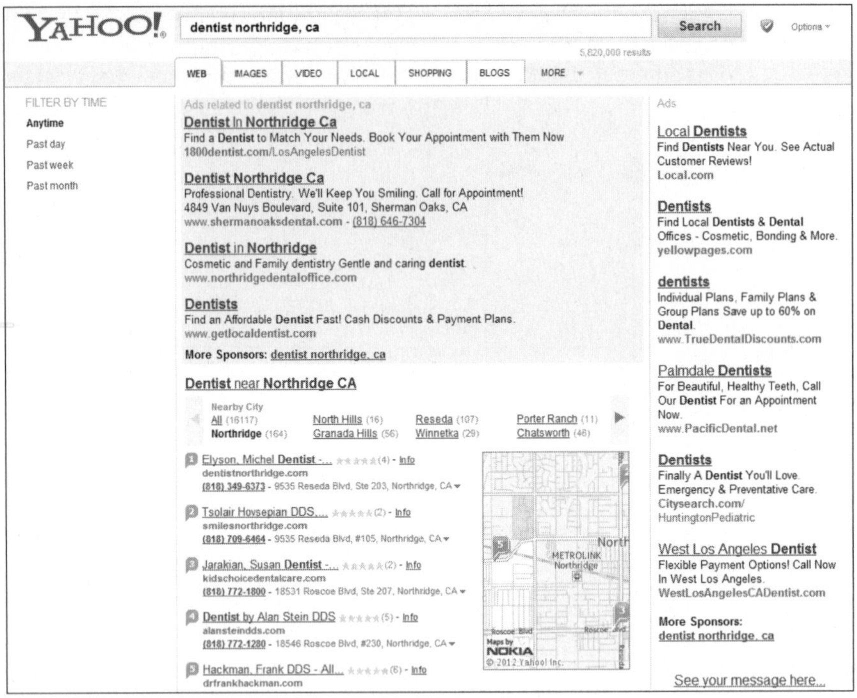

**Figure 17-3:**
A Yahoo!
search for
a dentist in
Northridge,
CA.

If you don't see your business name while performing a search, type your profession (or merchandise lines) and then your business name. When you do find your listing in this manner on the various search engines, immediately click to claim and edit the page. This way, you can add more information, photos, and details. Here are the links to look for after you have clicked through the links to your business name pages:

✔ Google (and Google+ Local): Is This Your Business? Manage This Page link

✔ Bing: Update This Page link

✔ Yahoo!: Edit Business Details link

# Find Listings on Review Sites

You covered your search results in the preceding section. The next step is to find your business on the review sites and claim your pages!

Yelp should be your first stop. When I went to Yelp and looked up my dentist's office, I found a page — and several reviews. But my dentist has yet to claim the page. In Figure 17-4, among the comments and data about the business, you can see an open invitation for the business owner to retrieve the page.

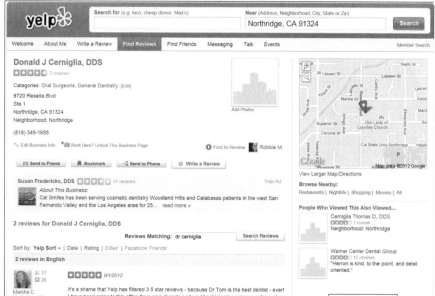

**Figure 17-4:**
Yelp puts
the business
contact info
front and
center on a
page.

Finding your page may take a bit more effort on the review sites than on a search engine, but knowing where and how you're listed are the first steps to "owning" your spaces. If your business has been miscategorized, people have difficulty finding you. Take the time to make the appropriate repairs to your listings so you can begin to build your reputation.

Check out the following review sites and see if your business is listed. Look for the words in quotes (next to the listed site name) when finding your business listing page to connect yourself as the business owner.

Find your page on these sites first instead of going directly to the site's business hub if possible. Your goal is to get the information correct on your page, not wade through advertising pitches.

✔ **Yelp.com:** Click the link titled Edit Business Info. Work Here? Unlock This Business Page. If you don't see that link, go to `https://biz. yelp.com/support`.

✔ **CitySearch.com:** Click the Own This Business? link.

✔ **InsiderPages.com:** Click the Claim Business link.

✔ **AngiesList.com:** Click the Business Owners link at the top of the site's home page — only registered users can search the site for business listings.

✔ **JudysBook.com:** Click the Claim Your Business link. If you can't find your listing, go to `http://www.judysbook.com/Biz`.

*26*

- ✓ **TripAdvisor.com:** Click the Manage Your Listing link at the bottom of your business page. If you're not listed, go directly to `www.tripadvisor.com/Owners`.
- ✓ **Zagat.com:** Click the Edit Info|Are You the Owner? link.
- ✓ **OpenTable.com:** Click the Restaurateurs Join Us link on your listing page.

If you arrive at your page and find a negative review, take a deep breath and step away from the computer. Remember that claiming your page and encouraging happy customers to post positive reviews will soon outweigh that unhappy person's post. Keep the following in mind as well:

- ✓ **Do not be tempted to write a fake review.** You run the risk of being banned from the site (your IP address marks your posts to servers wherever you go). Also, think of how embarrassing it would be if you were found out.
- ✓ **Remind happy customers to review your business.** Perhaps put a small sign on your counter.
- ✓ **Don't freak out if you have a less than stellar rating.** If you have more than one negative review, you can use this as a learning experience. Perhaps the commenters mention some weaknesses in your company that you have overlooked. If the site permits, follow up with unhappy customers to see if you can rectify the situation.

# Get Your Website Up to Snuff

If you have a website, consider my advice in Chapter 4 and add specific items to make your visitors feel more included and cared for. If your site isn't building a community of loyal customers, now is the perfect time to get the ball rolling.

Think also about adding some customer service widgets like those from SnapEngage or follow some of the suggestions in Chapter 13.

If you don't have a domain or URL address, immediately go to a company such as Network Solutions and secure a domain name in the name of your company. While you're at it, why not see if your own name is available? Owning a domain in your name may come in handy one day — even if you have no immediate plans for it.

Make the commitment right now to setting up a website. Call a friend for recommendations for someone to help you put one together, or go to `www.blogspot.com` and start a free site that you can build in the future.

(You can port your domain to any future site.) Chapter 4 gives you some more ideas.

Figure 17-5 shows you a website I quickly put up on Blogspot for one of my books. Because I didn't have a domain name, I went to bitly.com and secured a shortened custom URL: `bitly.com/custsrv`.

**Figure 17-5:**
A free and effective Blogspot site.

# Sign Up for a Facebook Business Page

Signing up for a business page on Facebook is a must. If you don't have a personal Facebook page, adding one is your first step. After your own personal page is up and running, clicking Add a Page for your business is just a step away.

The initial setup of your business page needn't take long. You no doubt have a couple of photographs and your logo. Put up a good photo like my friends did in Figure 17-6.

**Figure 17-6:**
Wig
Superstore's
Facebook
page.

When you've finished setting up your business page, read Chapter 9 for ideas on building your audience. After you have a following, go and visit Chapter 15 to see how to include some inexpensive advertising to drive more people to like your business page — and to visit your website.

# Study Your Competition

Use your search skills to find your competition on the Internet. Observe what they are doing in the social media arena to promote their business — and then follow suit. Also blaze new trails with your own creative ideas; outwit and outdo them.

# Identify Your Community through Keyword Searches

Go to a web search engine and type keywords that describe your business, along with your city name or ZIP code. You may find some of your competition; perhaps you may find businesses from out of your area that are actively seeking customers in your market.

Google also gives you the opportunity to search for blog mentions (there may be gold here). Type your keywords and your city, and then click the Blogs link on the left side of the search results (see Figure 17-7) to find people who have similar interests and news about your products in your geographic area.

Blogs are a super place to make connections. You may find prominent bloggers who are interested in your business category and would love to talk about your products.

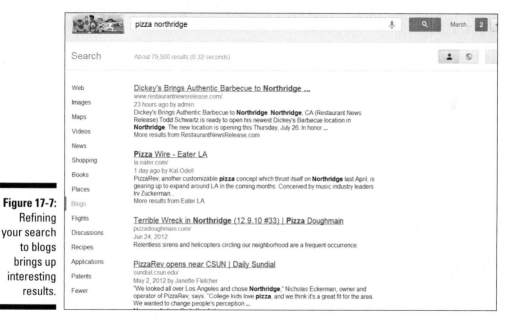

**Figure 17-7:** Refining your search to blogs brings up interesting results.

# Update Your LinkedIn Page

LinkedIn is your online resume, your calling card to others in any industry, who often search the web for experts and professionals in your field. Be sure to visit you LinkedIn page regularly to update the information. (If you don't, have a LinkedIn page, set one up *now*.) Figure 17-8 shows my LinkedIn page.

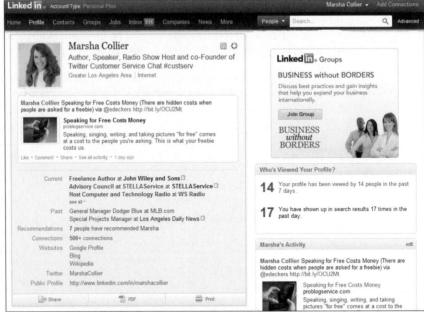

**Figure 17-8:**
The top of
my LinkedIn
page is a
calling card
for those in
my industry.

When your bio — complete with websites, blogs, and social media networks —
appears on LinkedIn, it establishes you as a denizen of the Internet. Connecting
with previous colleagues who you haven't seen in years is a perfectly acceptable practice on LinkedIn. They (or their online associates) may have solid
connections that can help you build your online presence.

# Promote with Friends and Associates

After you've set up your website and your personal and business Facebook
pages, it's time to call in favors. Connect with past and present friends and
business colleagues and let them know about your new involvement on the
Internet.

The more voices talking about your business (and reviewing it positively),
the closer you'll get to the coveted first-page results in search.

# Schedule Social Media Time

When you commit to some form of social media outreach, be sure to set aside time each day to visit your sites and connect with followers and prospective customers. In addition, when time permits, research by finding new social media participants in your community or check the trending demographics of the competition's sites.

But first and foremost, spend that time commenting and answering those who have reached out to you and your business online.

# Enjoy Social Media

Some of you may look at all this and consider it one big chore. Social media really won't be after you get into the swing of connecting. Every day, while drinking my morning coffee, I read my e-mails and post on social media sites. If I'm not in a mood to be working, interactions on Twitter get my mind moving and, 99 percent of the time, set my day up with a good attitude.

Social media is social. Take some time to enjoy the fun. Start now to engage!

# Chapter 18

# Ten Ways to Get Social Media Feedback

*T*oday's technology is changing the way we do business at lightning speed. Social media, too, moves at lightning speed, but by monitoring mentions and asking the community questions, you can get a pulse on how your market feels about upcoming changes. Others' posts as well can help you assemble critical feedback from the public to help portend change and plan for upcoming seasons.

In a recent interview, Marc Benioff, chief executive of Salesforce.com, commented on how the hidden nuggets inside social media can give you access to data. "At a very basic level, Facebook is the most popular application ever. With a billion people who know how to use it, the ability to access information is much better because it's easier to get to it."

As a small business, use your agility as an advantage; you can act on these opportunities without being weighed down by big business restrictions. Your social media network should consist of current customers, prospects, and industry influencers. In this chapter, I provide ten quick ways to leverage your social media audience and get to the heart of the current trends that are currently affecting your customers (and your business).

# Crowdsourcing Your Following

You may have heard the term *crowdsourcing* from someone in your industry or on social media. Crowdsourcing is a portmanteau, combining the words *crowd* (your online community) and *sourcing* for solutions. Crowdsourcing enables you to tap into the collective intelligence of others in your community.

The traditional way to garner opinions is to encourage customers to fill out comment cards. (This time-honored practice is still a good idea for hospitality businesses.) Solutions delivered via an online suggestion box often fall short in new media because they do not involve an open dialogue between you (the brand) and your customer.

Those with a bigger budget could hire an agency and run focus groups questioning actual customers. However, the people who actually purchase your product or services have a keen sense of what they want, and their advice is better than any research from a high-priced agency. Crowdsourcing though social media allows you to drive business-related decisions based on stated customer needs.

# Collecting Product Feedback on Twitter

Not surprisingly, due to Twitter's fast-moving conversation, you can ask questions related to your products or services and get answers quickly. Posting questions to your followers — or even sending public questions directly to individuals — can elicit responses.

Direct questions such as: "This holiday season, which is more important to you? Free shipping or Quick shipping?" generally net straight responses. I tested that question myself, and within ten minutes I received more than 20 answers. Figure 18-1 shows a few.

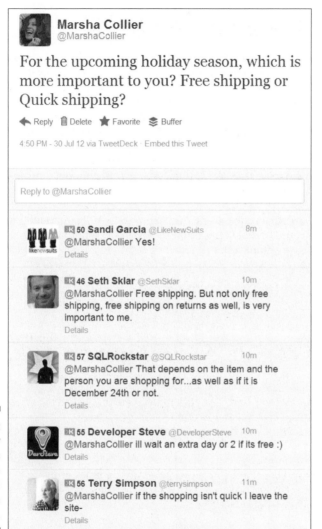

**Figure 18-1:**
A few
responses
to the
question I
posed on
Twitter.

Sending questions in the form of direct messages can often be misconstrued as spamming. People on Twitter (especially the more connected users) are touchy about the type of message they receive in private messaging. Transparency is pivotal in social media, so I recommend you keep your queries in open view.

# Study Sentiment on Social Mention

Social Mention can be used to monitor not only trends in your industry (as described in Chapter 14) but also public sentiment. For example, someone who owns a dry cleaning business would search for *dry cleaners* on the site. When I conducted that search, the results page showed recent posts from around the web from 113 unique authors. I can click to view each post individually, or pay more attention to the top keywords and sentiment ratings.

From the Sentiment box on the left, I can see that people are fairly neutral. But if I click the word Negative, I can view only negative posts, as shown in Figure 18-2. Use this research to get ideas for improving your business.

Get specific and search for areas that seem to be sticking points with customers. If one particular issue is popular, you'll know what area you need to keep your eye on at the front office.

**Figure 18-2:** Few things get a person's dander up about dry cleaners.

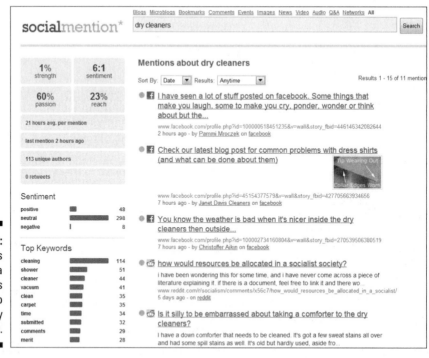

# Twitter Lists: Seeking Industry Experts

When you searched for people to follow on Twitter, I hope you looked for those across the country and around the world in your field of business. When you follow these people, you can get good insights as to the direction of your industry.

After you find people to follow, you can put them into a special Twitter list (which can be public or viewable only by you). You can ask these folks questions directly, and because you are in the same industry, their insights can be very useful. You do not necessarily have to follow people that you put on a list. Instead, you can just view them on a feed in Twitter (or in most social media applications).

I have a list of major brands on Twitter (shown in Figure 18-3) so that I can keep an eye on how they use their social media outreach. It's a public list and you can follow (or view it) at `http://twitter.com/MarshaCollier/brands-on-twitter`.

**Figure 18-3:** Set up a Twitter list with industry insiders to gain insight on trends in your market.

Here's how to set add a person or business to an existing Twitter list. (See the next set of steps for details on setting up a Twitter list.)

1. **Find the Twitter user you want to follow.**

2. **Click the small icon of a head and shoulders, and then choose Add or Remove from Lists.**

 Your existing lists appear.

3. **Select the list to which you want to add the user.**

 To select a list, click to put a check mark in the box to the left of the list. The person is automatically added.

Don't have a Twitter list? No problem. Follow these steps to set up a list and add a person or business to the list:

1. **Find the Twitter user you want to follow.**

 See Chapter 9 for tips on how to find people. A pop-up window or a profile page of that user appears.

2. **Click the small icon of a head and shoulders, and then choose Add or Remove from Lists.**

3. **Click the Create a List option.**

 The screen shown in Figure 18-4 appears.

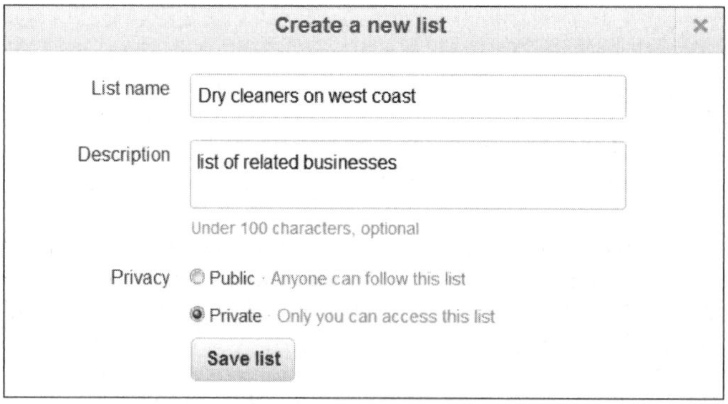

**Create a new list**                                    ✕

List name    Dry cleaners on west coast

Description    list of related businesses

Under 100 characters, optional

Privacy    ◎ Public · Anyone can follow this list
            ◉ Private · Only you can access this list

Save list

**Figure 18-4:** Creating a new user list in Twitter.

4. **In the List name text box that appears on the Create List pop-up box, type a name for your list.**

5. **(Optional) If you want to write comments about your list, type them directly in the description box.**

6. **Decide if you want the list to be available to everyone (Public) or for your eyes only (Private).**

You can change this choice at any time. Private Twitter lists can be followed in real time in any Twitter application.

7. **Click the Save List box.**

   The list appears in the lists portion of your profile page. (If the list is private, you'll see a padlock icon next to its name.)

# Creating Your Own Feedback Community

In Chapter 13, I delve into social media customer service on many levels. I suggest that you install a community platform on your site, if regular feedback is important to you.

The free app from Wufoo (www.wufoo.com) can be used to poll your visitors on specific questions. Keep in mind that the folks who visit your site are there because they love your product or are attracted by your content's personal slant. These people will more than likely want to participate. Take advantage of their loyalty. Your regular customers may understand your products as well as you do and have some great insights.

# Adding a Survey to Your Website or Blog

Many applications are designed to install polls or surveys on your website. Surveys allow you to ask multiple questions of the participants.

I like Polldaddy because of their ease of use and the fact that they offer a small account at no charge. They also have an iPhone and iPad app that can be used live at trade shows or on-demand in-person surveys.

Their customized survey builder allows you to put in your own queries, add pictures, and choose from a group of templates to best match your site or blog's design. After you've launched your poll or survey, your Polldaddy dashboard builds your reports in real time as your customers answer.

Polldaddy's free account allows you to receive up to 200 survey responses per month with 10 questions per survey. You also get basic reports for polls, surveys, and quizzes. Find out more on their website, at www.polldaddy.com/.

When asking a customer to participate in a survey (which involves more time than a poll), I recommend that you qualify the customer in advance and then offer those who participate a bonus, such as a gift card.

# Running a Poll on Facebook

Facebook has so many valuable tools for business. One easy-to-use tool is polling, or in Facebook parlance, Ask a Question. To initiate a poll, do the following:

1. **Sign in to your Facebook business page.**

2. **In the Update Status box, click the plus sign (+) next to Event, Milestone.**

   The screen shown in Figure 18-5 appears.

**Figure 18-5:**
Selecting the Question option on a Facebook status post.

3. **Select Question, and type your (brief) question in the box that appears.**

4. **Select Add Poll Options, in the lower-left corner.**

5. **Select Add an Option, and type an answer to your polling question. Repeat as necessary.**

   For example, in Figure 18-6, I typed two answers for my question.

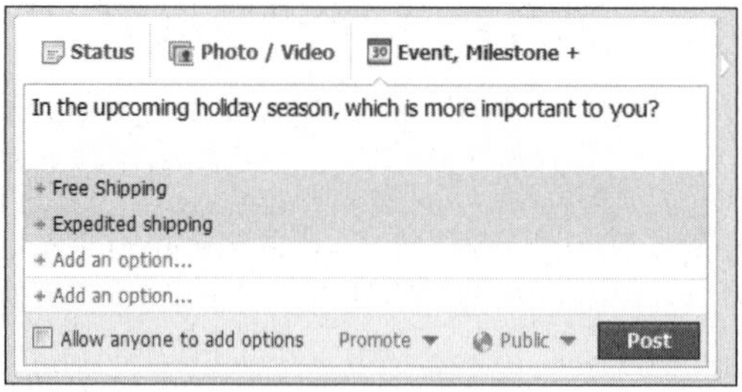

**Figure 18-6:**
Adding poll selections to your question.

6. **Select or deselect the Allow Anyone to Add Options check box.**

   You might get some interesting suggestions if you select this option.

7. **(Optional) To promote the poll, select Promote.**

   Refer to Chapter 15 for details on setting up a promoted post.

8. **Select Post to launch your question.**

   The poll appears on your page as a status update. As people vote, the votes for each option tally instantly within the post.

# Crowdsourcing a Video Focus Group

A face-to face focus group to gather opinions from consumers might sound old-school, but it could be a good idea. You can easily create a focus group through video chat. Solicit participants from your e-mail list, or ask for volunteers on your site or from your social media accounts.

In a video chat, you can show products, perhaps ask questions about product styling, and take a more visual approach to your crowdsourcing. You also get to see the expressions on your panel's faces when you ask and answer questions.

By using Google+ video hangouts, you can gather a group of up to nine participants. Another good alternative is to use free Skype video calls. A maximum of ten people can join in, although Skype recommends no more than five for the best quality.

# Crowdsourcing via YouTube Video

Continuing the video topic, you could record a video asking consumers questions, and then post the video to YouTube. YouTube allows viewers to post video responses as well as text comments. You might just get an idea from someone in a far-reaching part of the planet who is interested in your product or service. Chapter 7 gives you more insight into using YouTube to reach new customers.

Keep in mind that when polling publicly through social media in any form, you might be telegraphing your next move to your competitors. Design your questions so that you get the information you need without exposing your strategy.

# Asking and Answering Questions on LinkedIn

LinkedIn is the largest business network in the world, and many of the smartest people in any industry are members. LinkedIn Answers, a little-known area of the site, is designed for businesspeople to pose questions to their connections and get feedback.

After you've signed in to your LinkedIn account, go to the navigation bar and choose More➪Answers. (Or go directly to `http://www.linkedin.com/answers/`.) You see the screen shown in Figure 18-7.

On this page, you can read questions and post your own. Although you may not get a response on LinkedIn as quickly as you do on Twitter, you are addressing a targeted audience of professionals on LinkedIn.

Answering questions from other professionals in your industry is a great way to build new relationships.

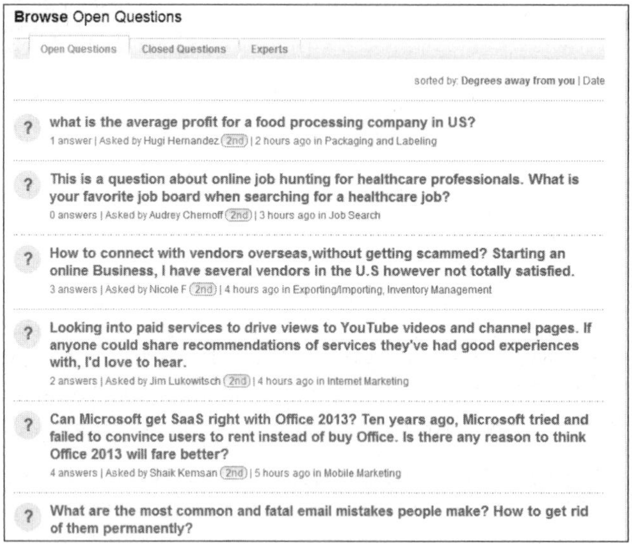

**Figure 18-7:** Today's open questions in LinkedIn Answers.

**Browse** Open Questions

| Open Questions | Closed Questions | Experts |

sorted by: Degrees away from you | Date

**?** what is the average profit for a food processing company in US?
1 answer | Asked by Hugi Hernandez (2nd) | 2 hours ago in Packaging and Labeling

**?** This is a question about online job hunting for healthcare professionals. What is your favorite job board when searching for a healthcare job?
0 answers | Asked by Audrey Chernoff (2nd) | 3 hours ago in Job Search

**?** How to connect with vendors overseas,without getting scammed? Starting an online Business, I have several vendors in the U.S however not totally satisfied.
3 answers | Asked by Nicole F. (2nd) | 4 hours ago in Exporting/Importing, Inventory Management

**?** Looking into paid services to drive views to YouTube videos and channel pages. If anyone could share recommendations of services they've had good experiences with, I'd love to hear.
2 answers | Asked by Jim Lukowitsch (2nd) | 4 hours ago in Internet Marketing

**?** Can Microsoft get SaaS right with Office 2013? Ten years ago, Microsoft tried and failed to convince users to rent instead of buy Office. Is there any reason to think Office 2013 will fare better?
4 answers | Asked by Shaik Kemsan (2nd) | 5 hours ago in Mobile Marketing

**?** What are the most common and fatal email mistakes people make? How to get rid of them permanently?

# Glossary

## A

**AddThis:** A service that provides a social sharing button placed on websites and blogs through a supplied code (see Figure G-1). By placing this button (built into many blogging services) on your page, you allow visitors to share your content on over 300 other social sites. AddThis (www.addthis.com) also supplies analytics so you know which of your content is shared and where it's shared.

**Figure G-1:** Get sharing code for your site from AddThis.

**AdSense:** The Google system of advertising for blogs and websites. As a subscriber to the service, you can agree to insert Google ads and earn revenue from the users who view or click the ads. The ads are targeted to the keywords in your content.

**algorithm:** A set of calculations developed for a computer to perform its functions. Algorithms are critical in social media for developing content-sharing strategies.

**app:** Short for application, a piece of software that performs a specific function. Apps can run on your computer, a web browser, the Internet, or on your smartphone or tablet.

**Application Programming Interface (API):** A documented interface that allows one software application to interact with another application or website.

**astroturfing:** To create the impression of support or popularity by paying individuals to promote and create buzz for a brand by posting on blogs, liking, or sharing content.

**avatar:** A picture or icon that represents a person online in new media venues.

# B

**B2B (business to business):** A company whose sales or services are directly targeted to other businesses.

**B2C (business to customer):** A company that sells goods and services with end customers.

**back channel communications:** Messages sent by the organizer or between individuals during webinars to help guide the conversation.

**bitly:** A free URL shortening service used to condense long URLs to make them easier to share. Registered users have access to statistics to see the numbers of clicks and shares (see Figure G-2).

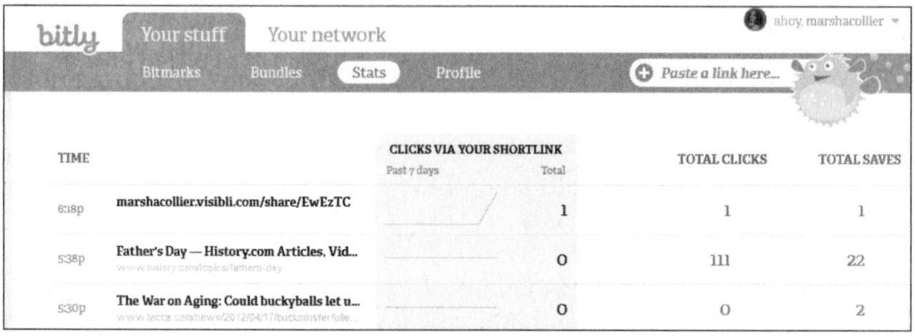

**Figure G-2:** bitly not only shortens your links but also supplies statistics.

**blog (web log):** A website that is posted with regular entries of commentary, descriptions of events, graphics, and video. To *blog* means the action of adding content to a blog.

**Blog Talk Radio:** A website and an application that allows users to host live online radio shows.

**Blogger:** A free and easy-to-use blogging platform that is part of Google. (Blogspot is Google's free domain provider that enables individuals and companies to host and publish a blog.)

**bookmarking:** A valuable tool for saving web content for later use (like a bookmark). Aside from bookmarking in your web browser, services such as Delicious, One Note, and Evernote allow you to keep a folder of content links in the cloud (available on any computer or mobile device).

# C

**campaign:** A set of marketing messages targeted to a specific goal, such as a Fourth of July sale. Organized to deliver on various platforms at predetermined times.

**chat:** Conversing on a web platform through text-based communication. Accomplished either through chat on Facebook, or an app installed on a website Chats also occur on Twitter, with all participants following the hashtag assigned to the group (such as #custserv, which is the hashtag for the Tuesday night customer service chat).

**circles:** The Google+ format for organizing your friends, family, colleagues, customers, and more into specified groups. When posting on Google+, you can direct posts to any of these circles or to the general public.

**cloud computing:** Storing your data "in the cloud," or on a web server where you can access it from any device. A smallish (depends on what you call small) amount of space is available for free on platforms provided by several companies, such as box.com, skydrive.com, and Amazon Cloud.

**comments:** Responses posted to blogs or online posts that are nested under the original post that generates a feed. This is the primary form of communication on the social web.

**community:** People of like mind or passions who meet online to participate in discussions surrounding their shared interests. Often appear as part of a brand's website or more commonly a social media platform.

**content:** Pictures, texts, infographics, videos — any material of value that appears on the Internet.

**Creative Commons.org:** A not-for-profit organization that enables content sharing. They supply free copyright licenses that provide a simple, standardized way to give the public permission to share and use your creative work, with conditions of your choice.

**crowdsourcing:** Polling followers or asking questions of a group who volunteer to contribute content and help solve a problem. Crowdsourcing can be as simple as asking a question of Twitter followers or posting a poll on Facebook.

**culture:** Defines the philosophy of a business. Successful company culture today thrives in an atmosphere of communication and respectful collaboration.

**cyberspace:** Anything in the cloud or on the web.

# D

**Delicious:** Free online service that allows users to post bookmarks and save the web addresses for future reference on any web-enabled device. Users can make their link collections public or private.

**Digg:** An online news aggregator with a social twist — members of the site submit and vote for online content and the most popular content appears on the home page of the site. Stories can be categorized by topic for curating.

# E

**e-book (electronic book):** Electronic versions of published books, printed materials, or a creation of your own that can be downloaded from the Internet. A PDF is a common form of e-book.

**embedding:** Adding code (provided by a website) to display content on another site. Commonly used when sharing YouTube videos or website widgets.

**Eventbrite:** If you plan a special event at your business and want to manage the crowd, you can send invitations and receive your RSVPs at www.eventbrite.com. There is no charge for the service if your event is free.

# F

**fair use:** A doctrine in U.S. law that permits limited use of copyrighted material without obtaining the permission of the copyright holder, such as use for scholarship or review. Fair use is delineated in Section 107 of the U.S. Copyright Code.

**feeds:** Allows you to share your online content or keep on top of posts from other blogs in a newsreader. Feedburner is a popular free tool that supplies feeds, titles, and links to posts from a blog.

**follow Friday:** A Twitter Friday tradition in which users use the hashtag #ff, or #followfriday, to recommend names of other Twitter members they find to be valuable to follow.

# G

**geotagging:** The technology that adds your location to online posts and other media. This location-based metadata is especially useful when targeting customers in your vicinity.

# H

**hangout:** Online video chat through Google+ that allows up to ten users to see, talk, and connect with each other (see Figure G-3).

**Figure G-3:**
My first
Google
hangout
with my
friends at
Mashable.

**hashtag:** A word or phrase preceded by # that is used on Twitter to annotate a tweet with a topic. A hashtag enables users to follow the stream.

**HTML (HyperText Markup Language):** The programming language for web pages and the Internet.

# I

**inbound marketing:** New age marketing that is driven by permission-based techniques from web signups and social media. The opposite of old-school, broadcast, cold-call client engagement.

**instant messaging (IM):** Real-time, direct text-based communication between two or more people. Popular platforms are Google Talk, Facebook Chat, Microsoft Live Messenger, and Yahoo! Messenger.

# K

**Klout:** The original online influence platform, at `www.klout.com`. Scores are based on the capability to drive engagement through various social media networks.

**Kred:** Measures social influence both online and offline. "Everyone is an influencer somewhere." A KredStory is composed of two scores: influence and outreach. When hiring someone as a social media consultant, check the person out at Kred (`www.kred.com`) first.

# L

**like:** Showing approval of a post by clicking the like button in Facebook. Similar to the +1 button in Google+.

**links:** Highlighted text on web posts or blogs that, when clicked, redirects to another web page. Also called hyperlinks.

**logging in:** The process of signing in to a website that requires prior registration. A login includes the user name and a password.

**lurkers:** People who hang out and read posts in online communities and do not comment or participate.

# M

**meme:** A concept, idea, or joke shared virally online. Typically a catchphrase ("Don't Tase Me Bro"), a video, or an image with text superimposed. Find current memes at `http://knowyourmeme.com/`.

**MT (modified Tweet):** When another user on Twitter repeats your Tweet and abbreviates it for brevity. *See also* RT.

# N

**newsreader:** A website or software on your computer that gathers content from sites to which you have subscribed (see Figure G-4). Commonly known as a *feed reader*, *RSS reader*, or *news aggregator*.

# O

**OpenID:** A login standard that allows Internet visitors to sign in to different websites using a single digital identity. OpenID eliminates the need for a new user name and password for each site.

**organic search:** A search that returns results based on site content and keyword relevancy. Organic search is untainted by advertising, and results rank highly due to relevance and popularity.

# P

**permalink:** The Internet address (URL) of shared web content. Because blogs contain multiple posts, each individual post has its own link as well. Often found at the end of a blog post on the share page.

**podcast:** Episodic audio content in the form of a digital file made available so you can listen online or download for listening offline. Think radio in the cloud.

**post:** An item on a blog or social media site: on Facebook, a status update; on Twitter, think Tweet; on a blog, think comment.

# R

**RSS (Really Simple Syndication):** Enables you to subscribe to online content that is delivered to read later in a newsreader.

**RT (reTweet):** When someone on Twitter quotes one of your Twitter posts verbatim and reshares it with their followers.

# S

**sentiment:** The attitude — positive or negative — reflected in user comments. Monitoring tools often measure sentiment of posts.

**SEO (Search Engine Optimization):** A way of improving search engine visibility and improving the quality of traffic to a site through organic (nonpaid) means.

**silos:** Departments within an organization that do not integrate with others and have defined territories.

**subscribing:** The process of adding an RSS feed to your aggregator or newsreader.

# T

**tag cloud:** A group of words reflecting the topic of posts in a graphic format (see Figure G-5). A visual depiction of user-generated tags, used to describe the content of web sites.

**tags:** Keywords attached to a web content item so others can find such content easily through searches.

**Terms of Services:** An agreement you must agree to before signing up or joining a website. Be sure to read before signing up to see what rights the site may claim over your content.

**thread:** Continuing posts in a conversation online.

**Tweet:** A status update on Twitter.com, not to exceed 140 characters.

**Tweetup:** A gathering of Twitter users at a prescribed place and time.

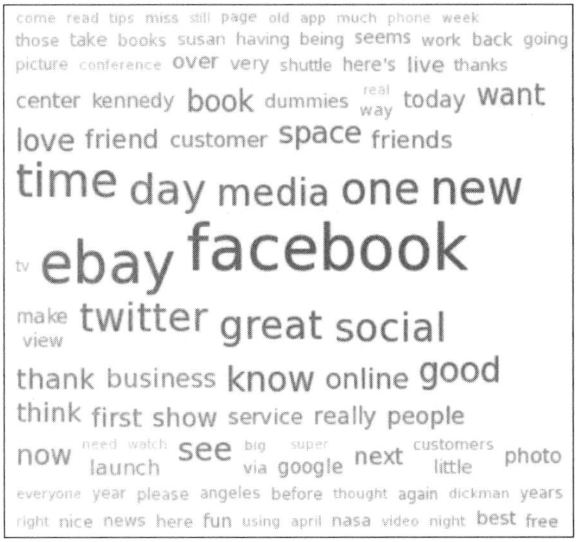

**Figure G-5:** Tag cloud based on my past 1595 Facebook wall posts from Wolfram| Alpha.

# U

**upload:** To transfer a file or other content from your computer to the cloud or an Internet site.

**URL (Universal Resource Locator):** The address of a page on the web.

# V

**viral marketing:** A marketing technique that uses social networks to meet objectives and increase online buzz through shares.

# W

**webinar:** Conducting presentations or live meetings with multiple participants over the Internet.

**widget:** An element on a web page that displays information, generally connected and ported from another website.

# *Web Initialisms*

- **BTW:** By The Way
- **CC:** Carbon-copy
- **DM:** Direct message; a private message sent user-to-user through Twitter
- **F2F:** Face to Face
- **FOMO:** Fear Of Missing Out
- **FTW:** For The Win
- **FWIW:** For What It's Worth
- **H/T:** Hat tip; attributing content or a link in your own post, update, or Tweet to another online user
- **IDK:** I Don't Know
- **IMHO:** In My Humble Opinion
- **IRL:** In Real Life
- **LMAO:** Laughing My A** Off
- **LMK:** Let Me Know
- **LOL:** Laugh Out Loud
- **MT:** Modified Tweet
- **NBDL** No Big Deal
- **NSFW:** Not Safe For Work (usually precedes a link that's best not opened in a public environment)
- **OH:** Overheard.
- **OMG:** Oh My God
- **QOTD:** Quote Of The Day
- **ROFL:** Rolling On Floor Laughing
- **RPM:** Revenue Per Mil (revenue for a thousand impressions, used in web advertising)
- **RT:** ReTweet
- **SMH:** Shaking my head
- **TMI:** Too much Information
- **TY:** Thank you
- **WTMI:** Way too much information
- **YW:** You're welcome

# Index

• **F** •

# • U •

## ...e & Mac

...d 2 For Dummies,
...Edition
...-1-118-17679-5

...one 4S For Dummies,
...Edition
...-1-118-03671-6

...d touch For Dummies,
...Edition
...-1-118-12960-9

...: OS X Lion
...Dummies
...-1-118-02205-4

## ...gging & Social Media

...Ville For Dummies
...-1-118-08337-6

...ebook For Dummies,
...Edition
...-1-118-09562-1

...n Blogging
...Dummies
...-1-118-03843-7

...tter For Dummies,
...Edition
...-0-470-76879-2

...dPress For Dummies,
...Edition
...-1-118-07342-1

## ...iness

...h Flow For Dummies
...-1-118-01850-7

...esting For Dummies,
...Edition
...-0-470-90545-6

Job Searching with Social
Media For Dummies
978-0-470-93072-4

QuickBooks 2012
For Dummies
978-1-118-09120-3

Resumes For Dummies,
6th Edition
978-0-470-87361-8

Starting an Etsy Business
For Dummies
978-0-470-93067-0

## Cooking & Entertaining

Cooking Basics
For Dummies, 4th Edition
978-0-470-91388-8

Wine For Dummies,
4th Edition
978-0-470-04579-4

## Diet & Nutrition

Kettlebells For Dummies
978-0-470-59929-7

Nutrition For Dummies,
5th Edition
978-0-470-93231-5

Restaurant Calorie Counter
For Dummies,
2nd Edition
978-0-470-64405-8

## Digital Photography

Digital SLR Cameras &
Photography For Dummies,
4th Edition
978-1-118-14489-3

Digital SLR Settings
& Shortcuts
For Dummies
978-0-470-91763-3

Photoshop Elements 10
For Dummies
978-1-118-10742-3

## Gardening

Gardening Basics
For Dummies
978-0-470-03749-2

Vegetable Gardening
For Dummies,
2nd Edition
978-0-470-49870-5

## Green/Sustainable

Raising Chickens
For Dummies
978-0-470-46544-8

Green Cleaning
For Dummies
978-0-470-39106-8

## Health

Diabetes For Dummies,
3rd Edition
978-0-470-27086-8

Food Allergies
For Dummies
978-0-470-09584-3

Living Gluten-Free
For Dummies,
2nd Edition
978-0-470-58589-4

## Hobbies

Beekeeping
For Dummies,
2nd Edition
978-0-470-43065-1

Chess For Dummies,
3rd Edition
978-1-118-01695-4

Drawing For Dummies,
2nd Edition
978-0-470-61842-4

eBay For Dummies,
7th Edition
978-1-118-09806-6

Knitting For Dummies,
2nd Edition
978-0-470-28747-7

## Language &
## Foreign Language

English Grammar
For Dummies,
2nd Edition
978-0-470-54664-2

French For Dummies,
2nd Edition
978-1-118-00464-7

German For Dummies,
2nd Edition
978-0-470-90101-4

Spanish Essentials
For Dummies
978-0-470-63751-7

Spanish For Dummies,
2nd Edition
978-0-470-87855-2

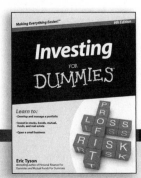
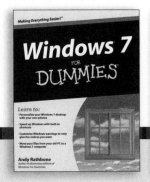

## Math & Science

Algebra I For Dummies,
2nd Edition
978-0-470-55964-2

Biology For Dummies,
2nd Edition
978-0-470-59875-7

Chemistry For Dummies,
2nd Edition
978-1-1180-0730-3

Geometry For Dummies,
2nd Edition
978-0-470-08946-0

Pre-Algebra Essentials
For Dummies
978-0-470-61838-7

## Microsoft Office

Excel 2010 For Dummies
978-0-470-48953-6

Office 2010 All-in-One
For Dummies
978-0-470-49748-7

Office 2011 for Mac
For Dummies
978-0-470-87869-9

Word 2010
For Dummies
978-0-470-48772-3

## Music

Guitar For Dummies,
2nd Edition
978-0-7645-9904-0

Clarinet For Dummies
978-0-470-58477-4

iPod & iTunes
For Dummies,
9th Edition
978-1-118-13060-5

## Pets

Cats For Dummies,
2nd Edition
978-0-7645-5275-5

Dogs All-in One
For Dummies
978-0470-52978-2

Saltwater Aquariums
For Dummies
978-0-470-06805-2

## Religion & Inspiration

The Bible For Dummies
978-0-7645-5296-0

Catholicism For Dummies,
2nd Edition
978-1-118-07778-8

Spirituality For Dummies,
2nd Edition
978-0-470-19142-2

## Self-Help & Relationships

Happiness For Dummies
978-0-470-28171-0

Overcoming Anxiety
For Dummies,
2nd Edition
978-0-470-57441-6

## Seniors

Crosswords For Seniors
For Dummies
978-0-470-49157-7

iPad 2 For Seniors
For Dummies, 3rd Edition
978-1-118-17678-8

Laptops & Tablets
For Seniors For Dummies,
2nd Edition
978-1-118-09596-6

## Smartphones & Tablets

BlackBerry For Dummies,
5th Edition
978-1-118-10035-6

Droid X2 For Dummies
978-1-118-14864-8

HTC ThunderBolt
For Dummies
978-1-118-07601-9

MOTOROLA XOOM
For Dummies
978-1-118-08835-7

## Sports

Basketball For Dummies,
3rd Edition
978-1-118-07374-2

Football For Dummies,
2nd Edition
978-1-118-01261-1

Golf For Dummies,
4th Edition
978-0-470-88279-5

## Test Prep

ACT For Dummies,
5th Edition
978-1-118-01259-8

ASVAB For Dummies,
3rd Edition
978-0-470-63760-9

The GRE Test For
Dummies, 7th Edition
978-0-470-00919-2

Police Officer Exam
For Dummies
978-0-470-88724-0

Series 7 Exam
For Dummies
978-0-470-09932-2

## Web Development

HTML, CSS, & XHTML
For Dummies, 7th Editio
978-0-470-91659-9

Drupal For Dummies,
2nd Edition
978-1-118-08348-2

## Windows 7

Windows 7
For Dummies
978-0-470-49743-2

Windows 7
For Dummies,
Book + DVD Bundle
978-0-470-52398-8

Windows 7 All-in-One
For Dummies
978-0-470-48763-1

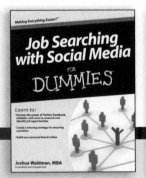

Available wherever books are sold. For more information or to order direct: U.S. customers visit www.dummies.com or call 1-877-762-2
U.K. customers visit www.wileyeurope.com or call (0) 1243 843291. Canadian customers visit www.wiley.ca or call 1-800-567-4797.
**Connect with us online at www.facebook.com/fordummies or @fordummies**

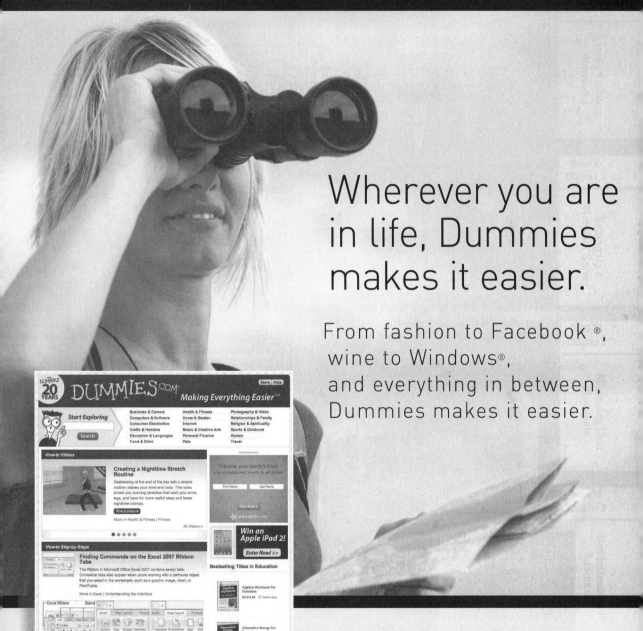